Singapore Diary

The Hidden Journal of Captain R.M. Horner

SINGAPORE DIARY

THE HIDDEN JOURNAL OF
CAPTAIN R.M. HORNER

Edited by Sally Moore McQuaid

SPELLMOUNT

British Library Cataloguing in Publication Data:
A catalogue record for this book is available
from the British Library

Copyright © Captain R M Horner 2006
Copyright © Ronald Searle 1939–45 as per individual drawing,
by kind permission of the artist and the Sayle Literary Agency

ISBN 1-86227-339-1

First published in the UK in 2006 by
Spellmount Limited
The Mill, Brimscombe Port
Stroud, Gloucestershire. GL5 2QG

Tel: 01453 883300
Fax: 01453 883233
E-mail: enquiries@spellmount.com
Website: www.spellmount.com

1 3 5 7 9 8 6 4 2

Printed in Great Britain by
Oaklands Book Services
Stonehouse, Gloucestershire GL10 3RQ

Contents

I am sure my father would, had he been alive, wish that this
Diary be dedicated to those friends who returned
and those who did not.

* * *

But the big courage is the cold-blooded
Kind, the kind that never lets go even
When you're empty inside, and your
Blood's thin, and there's no kind of
Fun or profit to be had, and the
Trouble's not over in an hour or two
But lasts for months and years

Extract taken from within the Diary from
John Buchan's 'Mr. Standfast'

Acknowledgements

The compilation of this book could not have been achieved without the support and encouragement given to me by family and friends.

Firstly I have to thank my son Anthony whose valued input and ideas helped me so much in producing the book, and also for showing me how to do 'short cuts' on the computer which made things a lot quicker – unfortunately I only learnt as I was getting to the end of the task! And to Emma, his wife, for putting up with the hours Anthony and I spent on the phone.

To Malcolm Chisholm who put all the illustrations onto disc for me and Mike Dodd who, in 1999, helped with the first draft edition, together with my brother, Iain, who proof read that edition, and my sister Elizabeth for one of the stories contained within the book itself. I was also given additional information by Sir Henry Every, Dr Nigel Stanley, Sydney Humphries and Frank Champkin and I would like to thank them for this.

I am also extremely grateful to Ronald Searle and the families of George Sprod, Desmond Bettany, Ken Archer and E B Holmes for allowing me to use their illustrations and letters. Unfortunately, despite my endeavours, I have been unable to trace some of those whose illustrations and letters have been used and I do hope they, and their families, feel that this book is fitting tribute to their work and the part they played during that time. Any omissions will of course be rectified in any reprint.

I would like to thank Chris Leather for the final proof read and the help and advice given by Elwyn Blacker, and Roderick Sudderby (Imperial War Museum), and, most importantly, Christopher Norris, Beth Macdougall of MGA (Publishing Consultant) and Jamie Wilson, Russell Butcher and Shaun Barrington of Spellmount Publishers; without whom this book would not have been published.

Nearer to home, I would like to thank my daughter, Nicola, for her support and practical help with some of the re-checking necessary, and of course my husband Neil whose advice, support and patience has helped so much during this time.

These Acknowledgements would not be complete if I did not mention the one person without whom this book would not exist. I am sure when he wrote on the first page; 'thoughts crop up, memories are revived and instances occur … these may, in later years, be of interest to myself, if to no-one else,' it had not occurred to him that they may be 'enjoyed' (if that is the right word) by others. I know he would be thrilled to see his 'odd jottings' in print. And I thank him so much for the privilege of helping this to happen.

Glossary

AA	Anti Aircraft
ADC	Aide de camp
ADS	Advanced Dressing Station
AIF	Australian Imperial Forces
ATTAP	Leaves and wood from the Attap Palm
BJ	Colonel 'Black Jack' Galleghan AIF
BOFORS	Type of anti aircraft gun
BOR	British Other Rank
Borehole	Rumour
BT	Bathythermograph
Coolies	Unskilled native labourers
Coy	Company
DAQMG	Deputy Assistant Quartermaster General
DO	Divisional Officer
DSD	Director of Staff Duties
DSO	Distinguished Service Order
DV	*Deo volente,* God willing
Dvr	Driver
ENSA	Entertainment National Service Association
ESO	Embarkation Staff Officer
GBS	George Bernard Shaw
GOC	General Officer Commanding
HQ	Headquarters
IJA	Imperial Japanese Army
IAOC	Indian Army Ordnance Corps
IMS	Indian Medical Service
IO	Intelligence Officer
Jap	Term for the Japanese, sometimed derogatory
KL	Kuala Lumpur
M&V	Meat and Vegetable (tinned)
MC	Military Cross
MCS	Malayan Civil Service
MO	Medical Officer

MT	Motor Transport
MTB	Motor Torpedo Boat
NAAFI	Navy Army and Air Force Institute
NBG	No Bloody Good
NEI	Netherlands East Indies
Nip	Nipponese. Term for the Japanese, sometimes derogatory
OC	Officer in Charge
OP	Observation Post
OR	Other Rank
P/O	Pilot/Officer
PB	Permanent Base
PBY	Flying Boat
PMC	President of the Mess Club
RAPWI	Recovered Allied Prisoners of War and Internees
RAOC	Royal Army Ordnance Corps
RASC	Royal Army Service Corps
RE	Royal Engineers
Red +	Red Cross
RIASC	Royal Indian Army Service Corps
RNF	Royal Northumberland Fusiliers
RSM	Regimental Sergeant Major
RTO	Railway Transport Officer
SCF	Senior Chaplain to the Forces
TAB	Typhoid A and B
Verb. Sap.	*Verbum sapienti sat est* – a word is enough to the wise
WO	Warrant Officer
Wop	Term for an Italian, sometimes derogatory

Introduction

In a letter to *The Daily Telegraph* in 1981, my father wrote about the diary he had kept during his time as a prisoner of war. He was contacted by Philip Reed, Deputy to the Keeper of the Department of Documents at the Imperial War Museum, and subsequently the diary was transcribed by myself; this transcript together with the original was handed over to the Imperial War Museum, for inclusion within their collection.

It was always the intention that we would eventually get the diary published, but we had, at that time, a private publication in mind for the family.

As so often happens the years rolled by and nothing was done. In 1999 I decided to update the diary, include some of the illustrations, and give it to my father as a Christmas present. As I only started in late November it did not give me much time, but together with the great help of Mike Dodd, we got the diary finished and ring-bound to form a book.

In January 2001 my father died. Somehow I never thought he would! This friend and father who had time for everyone, but never suffered fools gladly, a man of dignity and presence with a great sense of humour and a love of his family, surely couldn't leave us?

If it had not been for a conversation regarding the diary that my son Anthony had with his friend Chris Norris, I would probably not be at the stage of writing this Introduction. Chris suggested that we send a copy to Beth McDougall, a publishing consultant.

I cannot express how it felt when she told me that Tony Hammond, who had read the diary on her behalf, thought it was 'a fascinating and remarkable document ... simply terrific!' and that she would be pleased to handle it. To think that someone thought it was as special as we did was a very emotional feeling indeed. She offered the diary to Jamie Wilson of Spellmount Publishers and I was equally thrilled when he agreed to publish it.

It is hard to imagine how it must have felt when the realisation came that you were now a Prisoner of War, herded together and put in an alien situation, each man trying to deal with it in his own way.

Matters of importance soon came to light and the main concern was food, or the lack of it, and the major consequence of not having the correct vitamins to maintain any sort of healthy life, which meant that, as time went on, the men would eat anything that they thought might contain the all-important Vitamin B. 'We have had an issue of ground nut meal which was sent up as manure for the garden … made up as a biscuit I find it extremely difficult to stomach … [It is given] to cattle in England!'

The lack of communication from loved ones and friends became a dreadful drain on morale. 'Gosh, how I long for word from home, even a post-card.' Not knowing whether family at home knew that they were POWs was another worry that my father mentioned a lot. 'The greatest relief of all and the most joyous news that on 18 December [1942] they had been officially informed that I was a POW.' He received this news in December 1943.

Although the letters and cards were few and far between and always way out of date, it was a thrilling day indeed when he learnt in March 1943, eight months after the event, of the birth of his 'son and heir Ian.' (My mother used the Scottish spelling of Iain, but my father did not know that at the time)

The fact that the men were from a variety of backgrounds meant that there were many talents and abilities to draw on, which went such a long way to help provide articles, however basic, necessary to make life a little better. So that tooth powder was made from wood ash, soap from palm oil (when available) – there were even brush, nail and paper factories!

My father always enjoyed his pipe. When tobacco was too expensive they had to opt for making their own: dried papaya leaves cut up fine, boiled in tea and with a drop of Worcestershire sauce added was one concoction!

When my father was asked to take part in a play, I am sure he would never have imagined how many more plays, musicals, shows and concerts he would put on, produce or appear in (including a concert *two days* after returning from the Burma Railway). He was determined to help keep up the morale of his fellow POWs.

This diary tracks his day-to-day life from India Lines, Changi, the Burma Railway and back to Sime Road, Changi. It brings with it, determination, willpower, humour and friendship.

This is very much *his* story, as he wrote it, and I have now achieved the aim of our family in ensuring that it will never be forgotten.

Sally Moore McQuaid

* * *

Biographical Note

Born in St Albans, Ronnie was educated at Felsted School. His first job was working in a hat factory in Luton, but he later followed in his father's footsteps working for W & R Jacob & Co (Liverpool) Ltd., biscuit manufacturers.

He joined the Officer Cadet Reserve after Munich. Attested in September 1939 in the Royal Artillery, he transferred to the Royal Army Service Corps in December in response to urgent pleas for drivers.

He was called up in February 1940, commissioned in July 1940 to 292 Supply Company, 18 Division and embarked in October 1941 as Divisional Troops Supply Officer with the rank of Captain. He disembarked in Singapore (via India) on 29 January 1942 and became a POW at the capitulation on 15 February.

Initially held in India Lines, Changi, he proceeded to Thailand in May 1943 with 'H' Force 'on loan' to the Japanese Thailand Administration. He returned to Singapore in November on completion of the railway, first to Sime Road and latterly to Changi Gaol.

He rejoined W & R Jacob & Co. (Liverpool) Ltd. in 1946, living in St Albans and working in London. He was appointed Home Sales Manager in 1963, which necessitated a move to Southport, and on his retirement in 1976 he was director of Jacobs and Chief Executive, Home Sales, for Associated Biscuits Ltd.

He married Florence Langlands in 1936 and they had three children, Elizabeth, Iain and Sally. His main interests included cricket, rugby, the National Children's Home (his grandfather was one of the founders of the home), Kidney Research, Probus and Phoenix, hospital visiting and the local horticultural society. He was also an avid watcher of the television Channel 4 programme *Countdown*.

1. Ronald Moore Horner (RMH)

1942

I find that as the days go by (we have now been POWs for three months), thoughts crop up, memories are revived and instances occur that quite obviously will be forgotten if not noted down, and as these may, in later years, be of interest to myself, if to no-one else, I have decided to trace the path of events, with the aid of odd jottings from my diary, from the time I left Ahmednagar, India on 13 January 1942; and as events occur that I find of interest, intend to note these down so that the whole will be in the form of a glorified diary. This rather depends also on one important factor; whether or not I am able to get this home safely back to England!

I left Ahmednagar, accompanied by my batman Holt, at 0930hrs on 13 January. We had to change at Dhown, where we had a wait of two-and-a-quarter hours. I had lunch with the RTO and was extremely interested in watching the arrival and departure of a long-distance train. The filth of the third class carriages and their passengers: the turmoil and fascinating array of sweetmeats, cookies etc., that Tamils ran up and down the platform selling to the travellers. The station pump was put to good use, this being the sole washing facility available to the third class passengers. I had an hour's wait at Poona where, accompanied by an RIAOC Major, I visited a nearby Club whose name I have forgotten and eventually I arrived at Bombay at 2030hrs to be met by 'Trader' Horn and Denis Pearl.

Perhaps here I might sum up my impressions of our brief visit to India. If you say 'dust and smells', you have the whole thing in a nutshell. It seemed remarkable that the primitive methods of, one might almost say, BC, were working side by side with the ultra-modern; but that is what happens and I must confess that the attitude of regular units towards native troops riled us; as did the fact of having bearers, dhobi-wallahs, malis etc., running around all the time, cause us extreme embarrassment. However, our stay was interesting and I would have been glad had it been prolonged.

Brigadier EHW Backhouse had asked me to resume the duties of Ship's Baggage Officer which I had held since leaving Liverpool on 29 October 1941. I must confess I took a poor view of this as it's no easy job but as he pointed out when apologising for asking me to undertake it again, I knew all the ropes and a speedy unloading at our destination would be essential. Also, we were re-embarking on the USS *Wakefield* (the North Atlantic liner *Manhattan*) whose holds I knew, to my everlasting regret, like the back of my hand.

At 1230hrs on 14 January, the baggage train arrived and to make things more complicated had the USS *West Point's* (US liner *America*) baggage as well as our own. My job was to get ours to the two cranes loading our ship, see that 'Wanted' and 'Not Wanted' items were loaded separately, and also the ammunition had a dhow or dhows to itself with an armed guard. What a game! Endeavouring to control something like 100 coolies whose one fixed idea seemed to be to load our baggage on the *West Point*. However, by 2245hrs on the 15th I had all the dhows loaded, this was thirty-six hours without a break and with the heat and blisters that had formed on my feet, I was just about done in. By 1115hrs the following day we were alongside the *Wakefield* which was lying out in the Stream. Then came the rather tricky job of getting the correct dhows lashed alongside the correct holds. Once this was done all was set for the loading and away we went. We finally got the last item aboard at 0230 the following morning and I vaguely remember getting to my cabin, dropping on my bunk and knowing nothing else until tea-time.

Life aboard ship I have covered pretty well in my letters home, but perhaps the following odd jottings deserve mention. The combined Anglo–American concerts on 'B' deck aft, ending with the two National Anthems, and the community singing on Sunday evening – hearing 'Abide with me' go rolling across the ocean was very lovely.

It seemed fairly certain now that we were going to Burma, Java, Sumatra, Singapore or Australia, the first three being favourites in that order. For the initial part of our journey we were escorted by HMS *Hampshire* who left us to turn back to Ceylon, being relieved by HMS *Dorsetshire* whose camouflage, pink bow and one funnel blacked out, gave her the appearance of a destroyer rather than a cruiser. We looked at her with considerable interest, remembering the part she played in the sinking of the *Bismark*.

On approximately 26 January, the convoy was met by six destroyers and HMS *Exeter* of *Graf Spee* fame; the *Dorsetshire* left us and this was our escort to our port of disembarkation, which by now seemed to favour Singapore.

28 January
The convoy formed into line and entered the Banka Straits; shortly afterwards a single Jap aircraft came over and dropped a stick of bombs without hitting any of the ships. One AA burst lifted the wing off the plane and in view of the fact that we received no further attention from enemy aircraft until after we had arrived in port, we feel that it must have failed to reach its base, for in line in the Straits, as we were all day, we would have made an ideal target with no room for manoeuvre. The other ships in the convoy were the *West Point*, *Duchess of Bedford*, *Empire Star* and *Empress of Japan*.

29 January
We docked at Keppel Harbour, Singapore at 0900hrs and I was first ashore to contact the ESO (Baggage) to arrange about off-loading our cargo. The quayside and go-downs (warehouses) were crammed full of supplies of all sorts and our job was made very difficult owing to lack of space. However we managed somehow and eventually finished at 1630hrs on the 30th, having worked all night. We had to stop work at every 'alert' as both Chinese coolies and US Navy personnel downed tools.

We were very blasé until a stick of bombs that fell too close had us diving for cover: this was at about 2230hrs and we kept an eye and ear open after that. Two Jap bombers were picked up by searchlight and followed across the sky, but no fighter aircraft appeared and no AA either. This surprised us then, but would not have done later when the true state of affairs was made known to us.

30 January

At 1100hrs the Japs pattern-bombed (whole flight released its bombs at a given signal) the docks, and scored a direct hit on 'B' deck forward on the *Wakefield*; I saw the burst and thought it had gone straight down No.2 hold where I had my party working. John Day of the Suffolks who was my assistant and I doubled on board and were delighted to see most of the lads coming up the stairs black with smoke but uninjured. They said there was still one down there in the hold. We could now see that the bomb had penetrated the deck about 12 foot to port of the mouth of the hold, had burst in the Hospital underneath and started a fire. We couldn't get down the normal stairs but managed to get to the Hospital via an inside staircase. Here we found two US medical orderlies trying to get a stretcher case from the burning debris. We imagined that it was probably our man and anyhow, being unable to go any further owing to a wall of flame between the Hospital ward and the hold, we gave the two orderlies a hand to get the stretcher up the stairs. It was very hot and the smoke was choking, but between the four of us we managed to climb the debris-strewn floor, and the stairs, and got the fellow to the emergency hospital. Poor lad, he was a ghastly sight having little skin left on his body and I cannot believe that he could survive. On further investigation, I found that none of the six dead were mine and another check on the quayside saw all the party accounted for.

By now we had discovered that 53 Brigade had preceded us to Malaya and had been in action on the mainland; we met several of them on the quayside and the tales they had to tell made grim hearing. We learned that all forces were being withdrawn to the Island and the Causeway (the bridge joining Singapore Island to Johore) was to be blown. We were hardly reassured by hearing that defences on the North of the Island were negligible and certainly the sight of RAF personnel embarking as we were discharging cargo did not help either.

One of the saddest and most harrowing sights I have seen were the hundreds of women and children who were being evacuated on the ships that had brought us. They drove up in their cars and left them to go on board. Others were brought by their husbands who were staying behind. I helped one girl with her little daughter to get on to the *Wakefield* and met her husband later (Major Owens RIASC) and was glad to hear that he'd had a cable from Colombo just before capitulation to say she'd arrived OK. It made me feel pretty lousy; the kiddie was of similar age and colouring to Elizabeth and just at that time our future wasn't looking too good.

At about 1700hrs I joined the rest of HQ at Tanglin Barracks. Here, I found the resident regiment, the Manchesters, who seemed quite oblivious to the fact that there was a war on and in fact we were soon to realise that this was the spirit that imbued the whole of Malaya Command: the inability to grasp the fact that the Japs were at their doorstep. I am convinced that once it was obvious that we couldn't hold the Japs up-country, it had been decided to leave Singapore to its fate but this had caused such an outcry in the USA and Australia that, for the sake of appearances, they had sent in reinforcements (our Division and the Indian troops who came out with us) and although they knew it was a forlorn hope, were going to make a fight of it whatever the cost.

I cannot go into here the rather complicated structure that was the make-up of the civil and military organisation of Malaya, how they failed or were unable to make proper provision for the defence of the Island. At any rate, the situation when we arrived was such that, in spite of having 70,000 troops on the Island, our chances of holding were remote. In fact, to put it in a nutshell, we were being sacrificed to placate public opinion. The commonsense thing would have been to send us somewhere where we could have been used to full advantage, instead of sending our troops into battle unblooded and into a type of warfare to which they were totally unsuited and completely untrained.

31 January

At 0800hrs the Causeway was blown and the last link with the mainland severed. I was amazed later to see what a poor job they had made of this demolition, leaving, as they did, the piers intact!! I won't go into details as to my exact doings with regard to my work; suffice it to say that I was concerned largely with drawing and delivering to my units (Divisional Troops), reserve supplies so that all had a stock in hand of ten days' hard tack. Bukit Timah, Joo Seng, the Racecourse and Robertson Quay were all used as sources of supply. I had also to contact all Divisional troops; this was made more difficult by the fact that gunners, sappers, volunteers etc., were constantly being attached to 18th Division, then detached, so that I had to keep an up-to-the-minute tally so as to know just whom I was responsible for. And of course, last but not least, I learned to acquire the most speedy method of hugging mother earth when the Jap bombers unloosed in my vicinity.

They used to come over in formations of nine, twenty seven, or fifty four, and soon one got used to disregarding them if they weren't passing immediately overhead. They invariably 'pattern bombed' and used for the most part, a 50-kilo anti-personnel bomb that burst on impact and scoured deep grooves in the roads etc., instead of making a crater.

In time we evolved the plan of always having a lookout, as once I was nearly caught napping. I was going round Newton Circus, a roundabout junction of eight roads, when the first bomb fell in Clemenceau Avenue about 100yds in front of me; I was out of the 3-ton lorry in which I was travelling, before it had stopped and dimly remember seeing the nearside rear wheel missing my arm by inches. I got cut about the face and arms for my energy, but discretion is the better part of valour! The bombs fell all around but as far as I could ascertain there were no casualties. My driver and I helped an ARP Warden put out the flames in a bungalow in Scotts Road before we set off for home.

Back at Tanglin Barracks we found they had also had a packet, several near misses to the Officers' Mess, one of which set fire and completely gutted the car of one of the Manchester Officers.

4 February
We moved location to join Divisional HQ at the Singapore Plantation, Paya Lebar. This was all rubber trees and we were therefore under canvas. I shared a 40-pounder with Denis Pearl and although we were very cramped, we got a lot of fun out of it.

5 February
Those Units of 18th Division whom we had left behind in India, including two of our own Companies, arrived in Keppel Harbour. They had a rough passage, being bombed twice with hits on several ships and culminating in the *Empress of Asia* having to be abandoned on fire about 5 miles offshore. I had to deliver supplies to five of the units from the convoy, four of whom had been on the *Asia*. They were billeted in the Joo Chiat area and were a pathetic sight. It looked like Dunkirk all over again, bootless, hatless, but they were in grand spirits and never lost heart. I finished at 2230hrs and had a nightmare drive back to Paya Lebar with a driver who was quite blind at night: in the end I drove the lorry myself and must confess to a sigh of relief when I got back safely bearing in mind that the roads were very busy and that all Indian drivers have a craze for driving at high speeds without even side-lights in the dark. In all conscience they're bad enough by day, but let them loose by night and anything may happen.

The roadside had literally hundreds of abandoned cars, either crashed in ditches or resulting from bombs. There was no recovery work being done and they were just dumped.

8 February
We had our first dose of shellfire, mostly small stuff with an immediate detonation (Gray's fuse) which was particularly unpleasant used against troops under trees, as they splayed the surrounding ground with splinters and even a slit-trench gave only limited protection. The nearest fell 200yds away and splinters fell around us, but although there were a few wounded there were no fatalities. In consequence of all this fun and games, breakfast was rather an 'up and down' affair until we were able to guess by the whine of the shell whether or not it was going to land near us. I still refuse to be convinced, after hundreds of shells have come my way, that the one that gets you, you won't hear. I don't mind admitting that I found this first experience of shellfire rather unnerving and although I think I managed to hide the fact from others, I had the wind up.

Later, we got so used to it that we had to take, if work was to go on, a fatalistic attitude that if one had your name on it, there was nothing you could do about it. In consequence we would drive like hell wherever we were going, working on the assumption, quite obviously erroneous, that thereby we had a better chance of avoiding being hit.

The night of the 8/9 February was marked by a terrific artillery barrage from the west of the Island and although no reliable information was available, it was generally considered that this was a barrage from the Japs as a prelude to launching an attack with counter-battery fire from the Australians who held this sector. Our assumption turned out to be correct, the Japs landing at three points about 2300hrs. We have since learned that the landing craft were brought by rail down the mainland and that a full Division was landed during the night together with some tanks. At 0500hrs on the 9th, the Intelligence reports from Divisional HQ reported a landing force of about a brigade! This was the first example of incorrect reports emanating from Malaya Command. One glaring example that occurred when we had withdrawn to the Singapore perimeter, was an order from HQ for all petrol to be drawn from a dump in Thompson Road that was in Jap hands!!

On the afternoon of the 9th it was decided to move rear Divisional HQ to Hill 110 near the Kampong of Teck Hock. This was carried out during the afternoon and early evening and I left Paya Lebar at 2030hrs, with the last of our vehicles and equipment. The Japs were shelling pretty heavily and had the range of the road-fork at Somapah, also along the Tamperis Road. They had an OP on Palau Ubin, the Island in the Johore Straits off the NE coast and were making things pretty unhealthy for any vehicles showing even side-lights. However, we arrived without mishap even if I did think that the fireflies and phosphorescent fungus in the swamps through which we passed, were Jap eyes!!

The night of 9/10 February did not allow much sleep. We had gunners all round us; a 25-pounder battery was 400 yards abreast and a 75mm battery just to the south seemed to be skimming the treetops with its shells; however, Denis and I managed an hour or so in our 40lb tent which seemed in danger of collapsing with the vibration; The following day, I drew ammunition from one of the dumps and delivered it to those units who had had to abandon all their equipment on the *Empress of Asia*. The Joo Chiat area was twice visited by the Jap aircraft whilst I was there, presumably going for the Civil Airport, but none of their eggs fell nearer than 400yds away. I was glad to offload my burden as the thought of 100,000 rounds of .303 behind you on the truck was hardly conducive to a feeling of security with Jap aircraft overhead!

The night of 10/11 February taught Denis and me that whereas anti-mosquito ointment may be admirable in its primary use, it is a favourite food of red ants, particularly the large fellow that infests rubber plantations and is supplied with large pincers capable of taking out chunks of flesh and who will attack anything: they made no exception of us!

11 February

I went down to the Polo Ground first thing after breakfast. I might say here that this was the 18 Division's Supply Depot and was the best place to contact all units daily as their 'B' Echelons came back to draw rations from there each day. Consequently not a day would pass without at least one visit there. Perhaps an incidental detail was the fact that they always had iced lager on tap!

When I got there I found that Jack Feathers and Keith Bailey had decided to try to get through to the racecourse where we knew there were a lot of supplies and which the 4th Norfolks had re-captured in a counter-attack during the early hours of that morning. I asked Colonel Rossall who was down there whether I could go with them, but was told that he could only let two of us go as the position was somewhat obscure up there and he daren't risk the three of us. So we tossed up, Jack and I won and we set off. He and I were on 3-tonners with two other 3-tonners beside.

We had a pretty hectic journey both there and back but there was no excuse for the two lorries that did not have officers in the cab, turning back. Their excuse afterwards being that they missed their way…very thin! It was annoying because we only got 6 tons of supplies away instead of 12 as intended and this was the last possible chance we had of getting up, as later on during the day the road was blocked. On arrival at the Racecourse we learned that the 4th Norfolks, who were holding this sector, had been given orders to retire; as we loaded the lorries they were firing at the Japs advancing up the further side of the banking that overlooked the paddock, but luckily for us they didn't leave their positions until after we had retired. One way and another it was a pretty hot party; we were visited whilst we were there by nine bombers who unloaded on the petrol dump adjoining and we were sniped on both journeys there and back, by odd Japs or Malay 5th column-ists having filtered through, but there were no casualties and that iced lager never tasted better than when we arrived back at the Polo Ground!

At this stage it seemed almost inevitable, although one had to keep the fact from the men, that our ultimate fate was either capture or fighting on until we were all killed.

The former left room for doubt, as it has always been understood that Japs do not take prisoners in battle, and the latter seemed the more likely, particularly in view of a letter sent to General Percival (GOC Malaya Command) from General Wavell after his visit to us on Tuesday 3 February in which he stated that irrespective of civilian casualties we were to fight to the last man. I say that it 'seemed inevitable' because the Japs had been able to take half the Island and were now astride the Causeway and nothing could prevent them, with complete control of air and sea, bringing such pressure to bear that we were at their mercy and a large scale evacuation was out of the question.

On looking back, I find it remarkable how calmly one took this state of affairs, even joking about it amongst ourselves. Perhaps it was that we all gained courage from one another or perhaps it was the fatalistic attitude one had to adopt, that whatever the future held in store couldn't be altered. Whatever it was, I remember thinking to myself 'Here I am, the Japs are less than 2 miles away, bombing and shelling is almost continuous, our ultimate fate is obscure but grim; I ought to be feeling afraid and yet, apart from a disinclination to eat, I'm not'. I've talked this over with others since and find they had similar feelings at the time. I suppose it is all a question of nerves and whether or not you can get complete control over them.

During all this period, you were living on them all the time and if you let up for a single moment, then there was no knowing when, if at all, you would master them again. Added to this, if you were to retain the respect and command of the men, on no account could you show that you were rattled or worried as to the future. Certainly those officers and men who did lose control never recovered and were useless as far as their worth as active units is concerned.

12 February

I arrived back at location to find that all preparations were going ahead for a move after tiffin. During the morning, the Jap tanks had broken through on the North of the Island and it had been decided to form a perimeter round Singapore city. This manoeuvre was carried out during the afternoon and evening and hardly enhanced the reputation of Malaya Command owing to the chaotic traffic control. Two divisions, ours and 11 Indian Division had to utilise, quite unnecessarily, one X-road with the result that confusion reigned supreme! Rear Divisional HQ together with our HQ moved to Newton Road, (we were in No. 39) which was in fact about 400yds behind Advance Divisional HQ. We were in a house hastily evacuated by a good class Chinese family. It was heartbreaking to see the children's toys still on the floor. In actual fact, the owner returned after the capitulation; a charming man, his house is still occupied by the Japs; his fate, I do not know.

The fact that 80,000 troops were now packed in a perimeter with a radius of some five miles from Singapore, meant that, wherever you went in the 'half-way' zones, you were in the midst of the gunners. How we alternately applauded and cursed them. They did a grand job of work but naturally drew counter-battery fire that made movement in all areas beyond the actual front line extremely uncomfortable to say the least. And as they had to contend with mortar, machine gun and rifle fire as well, it was a gay party. There was one battery just behind us, 'Charlie' Battery of an Indian mountain regiment, who delighted us by the way they 'barked' back after each Jap barrage.

All night and all through the remaining time we were at Newton Road, in fact up to the capitulation, they gave back more than they received. Sometimes only three guns would reply and we'd say 'Hell, they've hit one of them', but they'd only be shifting position and would reply all together next time.

I don't propose to go into lengthy details during the period that followed, culminating in the capitulation at 1800hrs on Sunday, 15 February; some of the more interesting events I will relate however to give a rough picture.

On the night of 13/14 February a hurried conference of all officers was called and we were informed that a representative body of officers and men was to leave for the docks forthwith to rendezvous at Keppel Harbour at 2359hrs, with a view to making a getaway. Colonel Rossall, Bill Cowell (as Ammunition Officer) Majors Knowles and Hodgkinson were going from us and duly left at about 2330hrs. They returned the following day when they found that there was no properly organised party, although a considerable number of other officers in the division and other formations did actually get away.

Shortly after breakfast on the 14 February a shell penetrated the bedroom that Denis Pearl and I were sharing (bedroom is good!), just as I was leaving it. It burst on impact with the further wall and wrecked the room beyond. Fortunately no-one was there and there were no casualties, although I have a good impression of 'sailing through the air with the greatest of ease' by the blast. The house proper seemed, apart from this one shell, to bear a charmed life; hundreds of shells landed all round: in the garden, outhouses, road, but there were no further direct hits registered on the house itself.

Major Barber and I went about together on a 15cwt Fordson, driving all out all the time and hoping for the best that by so doing we'd avoid the shells which seemed to be falling thick and fast wherever we went.

During the morning we were temporarily turned into an ADS with our MO (Lieutenant Emery, a grand fellow who had been in practice in Kuala Lumpur before the war) tending casualties that occurred in the near vicinity. He did more grand work but he had some terrible and quite hopeless cases to deal with, as well as many which varied from deep scratches to broken limbs and badly ripped flesh from shell splinters. Our HQ cook Driver Palmer was quite amazing, producing lashings of hot sweet tea for the wounded and a meal for us at 1300hrs this in spite of the fact that shells were dropping all round the house and two fell each side of the cookhouse and plastered the outside walls with deep pitted holes.

Outside was a melancholy sight, many Chinese and Malays with all their portable belongings with them running hither and thither, not knowing which way to turn for safety. Dozens of fires, great columns of smoke rising whichever way you turned; death and destruction everywhere. I had the amazing experience of standing on the eighth floor of the Cathay Building, where 3rd Corps had their HQ and hearing shells whistling past *beneath* me and seeing their hits registered on the houses, roads etc., below. I watched until I was sickened by what I saw.

One trip I made to the docks through the Chinese quarter was the most nightmarish experience I have ever had and try as I may I cannot erase from my memory. It was surely not possible to allow this destruction and wholesale slaughter of civilians to continue: women and children, some whole, some in pieces lying all over the road and pavements.

15 February

Spent most of the morning with members of our HQ in a ditch potting at any Jap aircraft whenever in range of rifles. Although we saw one brought down by Bofors, we didn't have any luck ourselves, I wish I had thought of putting the fellows out before, as they were much better outside, seeing what was going on rather than stuck in the house all the time.

At the Polo Ground during the afternoon we learned that a Staff car bearing a white flag had passed through the 5th Suffolk lines to negotiate with the Japs for a cessation of hostilities at about 1100hrs – later a message from Divisional HQ said that 'cease fire' was to be called at 1630hrs. Actually this was a mistake, 1800hrs being the correct time.

It was rather extraordinary that twice after the 'cease fire' I came as near being killed as at any time during the battle. The gunners all around us were 'spiking' their guns and first half a shell and, later, part of the barrel of a 4.5 howitzer missed me by a few feet.

I must admit to a feeling of relief that I had managed to come through this brief but nevertheless extremely hectic campaign unscathed – I had always felt that rather than return home badly disfigured, I would rather have died, and having since seen officers and men of my acquaintance who were not so fortunate, I still hold to this opinion. Whilst later visiting friends in hospital up here at Changi, I have seen fellows so badly wounded that although many survived, they would always be quite helpless and, in some cases, so badly disfigured that recognition was difficult.

Had it seemed that there was any useful purpose in continuing this battle of Singapore, then I think we should have fought on, knowing what we do now about dispositions of troops, etc., and strengths at the time of the capitulation, I have no hesitation in saying that another twenty four hours would have seen a most awful massacre. Eventual surrounding was certain, the Japs had already broken through at Alexandra and down the Changi Road and on every front there were not suf-ficient troops to hold them.

There was also a serious shortage of water and ammunition (particularly 25-pounders) and the supply system was becoming chaotic. For two days we fed 11 Indian Division from the Polo Ground and the extra drain on our resources was becoming serious. I daren't let myself go on what I think of Malay Command. Perhaps one day I will, but for the present will simply say that they just didn't seem to have any idea what was going on.

It is rather a coincidence that I have just been lent the second copy of the 'Syonan Times' which is the propaganda newspaper printed in English and published in Singapore (or Syonan as the Japs call it) as it contains an eye-witness account dated 21 February of the period that I have been writing about. Allowing for journalese and omitting the purely propaganda paragraphs, I think it paints quite an accurate picture: 'Comparatively, she (Singapore) experienced both air and land bombard-ment greater than that which London, Moscow or Chunking had had to endure. In fact during the last three days of the battle, Friday, Saturday and Sunday, Syonan (Singapore) was bombed at intervals of every 15 minutes, while forming a terrify-ing background to this aerial activity was the intermittent crash of shell explosions (Jap estimate 200,000 rounds were fired during the battle).

It would be impossible for anybody who was not in Syonan at the time during those three days to picture the utter chaos that reigned in this city. Everywhere one turned the sight of mud and blood bespattered humanity met the eye. Civilians and soldiers alike died by their thousands (?), whilst thousands more were injured...there was also the clouds of smoke from the innumerable fires all over the Island which hung like a pall, blotting out the sun for most of the day…at night the glare from the fires lighted up the city shedding a brighter glow than from normal city lights.'

There it is for what it's worth. I query the 'thousands of soldiers' although I'm not in a position to do so with regard to the civilians [*later reported as 10,000 killed*] – I do know from what I saw in the Chinese quarter, that the casualties were appalling, but the exact numbers I don't know, nor perhaps will it ever be divulged. Anyhow it was a nasty sight and one that, as I've said before, I want to forget.

The night of 15/16 February seemed somehow rather fantastic; where was the drone of planes, the crackle of rifle and machine gun fire that had gradually been getting closer as the days passed, the whistle of approaching shells? For the first time for several days we were able to change into pyjamas (the SCF with Red + over-band attached, just in case!) and found my camp bed which had mercifully survived the shell blast. The room was a shambles, plaster, bits of brick and dust everywhere, but nothing really destroyed our side of the wall where the shell exploded. There was a certain amount of speculation as to whether or not the Japs would come through during the night although they were supposed not to until 0800hrs the following day.

Shortly after breakfast the following day, 16 February the Japs arrived and whisked us off in lorries to a field adjoining the Bukit Timah Road where we joined up with more of our troops. We only had our packs with us, but I obtained the use of a car from the Japs and made several journeys back to our billets to get rations, picking up more of my own and others' kits each time. By the time I got there, Tamils had broken in and looted everything but I got quite a lot away that I had given up for lost.

We stayed in this field in the open all that night and after tiffin the following day, the Japs took the fountain pens, watches, rings, pencils etc. from many troops, but I had stuffed all these down my puttees and was OK.

At 1400hrs on 17 February, we began our fifteen mile march to our POW area at Changi, on the NE corner of the Island. A nightmarish march under a blazing sun, passing unpleasant reminders in the way of corpses, destroyed buildings, burnt out vehicles etc., on the way; and it was a very footsore and weary party that arrived here at about 2100hrs.

Before going on to describe life here at Changi, I think one might pause to consider first how it was that Singapore, 'British bastion of the East', on which millions of pounds had been spent, had fallen after a fight of barely a week – I do not intend to go into lengthy whys and wherefores and, anyhow, this is hardly the appropriate time or place; suffice it to say that Malay Command had always held the belief that up-country, the mangrove swamps and jungle would always prove too big an obstacle for an invading army.

That the Japanese, with the aid of innumerable 5th columnists and complete air and naval superiority, did overcome these is now a matter of past history, and by so doing, they exposed Singapore's weakest feature, attack from the Mainland. A glance at the map will show that the island is surrounded by land on three sides with only an average of two miles of water, the Johore Straits, for an invading force

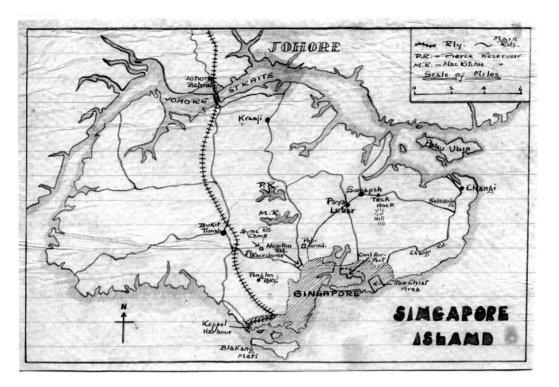

2. Singapore Island

to negotiate. Another factor that must be borne in mind, is that no attempt was made to clear any of the land, swamps, coconut and rubber plantations, in the immediate vicinity of the Straits, as they did not want to alarm the native population.

The one thing that would have facilitated defence, the clearing of half a mile of inland from the Straits, was not done and the invading army was able to infiltrate up the creeks in the swamps and get in amongst the thick foliage, completely unobserved. Again, with the exception of those troops who had been stationed in Malaya for some time (Leicesters, East Surreys, Argyles), all other British troops and most of the Indian (always excepting the Gurkhas) were completely untrained in jungle warfare.

That the Japs were fully trained in this aspect was made only too clear as the battle of Malaya and later Singapore continued; and as Singapore Island is for the most part thickly overgrown, with mangrove swamps, jungle, coconut and rubber plantations, again their superiority was only too painfully obvious. I have already mentioned their complete air and naval superiority (during the actual Battle for Singapore Island not one single aircraft was used in its defence) so that it will be seen that its fate was virtually sealed, long before we set foot on the Island.

One cannot help a feeling of bitterness when you see a complete division like the 18th, out of the war, probably for good, simply because of 'world politics', the fear of upsetting public opinion in America and Australia made it necessary for the British Government to sacrifice, and there is no other word for it, a complete Division to what was virtually a lost cause.

And what of the lighter side? One or two odd 'shots' come to mind, the rickshaw coolie transporting a portly Chinese, a shell lands in the near vicinity, down go the shafts, out tumbles the Chinaman with more haste than dignity.

On one occasion when the Polo Ground was being pretty heavily shelled, one seemed to be coming too close for safety and we all dived for cover; as I got up out of a ditch I was greeted by the sight of Jack Feather's bottom sticking out from beneath a mattress, under which he'd dived for cover. The end-on view that I got was reminiscent of an ostrich, but on such occasions you don't have time to think of appearances!

Again at the Polo Ground I was giving a supply sergeant instructions as to the dispositions of certain units in the Club House that served as an office; a too-close shell had us diving for cover and found us both on the floor together, still with our notebooks, and I continued my dissertation until we both burst out laughing at the absurdity of our positions.

Similarly at Newton Road we were having dinner (Palmer where did those chickens come from?!) when a shell seemingly missed the roof by inches and we were all on the floor in a flash, some still clasping their plates. Another occasion I wanted to find a certain field regiment, took the wrong road and after negotiating a long, uphill and winding track, eventually landed up in a leper colony – I didn't stay long! And finally, the sight of the SCF with Red + arm-band pinned to his pyjamas, getting up to shave the morning after the capitulation – safety first!

And now we come to the aspect of the Far Eastern visit of mine, in which I find myself as I write this, a prisoner of war. Obviously I can't write all I should like to, as there is no knowing into whose hands this might fall before, if ever, I get it back to England, but I will make a note of any items of interest and so try and give a true picture of the weeks, months, years (?!) that are to follow.

For fairly obvious reasons, we always have the feeling of being on the edge of a volcano and we find the mentality of our captors so complex when compared to our own that it is difficult to estimate just what is going to happen next.

I am writing this in the Officers' Mess, India Lines, Changi, situated on the NE corner of Singapore Island. We are in a barrack block that was formerly (as the name suggests) occupied by an Indian Regiment. Unlike German POW camps, we have not been segregated from the men, owing to the large number of prisoners taken in such a confined space, the four formations: 18 Division, 11 Indian Division, AIF and Command and Garrison's troops (known as Southern Area) each have their own locations and each do their own internal administration with Malaya Command as the link with the Japs. As RASC we have plenty of work to do, drawing rations from Singapore, sorting them out on the Gun Park for redistribution to the four formations (distribution is done by man-handled trucks, either two-or-four wheeled, made out of car chassis etc.) and generally being responsible for all pro-

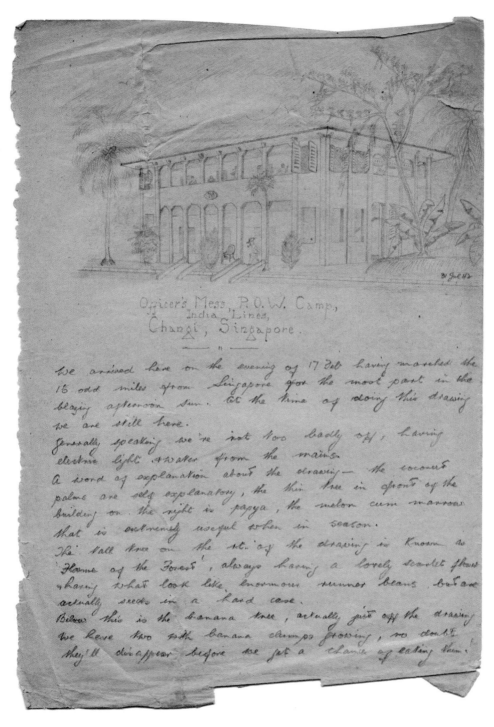

Officer's Mess, P.O.W. Camp,
India Lines,
Changi, Singapore.

We arrived here on the evening of 17 Feb having marched the 16 odd miles from Singapore for the most part in the blazing afternoon sun. At the time of doing this drawing we are still here.

Generally speaking we're not too badly off, having electric light & water from the mains.

A word of explanation about the drawing — the coconut palms are self explanatory, the thin tree in front of the building on the right is papya, the melon cum marrow that is extremely useful when in season.

The tall tree on the rt. of the drawing is known as 'Flame of the Forest', always having a lovely scarlet flower & having what look like enormous runner beans but are actually seeds in a hard case.

Below this is the banana tree, actually just off the drawing we have two sith banana clumps growing, no doubt they'll disappear before we get a chance of eating them.

3. Officers' Mess

duce whether local-grown or purchased outside the camp. Actually at the time of writing one of my jobs is to get the 18 Divisions' supplies from the Gun Park to our own DSD and see that (a) we get our fair share and (b) that it arrives intact – not so easy as it sounds.

A few words about our immediate surroundings – our mess faces a small padang (field, usually used for sports) which can just take a shortened football pitch. On the far side are attap huts and coconut palms. These are prolific round this area and the result is that coconut has a large say in our daily diet! There are a few rubber trees, but no specific plantations as in other areas we have been in on the Island. Mangrove swamps run from the fringe of our area down to the sea, with innumerable creeks winding through them. Altogether we are lucky; owing to the disposition of the barrack blocks and huts we have, comparatively, a good deal of 'leg-room', although with the thousands of troops up here, it is quite impossible to get away from one's fellow men.

The most discussed subject is undoubtedly 'food' – our daily diet is such that we cannot help but feel permanently hungry, we already hate the sight of rice, although we've got used now to its being the mainstay of every meal. Every book you read seems to have long descriptions of meals in it and a favourite occupation for Denis and I is to discuss meals we've had in the past and meals we intend to have on returning home.

Actually the cookhouses are getting quite enterprising in attempts to disguise rice and will continue the good work as time goes on – biscuits, buns, porridge, duffs, pasties, pies and so on, all with rice and ground rice bases. All help to disguise that white grain that I have never liked and never never will after this.

Had we not brought up a considerable portion of hand rations with us, we would have had nothing, as we got nothing from the Japs for a fortnight; now we get frozen meat twice a week, flour, tea, milk (tinned), ghi (Indian fat), salt, M&V or Irish Stew in lieu of vegetables – all in very small quantities.

Actually the complete lack of fresh vegetables is the more serious; deficiency diseases are already creeping in and as time goes on these will reach alarming proportions unless we're given a more balanced ration. As an example, here's today's menu: ground rice porridge, boiled rice and onion (?) gravy, tea (made Malayan style, weak and without milk and sugar to help the sweets out) – this is our breakfast taken at 0930hrs. Tiffin is at 1330hrs and today consists of: sweet boiled rice, coconut biscuit, and tea. Supper at 1830hrs is a 'bully'-and-rice pasty followed by a coconut rock bun. This is quite an average day's menu and you will see that rice plays an all-too-predominant part each day.

We have started our own gardens and will reap the benefit from these in due course. We have also bought some chicks and ducklings, but the former have some disease and we are losing some of them.

I have already said that coconuts play an important part in our daily menu, and although an extra flavour, familiarity breeds contempt! To sum up, we have now got accustomed to being permanently hungry. I have lost 2st since leaving England

and although in my case this was desirable, you need the extra stamina to help you out should you go down with dysentery or malaria – unfortunately there are no nourishing foods to build you up again if once you do get low in health.

And now for a word about climate – Singapore has an average yearly rain-fall of 93 inches, with the worst period around December and the lowest July. Tropical storms, thunder and lightning are a daily occurrence either near or far away.

The 'Sumatra', a sudden increase in wind followed by lashing rain is also fairly common. Consequent on the high rainfall, the humidity is considerable and one sweats with little or no effort. Before we got the water connected, our only way of having a bath was to stand in the open during the 'Sumatra'.

We are also now able to use a 'flush' WC, this is of Asiatic pattern and neces-sitates squatting, but is infinitely preferable to the out-of-doors 'thunder-box' with its myriad of flies!

Ewan Escritt is a naturalist and spends hours sketching spiders and various insects etc., that are of interest – praying mantis, giant grasshoppers, cicadas, atlas moths etc. There are numerous varieties of jumping spiders, who jump on flies and insects to make their kill.

I suppose that everyone has had that sense of relief on waking from a nightmare to find that it was all just a dream – naturally the everlasting wishful thinking means that one dreams of home and one's loved ones only to find on awakening that you are still 10,000 miles away, an unpleasant reversal of procedure.

The humidity out here makes everything that is not chromium or stainless steel tarnish within twenty-four hours – leather shows signs of mould from one day to another and the inside of suitcases or any clothes have a dank musty smell.

There are a number of interesting birds, parakeets, flying-fox (large bats), the 'tock-tock' bird or Malayan night jay, bee-eaters, woodpeckers and mynahs to name some of the most common. Until you get used to it, the 'tock-tock' bird, which is sea-sonable, keeps you awake at nights with the loud 'tock-tock' it makes in its throat.

Almost everything out here, butterflies, moths, ants, bees, crickets, spiders are much larger than those found in England.

There are millions of ants, from ordinary garden size to others that are three-quarters-of-an-inch long, and varying in their offensive spirit. The large red ant that Denis Pearl and I contacted at Teck Hock is by far the worst; he has large pincers which take a nip of flesh out quite easily. They usually nest at the top of coconut trees and make this by binding the leaves from the fronds into a ball about the size of a football. The undignified retreat of the RSM from half-way up a tree when attacked by swarms of these offensive little brutes, is still told and retold with great relish by the men.

Another variety of interest is the termite, white or black, which lives below ground, is quite blind and will eat the inside out of wood or even concrete. The queen is a fat slug of little or no shape and jealously guarded by its 'soldiers'. These have large mailed heads, which, like the red ant, can draw blood with their large

4. Officers' Accommodation

(life size)

Rough sketch of the larger type grass-hopper who helps to make the hours of darkness a rather noisy affair, using the barbs on his back legs to make a piercing noise which is only surpassed by the cicada, who produces a continuous note by rubbing his wings together, & can be heard at least 200 yards away.

———— — ————

(life size)

A praying mantis; this insect, known for its carnivorous qualities, as the "tiger of the insect world", lies on boughs & bushes & strikes suddenly with his barbed fore-paws via unerringly accurate. Lives on other mantis, crickets etc. — its wings resemble a leaf so closely that on one occasion a grasshopper we had incarcerated in the same glass-covered box, tried to eat the mantis' wings!

5. Praying Mantis

pincers. The 'workers' have small heads and normal bodies. If disturbed they make an amazing sight marching five-or-six deep from their old to their new homes in a long black line that wears a smooth path in the gravel or sand. They are policed by the 'soldiers' but being blind, many stray and are then easy prey for the small 'garden' ants who take a run at them, bowl them over and proceed to cut them in pieces for transportation to their own nests – there is even a jungle law amongst the insect world.

There are quite a lot of snakes and, when cutting down coconut trees, particular care has to be taken as they are often hidden where the fronds join the trunks. Of scorpions, little is seen here and the variety is much smaller than those we had in India. There are centipedes, long reddish-brown brutes that need careful handling should they get on you. A cigarette end in the centre of their back is the best way, any attempt to shake or brush them off means a painful sore where they have dug in all their feet.

Bull-frogs are much in evidence, particularly after rain, and their hoarse croaking resembles hundreds of snoring males in a crescendo of discord! They form a background to the incessant buzz and rasping notes of the crickets and cicadas that vie with the 'tock-tock' bird to make an unmusical chorus for the hours of darkness.

I have made a brief mention of deficiency diseases – the study of vitamins is usually credited to health food cranks, and vegetarians, but here it has become literally a matter of life and death. The almost complete absence of vitamin B and C will mean that unless rectified, 'beri-beri' and scurvy will soon be in evidence in their most serious form; there are already cases of the former in mild forms. We have had an issue of ground-nut meal which was sent up as manure for the garden, but being believed to contain vitamin B has been made up in the form of biscuits and eaten. I am not one to turn from food, but find these extremely difficult to stomach! Dick Vaughan who farms in England, says it is the same as the cake that is given to cattle in England!

Opposite our mess is a small padang (field) which can take a small 'soccer' ground. We also play hockey there. Consequently, I have watched more matches than I have ever seen in my life before and have, after a lapse of many years, started playing hockey again with a fair amount of success.

There are some first class soccer and hockey players; until a few razor blades were made available, it looked odd seeing fellows playing games wearing long beards!

On 29 April – the Emperor of Japan's birthday, we were given an issue of tinned pineapple and a day's holiday – they forgot to give us any vegetable or M&V so that the fruit was hardly an extra as intended. The reverence of the Japanese for their Emperor is all wrapped up in their religion Shintoism. It is said that a committee sat for three-and-a-half years trying to define this religion without success. Sounds like the British Government at work on one of their major decisions!!!

30 April

The Colonel's birthday, we had a slap-up 'do' for which we had been saving up for some weeks, with odd surreptitious purchases from Malays and Chinese. We had celery soup, salmon and rice fish cakes with tomato sauce, raisin duff made from all-wheat flour, cheese on toast and papaya and cream. Boy oh boy was it good?! No ground rice added to the duff. Papaya is a form of sweet marrow; known in India as Pawpaw, it can either be used as a vegetable or fruit.

Denis Pearl and I share everything we have, (tobacco, cash etc.) and have long discussions on food, pipes, tobacco and have fully decided on our 'reunion' dinner when we're home again. We have one cigarette after breakfast and one pipe after supper, and this will last until my stock lasts out.

There have been one or two open air concerts and a Divisional party functions to about 500 each night; units go to the 'theatre' which is a broken down attap hut – and a jolly good show it is too.

Adjoining our mess is a Mosque which has been converted into a very excellent church; altar, rails, pulpit (all made in the camp) go to make St George's Church a splendid centre for people to congregate, whether for services, discussions, lectures or debates.

However, I don't think I've ever attended a more impressive service than that held out on the padang on the first Sunday we were here. For pulpit there was a soap box, for organ, an accordion – but it was nevertheless an amazing and solemn gathering. Amazing, because everyone from the most senior officer to the most junior private was so obviously devout in offering thanks that he had survived the ordeal we all had had to face – and solemn, because few if any hadn't lost friends in the battle.

I know in my mind, and I expect in many others, was the one hope that the time would not long be delayed when our loved ones at home would be advised that we were safe and sound even though prisoners of war. At the time of writing this, the beginning of May, we don't know whether news has yet reached home.

There are various ailments peculiar to tropical climates that beset us – 'prickly heat', a rash that is brought on by continuous sweating and for which talcum powder is the only corrective, is the most common. 'Singapore Foot', a sore that usually starts between the toes and is apt to spread unless promptly treated. Tropical ulcers, usually emanating from a slight scratch or cut. Ringworm that attacks any part of the body, not usually the head as at home. There are at the time of writing 1,000 cases of dysentery in the hospital; several deaths have occurred from this. Malaria and dengue, both brought about by mosquito bites, the latter mosquito having a distinctive striped or rather hooped body.

Barnett, the Australian Test Cricketer is a POW in the AIF (Australian Imperial Forces). *(Editor's note: Ben Barnett, wicketkeeper who toured England with Bradman in 1938.)*

6. St George's Chapel (a converted mosque)

5 May

Our meat ration has been reduced; three-and-a-quarter ounces of meat including bone, fat etc., to last three days, and four ounces of tinned onions most of which were 'blown' having obviously been in a fire (probably at the MSD Bukit Timah which was hit by bombs on Tuesday 10 February). There are no further issues of tinned milk, which had been invaluable in making rice porridge and puddings palatable. There is a possibility of an issue of fresh veg. I hope to God it comes as this cattle food nut cake is our only means of getting vitamin B and although I manage to get it down it nearly makes me sick.

Some of the slimmer fellows are getting rice 'pods' or bellies. People of my portly build have all lost weight. Ken Charnock has lost 3st; Wilkinson of the Northumberland Fusiliers 2½st. I am just over 11st stripped, which is 2st lower than when I was attested in September 1939.

This continual humidity makes concentration difficult and explains the lethargic way in which most people out here went about things. A state known as 'Singapore Mind' is apt to make one forgetful and makes quick thinking difficult.

ATLAS MOTH

7. Atlas Moth

I am getting used to being in a permanent 'bitten' state; everything that flies or crawls seems to bite. Bed bugs, fully-grown about the size of a lady-bird, only flatter and transparent until they've got a bellyful of blood, are prolific. The charpoys (Indian-type beds with wooden frames and rope springs) that were left here by the Indian troops, were alive with them, as is every chair or form you sit on.

An Atlas Moth was caught yesterday. With a wing span of 9 inches, they are beautifully coloured in shades of brown and have feelers like miniature feathers.

6 May
Some fresh vegetable has arrived, Kangkory (a form of green) papaya, cucumber and pineapple. They are most welcome and we hope contain lashings of vitamin B.

8 May
Denis Pearl going down to Singapore today on a six months' working party detail. Several parties have already gone and are doing various jobs from cleaning debris, to building huts and breaking up vehicles for scrap, of which there are thousands on the Island, many lying by the roadside abandoned.

As Denis is my particular pal and we went through the battle together a great deal, I'm very fed up that he's going – I wonder if I'll see him again before we reach home? Have been made PMC of this mess, there will be some eighty officers left made up of Sapper, Northumberland Fusiliers, RAOC and RASC.

Odd shot – the cheechas or chik-chaks (wall lizards) are never killed as they live on flies and mosquitoes. If you tap their tails they discard them in fright and leave them wriggling on the ground without any harm to themselves.

15 May

It has been very hot these last few days and at nights the sweat has run off in streams even tho' you are lying still. There is no doubt that a mosquito net increases the heat, but owing to the prevalence of that insect they are intended to defy, their use is advisable. Actually I take a towel to bed with me, wear only pyjama trousers or a sarong and mop up my back, chest and arms as the night progresses.

The Japs are being difficult – General Percival the GOC in C has had to serve a term of imprisonment for refusing to supply radio announcers and technicians for repairing AA guns. General Heath has just finished a 'term' for refusing to discuss the defences of India. He was knocked unconscious while bending down, kept without food, water or proper sanitation for forty-eight hours in a dark cell, then on his way back here was taken into Changi Gaol where he was allowed to see Lady Heath and given food and wine! How can one attempt to explain such treatment?

An iguana was killed in the gardens the other day, a cross between a huge lizard and small crocodile, measuring 4ft from snout to tail tip. When skinned and cooked it tasted rather like hare.

Another interesting specimen I saw the other day was a flying lizard; actually, like the flying-fish they only have the power to glide, but have a definite wing formation on their backs.

17 May

Have got a bad dose of 'prickly heat' that keeps me awake at nights. We are able to obtain a few cheroots in Singapore; they're quite good and the butts can be smoked in your pipe. What a sign of the times!

19 May

Doing fine! Have got prickly heat, Singapore Foot, cut on the finger and crack on the shins at hockey that has turned into a tropical ulcer!!

Japs very active these days, extra patrols and general air of excitement.

21 May

It is an unpleasant but nevertheless true fact that the life of a POW has turned hitherto decent officers, particularly in the case of field rank, into selfish, mean and unscrupulous beings who will stop at nothing as long as their own ends are satisfied. At the moment I don't think it propitious to mention names, but the utter illegality of many of their actions deserve to be brought to light when the time is suitable. The old Army gag 'F--- you John, I'm all right' is very apt.

I have been able to get hold of a few sacks, about a dozen in all, of cargo of unmilled rice. It has part of the outer husk remaining, and this contains the now all important vitamin B – I don't think I've mentioned previously the prevalence in both rice and flour of thousands of weevils; a good many are picked out before cooking (by letting the heat of the sun drive them out), others we pick out before consumption, the others go the way of the rice; maybe they have a vitamin content. I hope so, as we must eat hundreds a week.

Tomorrow night the general is coming to dinner and I am arranging a 'do' for the occasion. By extra purchases made by those going to Singapore on ration parties, I've got a good menu together: tomato soup, braised beef, peas and potatoes; doughnut and cream and sardines on toast. The doughnut is made of wheat and rice flour and is pretty good; the toast is made from bread made at the Field Bakery that we have now got working and for which a portion of our weekly issue of flour is deducted to give us three issues a fortnight of one slice each, about three-quarters of an inch thick.

23 May

The dinner party went off well last night and 'Becky' [*Lieutenant General MB Beckwith-Smith DSO, MC, GOC 18 Division*] was very appreciative. He was late and came tearing over to the 'A' Mess on a lady's bicycle! There were eleven at table, 'Becky,' ADOS, CRE, CRASC, our four Company Commanders and 'Wilks' of the 9 NFs who is in charge of their small detachment remaining in Changi and of course myself as PMC.

Had heavy rain today, the first for over a fortnight. This will, I hope, put paid to the thousands of flies that have pestered us of late.

25 May

Whit-Sunday, I went to communion at 1130hrs and to evening service – this is always well attended and ends with the hymn 'The day thou gavest Lord is ended' and after the blessing 'God be in my head' which I don't think I'd heard since Arthur and Denise's wedding. [*Brother and sister-in-law*]

The Divisional RASC are to find 300 men and twelve officers for an up-country or overseas detail, destination unknown.

Have considerable difficulty with the 'Aussies' when collecting our rations from the Gun Park. They're past masters at pilfering and their own officers seem quite unable to control them. They're mostly the reinforcements that were sent out, untrained, shortly before the Far Eastern war started and are riff-raff of the lowest order. The regular and MT units are grand chaps or 'cobbers' as they call them.

The sunsets out here are beautiful, producing the most lovely colours; blues, reds, golds, copper and many undescribable tints.

30 May

Have just read an article in the No. 41 number of the National Geographical Magazine dealing with Singapore. It is amazing how everyone seemed convinced, or was it wishful thinking, that Malaya was packed with troops and planes to meet any eventuality, instead of the totally inadequate force we now know was here with obsolete aircraft for its Air Force. The accompanying photographs, some in natural colour, were excellent.

My Singapore foot is taking a long time to clear up. That is one of the worst features of any sore or cut in the tropics, the length of time it takes to heal. Many fellows are still in hospital with wounds that could have healed long ago in England.

31 May

A Division's team played hockey against the hospital staff today, they had two 'all Malay' players and several very good Anglo–Indians – we lost 3-0. I'm told I played well, although at times I felt completely outclassed.

We had not long finished our game when we had the most severe 'Sumatra' that we have witnessed. We are used to tropical rain, but this was something quite remarkable. All drains were flooded in a matter of seconds (Malarial drains such as intersect the lines are 3ft deep) and in no time all flat surfaces were underwater. It was coming in from the NW, driving straight on to the back balcony of the Mess, and the floor was soon one large pond.

The job of PMC is most exacting; it is virtually impossible to please all the seventy odd officers that constitute our Mess and altho' I have quite a good Messing Officer, there are many grumbles and considerable criticism. I find that the tactful handling that dealing with senior officers necessitates, when quite absurd and frivolous complaints are made, are very trying to one's patience. Which brings to mind the unfortunate but nevertheless certain fact that this climate and I suppose confinement as a POW has played havoc with all our tempers. Mere incidentals have one seeing red and a very firm grip is necessary to prevent outbursts.

2 June

Have just come in from a walk round the area with the MO including excursions into the mangrove and coconut plantations surrounding us, but still within the boundary wire. The object was to seek out and destroy all prospective or actual mosquito breeding places. It is amazing that their larvae can grow in any receptacle that contains stagnant water. The tops of bamboo stakes, empty coconut husks, old tins, puddles etc.

We had to beat a hasty retreat from one coconut grove that was full of red ants and dengue-carrying mosquitoes. Saw one or two snakes, but they were only-too-keen to slip out of sight on approach rather than try anything offensive.

4 June

The Japs have sent up some live bullocks for consumption in lieu of frozen meat, and this morning watched the demise of the Division's portion by pole-axing. Did not enjoy the spectacle, being witnessed on an empty stomach before breakfast, but having been ordered to be in attendance, had no alternative.

I wonder what a 100% riceless meal would taste like?! We're fed to the teeth with rice as our main source of supply and even the extra vegetable we get doesn't obviate the necessity of having a large dollop of boiled rice to add the bulk.

7 June

Corps Sunday – had special service at 1100hrs. In afternoon officers played NCO's at soccer. I played in goal and got in one or two good 'rugger' tackles in a game that was marked more by its vigour than its skill. We lost 2-0.

Strong rumours that we're moving to Singapore – expect I'll go as I had a 'set-to' with the Colonel at breakfast from which he so far got the worst of it that he apologised before the meal was finished. He has not done anything to commend himself to us since being in Changi, very much the reverse. I only hope that one day there will be a day of retribution; he has ruined our reputation as Divisional RASC.

8. Changi Gaol, or 'Suburbia'

10 June

Denis Pearl looked in for a short time today – one of his party, who are breaking up vehicles at a dump near Changi gaol, had got badly burned and had to be admitted to hospital. There is talk of a serious food shortage in Singapore, certainly no meat is being imported so that the exhaustion of present stocks is only a matter of time and then – ? Still sufficient unto the day! In all conscience, a further reduction seems hardly possible.

13 June

[*Our Wedding Anniversary.*] And a Saturday too! I'm feeling pretty blue, remembering this same day six years ago and feeling the many many miles that separate us. If only we had got some letters. Not one word since leaving England at the end of October last year; still I'm not the only one. Today is marked by our receiving an Amenity Grant of $7.50 from the Japs – including 20 days back-pay we get $2.50 per 10 days. Now for some purchases at the canteen!

In the evening went to see *Hellsabuzzin* given by Southern Area. They use the old open air cinema. An excellent show including a female impersonator who couldn't be told from the real thing. Were the men's eyes popping?!!

14 June

First fruits from canteen purchase. Shared a tin of pilchards with the remainder of the table to help the plain rice down at breakfast. What a sign of the times, to find a real delicacy in tinned fish and boiled rice! Yet it's a fact. It is impossible to put down on paper the enjoyment that that tin of fish gave and possibly on re-reading this in later years it will be difficult to believe – but the fact remains that after weeks of plain rice and watery stock, that fish tasted superb.

Have been made IO for India Lines, nuffsaid! – The canteen are selling Chinese and Malayan cigarettes – they're pretty shocking and make their sale by imitating as exactly as possible packets of well known English brands. Gold Flake, Capstan etc. The cheroots are good, particularly when you can get Burma.

Have scrounged a dart board and darts and in its inaugural competition, Paddy Sykes and I went out to Joe Clymer and Eric Martin – who incidentally, are the main stalwarts, being both county players, of our still unbeaten (by teams in the Division) India Lines hockey team.

We hear from Ken Charnock that Eric Hinde, being pompously tactless as is his wont, was beaten up by the Japs and tied blindfold to a tree for six hours. They're pretty unpleasant in their camp at Thompson Road, but have been fairly orderly up here.

The Japs send us as latrine paper, bales of old American newspapers which make interesting reading with views, particularly with regard to the position in the Pacific, expressed twelve months ago. They also include 'Comics', supplements to their Sunday editions with coloured strips of Jiggs, Blondie, Donald Duck etc., and in fact, many of the strip cartoons that are found in English papers.

17 June
One of the four bulls that we had collected for slaughtering and eventual consumption, broke loose, charged Dick Vaughan and eventually led the RSM and his rescue party a merry dance for ten hours before he was run to earth, too exhausted to fight any further.

18 June
A day of days – we were all given a postcard and allowed to send a message home, I do so hope it gets through OK so that they'll know we're in good health.

'Paddy' Sykes and his company left today to go up-country. I was very sorry to see them go, for, having spent twelve months with the Company from its formation in July 1940 to July 1941 when I joined HQ all the officers and men were known to me and I still think that my old 'D' Section were the best bunch of boys you could wish to have. Corporal Sainsbury was the only one to fall in battle and we all felt his loss very much.

20 June
Eric Martin, our DO left for up-country today. Since Denis Pearl left, I had got very pally with him and was sorry to see him go.

Had a most interesting lecture on the sinking of the *Bismark* by a Royal Marine Captain who was on board the *Prince of Wales*, surely an ill-fated ship if ever there was one.

21 June
Have a dose of Tinia, a disease of the skin due largely to vitamin deficiency in a 'sweaty' climate.

23 June
The Japanese are difficult to understand – the story of the wounded MO at the Alexandra Hospital just after the capitulation illustrates my meaning I think: As he lay a Jap soldier gave him a tin of milk; as he drank it another knocked it out of his hands. Another gave him a cigarette, which a fourth soldier stubs out on his neck! Jolly little playmates! I wish I dare write now all I could and would like to on this subject. I only hope that time will not dull my memory.

I have already mentioned the extreme selfishness and unscrupulousness of most of our senior officers. There seems no end to it and we have to sit back and watch in silence. It certainly takes a POW camp to show who are the pukka sahibs and who the complete and utter outsiders!

25 June
Bought some Gula Malacca from the Canteen; rather like fudge it was good, but expensive. It is the tappings from the palm tree flower and makes, I'm told, an excellent sauce.

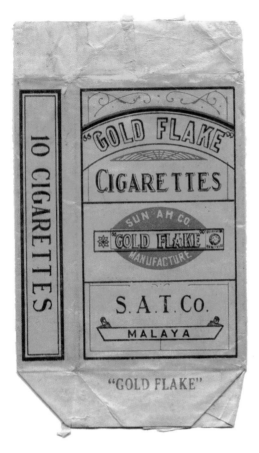

9. Cigarette packets

There are some grand books in the library. Three that I've read recently are Duff Cooper's *Haig*, Philip Gredella's *The Duke* and Roger Keyes on the Gallipoli Campaign.

2 July
Both Dick Vaughan and I have been troubled with insomnia. Often we chat on the balcony between 1 and 2 am and sometimes even later. I suppose it is due to the heat; I only wish I could discard my mosquito net.

The RE have constructed a fishing pagar which Mike Kennan visits each day in hopes of a good haul. So far the results have been very disappointing and I suspect that Malay fisherman might be able to give an explanation.

3 July
Beat 23 Brigade 2-0 today at hockey, thus avenging an 11-2 defeat a fortnight ago. Mostly comprising Gurkhas, they're a cheery lot of lads and have some good players.

4 July
Smoked a palm leaf cigarette today. This form is popular with Malays, but I found it very hot. Dried and bleached in the sun, it curls up naturally and is either smoked in its raw state or with a tobacco insertion.

5 July
Tasted today the famous fruit Durian, which many people say has the choicest flavour of any fruit in the world, once you have got used to its smell! The casing looks like a huge 'conker' and they grow to the size of a 'rugger' ball. The spikes are hard, as I learned to my cost when, unthinkingly, I went to catch one that was falling from a locker! The smell and in fact the taste as well, is a mixture of garlic, onions and strawberries and cream – a lot of fellows think they're first class, but we've made it a rule that anyone having one eats it on the roof, so powerful is the smell!

This evening we had a gala dinner, killing ten of our drakes – the MOs deciding that their pen was a breeding place for flies – good enough! They were grand, with roast sweet potatoes, bread and garlic stuffing and Kangkong – shades of home fare! To follow we had doughnuts and cream, not quite the real thing, but very enjoyable.

Actually, on our table we finished off the meal with a huge fresh pineapple that was purchased in Singapore by one of the ration parties. It is little wonder that as I sit writing this, smoking a Burma cheroot, life seems rather rosier than usual!

6 July
When drawing rations from Singapore today, we were greeted by the sight of the heads of three Malays or Chinamen placed on trays at the top of poles. We were told that that was the penalty for pilfering from the Japanese and that altogether there were eight of these placed at various vantage points in Singapore, as I've said, we

only saw three. The psychological effect of putting the head on one side of the tray, thus implying that there was plenty of room for more, was the most striking feature of a sight that is best not seen on a near-empty stomach, as was our case.

8 July
Interesting lecture by GOC-in-C. Lieutenant General Percival on European phase of war, one or two points were brought out that I did not know of previously.

11 July
Weighed myself today, 10st 13lb, the first time I've been below 11st for many years. Still, apart from blackouts when rising suddenly, I feel pretty fit. I would prefer to get rid of this confounded prickly heat, but that has only to do with the climate, not to our diet.

Had the first of two anti-cholera injections today – there is a scare in Singapore and the Japs are terrified of an epidemic.

12 July
Remarkable people our captors: for no apparent reason they've made a present to each general of stout, whisky, tinned butter and cheese, whilst for the troops there are 13,000 tins of pineapple to be split up amongst all formations. 'Becky' has made a gift to each of his staff officers (including RASC) of six bottles of stout and one tin each of butter and cheese – so that today's tiffin should be a 'dinger'. Perhaps the stout will put me up to the 11st mark again.

15 July
Went to see the 18 Division's presentation of *The Dover Road*, a really first class effort that helped to make one forget one's surroundings for a short time. Held in the new Windmill Theatre (the centre floor of an old battle-scarred NAAFI block), it really recaptured the true theatre atmosphere.

16 July
Dick Vaughan and I found the heat so oppressive last night that we were smoking on the balcony at 0115hrs, 0230hrs, and 0430hrs; finally when I was all set for sleep soon after 0500hrs, a 'Sumatra' broke with thunder and lightning – what a helluva country! I'm fed up with this continuous humidity, every effort making you sweat – I can't imagine anyone living out here from choice, altho' I suppose in a modern bungalow, with electric punkahs and a well stocked ice box, one wouldn't worry so much.

It is rumoured that all senior officers are going overseas, either to Formosa or Japan, together with several thousand others. I wonder?!

17 July
Two fruits that are just coming into season which I think are worthy of mention. The first, mangastines [*mangosteens*], a round, hard-cased fruit with a sectioned

interior, usually six sections, two of which are double-sized and contain a soft stone, they are very pleasant. The other, rambootans [*rambutans*] – looking rather like and about the same size as 'conkers', inside they have an opaque fruit covering a hard stone. Again, very pleasant with a characteristic flavour.

A vegetable I tried today for the first time was towgay. This can either be eaten in seed form, rather like small peas, or as was the case today, germinated – in which case it's like cress, with a juicier stalk and a flavour of a mixture of cress and asparagus. It is supposed to be full of vitamin B!

Today we had an historical ceremony enacted in our St George's Church adjoining this Mess. The Bishop of Singapore came to confirm several hundred candidates from the Australians, 11 Indian Division, 3 Corps, Fortress Troops and 18 Division postponed from the 15th, when the Bishop failed to turn up; it was my job to provide tea afterwards. This consisted of sandwiches and cakes with, wonder of wonders, tea and milk and sugar! Using a special grant I was able to get a good variety of sandwiches: banana, cheese, kangkoy, chutney, cucumber, egg and sardine! A very colourful spectacle with the Bishop in his robes (accompanied by a Christian Jap escort) four Generals, ten Brigadiers and all the senior Colonels. They complimented me afterwards on the tea and decorations. A memorable and I should think historic occasion, as there can surely have been no other case where men were confirmed whilst prisoners of war. [*St. George's Church was a converted mosque. The Minister was Reverend E W B Cordingly, padre to the Northumberland Fusiliers who, after the war became Bishop of Thetford in Norfolk.*]

21 July

Today we had to line the roads for inspection by a new Jap General who is taking over command. I did not mention earlier in this narrative that during the first month or two of our captivity we had to do this for various Jap dignitaries. The conquering GOC (Lieutenant-General Yamashita) with photographers, cinematograph apparatus and all the paraphernalia surrounding a good propaganda write-up. Then later for Air Force and Naval commanders – always the same routine, a wait of at least an hour in the blazing sun!

23 July

Included in the party of senior officers going overseas are others who have been brought specially from Kuala Lumpur, Java and Sumatra. They have brought some 'interesting' stories of which I think more may be heard at a later date.

I have now taken over the job of Messing Officer as well as PMC, the Sapper subaltern who was doing it lacked any imagination and was bone lazy. So I've now got to try and think of as many different ways of camouflaging rice as I can! What a life!!

One of my other jobs is Officer in charge of Rice Supplies, and every Monday and Thursday I take a convoy of lorries to Changi Pier to collect our divisional supplies from the go-downs there. Whilst there I have visited the magazines that are situated

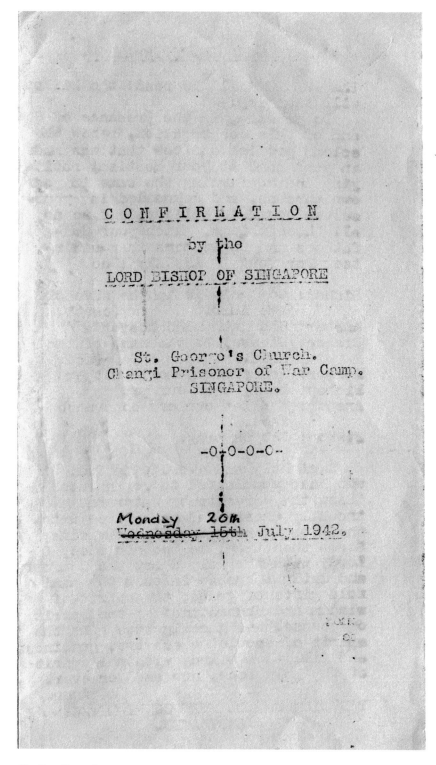

CONFIRMATION

by the

LORD BISHOP OF SINGAPORE

St. George's Church.
Changi Prisoner of War Camp.
SINGAPORE.

-0-0-0-0-

Monday 26th
~~Wednesday 15th~~ July 1942.

10. Confirmation

100-odd yards back from the mangrove and which, six in number, were supposed to be demolished before the capitulation.

Just one more example of Malaya Command's inefficiency – they were all fused separately and when the first magazine was 'blown', leaving a huge crater that would easily take this Mess and which hurled chunks of reinforced concrete 20ft x12ft a quarter-of-a-mile away – all the other fuses were put out of action – there were a few minor explosions due to 'sympathetic detonation', but otherwise the other five, including at least 30,000 rounds of 25-pounder were left intact.

27 July
Had a Mess meeting today, at which I was complimented on the improvement in meals since I took on the job of Messing Officer. Actually it's the cooks who produce the stuff and if you show that you have ideas and are keen to hear suggestions from them, they really get down to the job. By liaising with other Messes, I've introduced more variety; Indian pilaus and chapatties, pancakes, egg and rice dishes etc., etc.

29 July
Beat an Australian Medical Corps XI 5-0 at hockey today – they were very keen but lacked practice. For the second game in succession Colonel Hingston in goal didn't touch the ball! Colonel Wilkinson and I say it's owing to our impenetrable defence as backs, but rumour has it that the opposing forwards have been weak!

31 July
And my thirty-first birthday – should be rather a noteworthy occasion, but I fear that the conditions and surroundings are hardly conducive to a really hilarious party! (even if we had access to alcohol). Am having a supper party of bully beef, with a salad of kangkong, cucumber, two tins of beetroot and two tins of asparagus – followed by the now rather inevitable tinned pineapple. It's a good thing I like this fruit as it is the only one that we see in really large quantities, both tinned or fresh – tins are roughly 35c and fresh vary from 40c – 60c.

4 Aug
Am reading a very interesting book by a Captain MD Kennedy – *The Military Side of Japanese Life*. Written between 1918–1923 it is only naturally rather more pro-Japanese than otherwise, but is not devoid of criticism where he thinks it necessary. Some of his conclusions or, perhaps more accurately, comparisons, we can appreciate fully and agree with seeing them daily as we do. Their untidiness and unshaven appearance compare unfavourably with our own troops but do not in any way impair their discipline or fighting qualities, for which I have the greatest admiration. Japanese officers and WOs go into action with a heavy two-edged sword. It looks clumsy, but I could relate several instances which prove their efficiency. Their feeding is frugal and for this reason they are more easily able to infiltrate in small bodies through jungle etc., carrying a little rice and barley (to prevent beri-beri) and

living on products of the country. In Malaya, their guerilla troops were stripped to the waist, had a belt with food and ammunition and carried a 'tommy' gun – and it was these troops who caused such havoc and ambushed so many troops in the Malayan campaign.

5 August

Had quite a potent drink today of: raisins, gula malacca, coconut water (or milk), cashew, apples and sugar. Incidentally, I don't think I've mentioned previously that the cashew nut grows on the end of an apple-like fruit which has a characteristic 'acid' taste. The nut itself is surrounded by a sticky dye, also having strong acid properties, which needs baking in the oven before opening. They make a useful addition to curries.

6 August

Went last night to concert at Divisional Signals – quite a good show! Archie Bevan, 'Becky's' ADC has asked me to take part in I Killed the Count, which is the next play to follow The Dover Road when it comes off in a week or two's time. I've agreed to take the part of Samuel Diamond, a cockney salesman, which should be good fun! I only hope that I won't find memorising the lines too difficult; this climate will not help matters and I never was too good at this.

7 August

Have shaved off my moustache, the cavalry affair that I think I'd mentioned I'd grown. It was a damned nuisance; anyhow wouldn't suit the part of Samuel Diamond and I'm certain that Flossie's first remarks on returning home would have been 'For heaven's sake remove the foliage before I kiss you.' I feel much cleaner now.

11 August

Our contacts with the Japanese, and reading several books about them, have shown how differently they and Europeans think. They for instance, thought that the stripping of English women during the China 'incident' was not disrespectful. Their attitude to women is that they are in the world to serve – to produce children, look after the homes etc., and a wife has no cause for complaint if her husband goes off for a holiday with a geisha girl. However, to see a European kissing his wife or girlfriend 'goodbye' at a railway station is considered shocking. In Japan it is a compliment to the food you've consumed to belch after the meal, and to clear one's throat and spit in public is thought, as it is in India, quite a normal procedure.

12 August

Feeling homesick today, this being my Flossie's birthday. Oh how I wish I was home again; it all seems somehow so very far away. Have put on a special sweet this evening in her honour 'Florence Cream Sandwich' – a 100% whole wheat flour pastry sandwich with a lemon cream filling. I stress the 100% as usually the larger proportion is ground rice flour and the quality of necessity is not so good.

Last night dined with the 6 Norfolks at the invitation of 'Doc' Jackson. After dinner we played some comic card game that fortunately didn't need too much concentration – altho' a lot of bridge is played in the Mess, I still have no desire to participate.

17 August

All Generals, Brigadiers and full Colonels together with sundry staff officers and about 2,000 ORs left today for either Formosa or Japan. We lined the route and cheered 'Becky' and our Brigadiers on their way. Poor 'Becky' was terribly affected; he was a grand man and I think blames himself quite unnecessarily for our being brought here when the general consensus of opinion was that the chances of holding the Island were pretty remote.

I think he had a very rough break, two-and-a-half years training a division and then not only see it put into front line action straight from landing and fighting a type of warfare in which they were completely untrained, but also seeing the various brigades and battalions under his command taken away by Malaya Command so that he hardly could be aware who he still had left under his command.

Without going into details, a number of the battalions were removed from their brigades and helped to form independent forces under completely 'strange' commanders – one brigadier for a short space had no troops left in his brigade and eventually finished up with one battalion and a mixture of Dhogras, Gurkhas, Punjabies etc., whom he'd never seen before!

Dickie Ritchie the ex-Davis Cup player has just come into the Mess to see me; poor Dicky, used to a very active life, he has put on a lot of weight and with such a large proportion of rice in his diet will continue to do so. He visibly writhes when we call him 'Tubby'. He's adjutant of one of our field regiments which has quite a cluster of sporting celebrities. Their CO is Lieutenant Colonel SW Harris, English Rugger International and South African Davis Cup player as well as representing them at boxing, athletics etc. EW Swanton who is on the BBC staff as cricket commentator, is a first class player himself and also writes for the *Evening Standard* on cricket and rugger and then there's Roger Sparks, Bedford, E Midlands and Trials rugger captain as well. Ian Peebles was also in the regiment but didn't come overseas.

Beat the British Battalion 1-0 at hockey today. They were formed from the remnants of the Leicesters and East Surreys who had a rough passage up-country and who were some of the few troops in Malaya who had really been trained in jungle warfare.

It is now six months to the day since we came to Changi and possibly a comparison of conditions then and now would not be out of place. In the early days food was very scarce and had we not brought tinned goods up with us we would have had nothing for the first fortnight. When this was used up and we had to subsist on IJA rations we were very hungry. Now we are able to supplement in some degree by

*Special order of the day by MAJOR-GENERAL M.B. BECKWITH-SMITH D.S.O., M.C.

On my departure for Japan I wish to take what may be my last chance to thank all ranks of the 18th Division for the cheerful service and loyal support on many shores & seas during the two years in which I have had the honour to command the Division.

I regret that I have been unable to lead you to success in battle to which your courage & sacrifice is entitled and although I leave you with a heavy heart I carry with me many precious memories and a real sense of comradeship such as could only have been inspired by the trials & disappointments which we have shared in the last few months.

Difficult days may still be ahead, but I hope that the spirit which today animates all ranks of the Division will prevail, and will form a corner stone on which, one day, a just and lasting peace will be founded.

God grant that the day will not be long delayed and we may soon meet again; meanwhile good luck, Head up, Keep smiling.

(Sgd.) M.B. Beckwith-Smith
Maj-General
Commanding 18th Division

16 Aug 42

* Major General Beckwith-Smith died at Dai-Hua (Formosa) on 11 Nov. 42 from diphtheria.

11. Letter: Maj.Gen. M B Beckwith Smith

canteen purchases and as far as messing is concerned (this is my province) the job is to dish up the same old thing in as many ways as possible so that altho' the basic ingredients are the same, a variety is offered by different shapes and flavours.

We have electric light now, which we didn't have before, and showers laid on from the main. So, on the whole I suppose we shouldn't grumble.

I fear that sometimes I get infernally homesick – particularly when a vivid dream has brought one's loved ones close to one, only to find on waking that they're still 10,000 miles away.

If only we could hear from home, even a postcard to say that everything was OK. Not having had a word since we left England at the end of October 1941, I feel so very remote and out of touch. I don't even know whether there's an Ian Horner in the world!

Still, whole in limb and unless I go to Formosa or Japan I do know that my present wardrobe will see me through from one year to another. The heat and humidity gets on one's nerves, but as I've said before, we're used now to a perpetual state of sweatiness. Deficiency diseases are on the increase however, and will, I fear, continue unless there is a change of diet, which will include a proper proportion of all vitamins.

19 August

What a do! First we have to line the roads for inspection by the new Jap general, one General Fukuye. Then we have to march to the padang in the 11 Indian Division's lines, form a hollow square and have a speech made to us by said general, which is afterwards interpreted – the rough idea seems to be that as long as we behave ourselves, he thinks he will be kind to us in the manner laid down by the IJA for POW administration. Somehow all this palaver for so short a speech seems rather 'phoney' – we wonder whether the fact of lining the route to give 'Becky' a send-off, and which we were fully aware would hardly meet with the approval of our captors, had any bearing.

A repatriation ship, returning Jap nationals has arrived in Keppel Harbour with Red Cross supplies – boy o boy, how welcome they'll be: milk, maize flour, jam, kaffir corn, bully, M&V, mabela (malted porridge), sugar, cocoa, tinned vegetables and fruit, vitamins A and C, sweets and biscuits in the food line and as well as medical supplies for the hospital, boots, hats and various other ordnance supplies.

I am reminded of an occasion on St Pancras' platform, when Frank (my father) suggested that I was going a 'dinger' when I gave 2 shillings for a Red + flag (actually I think it was the smallest change I had) and I remember answering 'Who knows, some day I may be grateful for Red + help' – there's certainly many a true word spoken in jest.

25 August

Had the last of three lectures today on the Eritrean campaign by General Heath, who was 'the' man at the capture of Keren. Incidentally, he is still here, owing to the serious illness of Lady Heath, who is interned, along with 3,000-odd civilian men, women and children in Changi Gaol. His lectures have been most illuminating and brought home the difficulties of terrain that had to be overcome. Incidentally, he stressed how in this campaign, it was found necessary even with regular infantry to 'blood' them before going into the fiercest fighting, an aspect of general tactics that I have found in books on the last war and which, as far as 18 Division was concerned, was so sadly lacking in Malaya.

Diphtheria is on the increase and is seriously alarming medical authorities, particularly as there is no anti-toxin serum.

Have got a chameleon that I'm hoping to tame; they have huge tails and change colour according to what colour they rest on. They also have long tongues that they flick out at terrific speed to catch flies etc. He's bitten me once and so far shows no sign of wishing to be pals, but I'm hoping. I've christened him, for no reason at all, Oscar.

The Japs have sent round a screed for everyone to sign in which you state that you give an honourable undertaking not to escape. We are naturally refusing *en bloc* and as they have already said that should we refuse, severe measures are to be taken against us, we are asking ourselves 'what now?!'

It is hardly the time or place to discuss escape possibilities – the Japs have said they will execute anyone who tries and in fact there have already been several cases – severe restrictions are also placed on all other POWs should anyone try to escape, so there you are!

31 August

Am giving Oscar up as a bad job, he refuses to be tamed and usually bites my fingers.

There are several 'Escape' books in the library dealing with POWs in Germany and Turkey in the last war. Of course conditions and the general layout here are very different. By reason of the large numbers here and disposition of blocks of buildings, we are far better off from the point of view of 'leg-room' – but where they scored was in being in constant touch with home by letter and postcard, as well as receiving parcels which meant that their food was much better than ours here.

At the moment, with the Red + supplies we're living comparatively well, but when they're gone, the basic Jap ration even with Canteen purchases is pretty putrid.

In the *Road to En-don*, dealing with POWs in Turkey, EH Jones the author, deals with the aspects of life in a POW camp that one finds so marked here. The close and regular proximity to the same people month after month makes one long for solitude.

The selfishness and unscrupulousness of some officers to further their own ends, solely concerned with their own comfort and devil take the rest – is so marked in many of our senior officers I'm sorry to relate. And in fact the hopeless feeling of being in an enclosed space, outside of which, as far as we are concerned, it's a firing party and shallow trench if you're caught. Stay steady laddie, you're getting morbid – there's no doubt that it's the best thing to have a job of work to do to keep your time occupied; that's why I'm enjoying rehearsing for *I Killed the Count*, it takes up all my spare time.

We hear we are to be paid. So far we have been receiving an amenity grant that is actually pay for labour (no sick or light duty men get any) – after deductions for hospital etc., we are to receive $20 per month. Boy, we're rich!

1 September

I haven't mentioned previously the prevalence of hornets and bats – at sunset each night the latter come out literally in their hundreds, mostly from amongst the palm fronds. There is also the Mason Bee, who builds a nest in any enclosed space, corner of a wall or cupboard, or the open end of a towel rack. Rather like a miniature swallow's nest, she lays her eggs and then comes back with spiders and caterpillars for the young to feed on when hatched out.

I've bought a pair of Chinese sandals made of wood with a rubber toe cap. They only cost me 25c, and when I've got used to them will be invaluable for saving shoe and boot leather – *comme ça*:

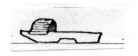

12. Sandals

3 September

The war, starting today on its fourth year, has been brought home to us with a bump! Events have been moving with some considerable swiftness during the last thirty-six hours. At 2300hrs on 1 September, Colonel Holmes of the Manchesters, who is acting GOC since General Percival left, was sent for by General Fukuye [sic] and told that unless we signed the Parole Paper by 1500hrs on 2 Sepember the whole area of 15,000 troops would be concentrated in Selerang Barracks in the AIF lines, a group of 7 blocks (three-tiered) around a bomb-pitted square, and used in peace time to house only one battalion (about 800). As this threat has in no way made us alter our minds, I am writing this at 1000hrs on the 3rd, on the second floor of one of these blocks.

The expression 'herded together like cattle' is certainly being enacted around me; this block has 2,500 in it, whereas it was designed to accommodate 300. I have my camp bed and we are on the balcony facing the road, beds touching one another all along and others long ways at the base All good clean fun!

Our move here was an amazing sight, fleeing evacuees wasn't in it! All our possessions, even livestock (I carried one duck!) with trailers pulled along piled high with valises, kit-bags, cooking utensils etc.

The amazing thing is that the morale of the troops is higher than ever. The Jap guards have orders to shoot anyone who puts a foot on the road surrounding the blocks [*see plan*] – there are also Sikh guards. These latter are some of those who have gone over to the Japs; we don't know how many there are, they do sentry-go between areas and we have to salute them. Failure to do so means getting your face slapped, press-ups or some such indignity – *Elephas nunquam oblivet*.

C O P Y

TO:- All Units, 18 Div Area.

Copy of SELERANG SPECIAL ORDER No 2 BY COLONEL E.B.HOLMES MC., is forwarded to all units for information:-

"1. The requirement by the Imperial Japanese Army, issued under their Order No.17 dated 31 Aug 42 that all ranks of the POW Camp Changi, should be given the opportunity to sign a certificate of promise not to escape, has now been amended in a revised Imperial Japanese Army Order No 17 dated 2 Sep 42 to a definite order that all offrs, NCOs and Men of the POW Camp shall sign this undertaking.

2. I therefore now order that these certificates will be signed by all ranks, and handed by Area Commanders to Command Headquarters by 1100 hrs on 5 Sep 42.

3. The circumstances in which I have been compelled to issue this order will be made the subject of Selerang Special Order No 3 which will be issued later.

(sgd) E.B.HOLMES.
Colonel Commanding British & Australian Troops.

SELERANG.
4 Sep 42.

In view of the above I direct that all Officers , NCOs and Men of the 18th Divisional Area sign the above mentioned undertaking.

(sgd) S.W.HARRIS.
4 Sep 42.   Lt.-col Commanding 18th Divisional Area.

Selerang 1/A

3 Corps,S.Area,11 Div,18 Div,AIF.,OC Hospital.

Reference Selerang Special Order No 3, dated 4 Sep 42.
My attention has been drawn to some concern which is being felt that there may be adverse financial consequences on individuals as the result of the signing of the non-escape certificate.
It is obviously impossible for me to give a ruling in this matter, which must rest in other hands than mine. I wish, however, all ranks to be informed that this point had my full consideration at the time of decision, and I am convinced that no such adverse consequences on pay, pension or allowances will result to any individual. It will naturally be my first endeavour also to ensure on release that the position is made clear to His Majesty's Government.

(sgd) E.B.HOLMES.   Colonel;
Commanding British & Australian Troops.

CHANGI.
4 Sep 42.

13 & 14. Special Orders from Col. E B Holmes and Lt Col. SW Harris

Opposite:
15. Sketch of Barracks
16. Sketch of Quarters

1942

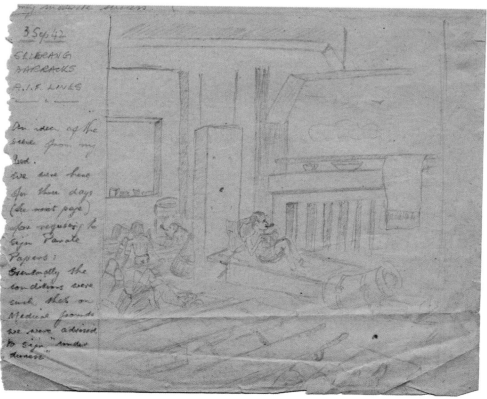

All Area commanders had to witness the death sentence carried out on four would-be escapees who were recaptured last week. The firing party consisted of Sikhs but other details I do not know at the moment.

Last night the Japs pleaded with Command to sign owing to the likelihood of disease – they are afraid of diphtheria spreading owing to the fact that everyone is herded together and of dysentery due to the fact that latrines are having to be dug in the asphalt square and will be on top of the cookhouses – the outlook does not look exactly rosy – the wood problem for keeping fires going is acute, doors and all woodwork are rapidly disappearing – malarial drains are having to be used for urinals in the absence of anything else.

With regard to the firewood, all interior doors, windows etc., are being disman-tled and chopped up; aren't we having fun! The position with regard to rations is obscure. No water allowed for washing or shaving as there are only two available water points and these are required for cooking. I fear skin diseases will increase.

Have just watched the Japs changing guard. The new and old sentries bow to one another and when the troops march off they do a few paces in a form of 'goose-step', only with a bended knee.

As I write, the Japs are digging furiously a machine-gun post on the corner oppo-site our barrack block, they certainly get going on a job. Just to show our contempt, we're erecting a chicken-run on our side.

4 September

Apparently we are to be starved into submission if the overcrowding doesn't produce an epidemic. It appears that the orders emanate from Tokyo and for that reason, no alteration can be made in the wording and we've got to sign whatever the cost in men's lives.

Medical authorities are very pessimistic about the spread of disease and dysen-tery and the general feeling is growing that if we've got to sign in the end, to save unnecessary loss of life, we had better sign soon, with the full knowledge that it is being obtained by duress. Hell's bells, if we do have to sign, it's another humilia-tion; first the capitulation itself, then our orders to salute Sikhs and Jap privates. Failure to do so means face slapping and kicking, then last Wednesday's firing party and now this.

One feels one has little pride left, but the men's lives are the main consideration, and remembering that the signature is given under duress to save large scale loss of life, is worth a little pride swallowing.

1900hrs – Have just signed the Parole Paper and am feeling depressed in con-sequence. The eventual order was given by Command, after Colonel Holmes had obtained (with difficulty) a written order from the IJA ordering him to do so.

We all started with our tails well up, in fact the men have been first class all the way through and are as disappointed as we are.

5 September

There's talk of our moving today altho' so far nothing official. The scene of this square from the top of our barrack block is quite amazing. I can only liken it to some crowded continental market square on market day – the latrine trenches hewn through the asphalt are in the centre and all round are cookhouses, tents, sheds, water trucks and thousands of men. It has been an amazing experience, altho' hardly one that one can relish. Even if the signatures have been given, the men's morale is higher than ever.

1500hrs – Here we are, back in India Lines again – I should never have believed that one could be *glad* to get back here, but after the packed conditions of Selerang, this seems like heaven. The shower that I've just had was one of the most refreshing I've ever had.

My cookhouse staff are now hard at it preparing a meal for tonight; we're putting on cold bully beef and chipped sweet potatoes with a course of boiled rice to fill in the gaps and duff and jam sauce to follow, so I don't think there'll be any complaints. My cooks have done wonders during the sojourn in Selerang, producing meals over an open trench fire and generally keeping the flag flying under most trying conditions.

6 September

Have just heard from Colonel Harris some of the details of the execution he had to witness of the four escapees. The firing party consisted of one Sikh officer and three Sepoys, all with rifles. They were so shaky that in all, twenty-one shots were needed before the four men were declared dead. After the first volley, all the men fell down; one, an Australian, got up and pointing to his arm which had been hit said 'For God's sake aim at my heart, not my arm' – the next shot got him in the thigh! Eventually he was finished off with the firing party standing over him with their rifles almost touching his body. Not a very pretty picture!

9 September

The Sikh guards have been proving even more unpleasant than previous to Selerang – incidents are numerous and one fears a serious one might occur at any moment. Representations have been made to the Japs – *I Killed the Count* opens on Thursday next, the brief break hasn't seriously affected production.

13 September

The number of people admitted to hospital with vitamin deficiency diseases is on the increase in spite of the extra medical supplies that have now arrived. Personally I eat a good number of peanuts that at 30c per Kati (one and a third pounds) are good value as being a source of Vit B, which is necessary to combat most of these diseases. My weight is down to 10st 8lb – generally speaking I don't feel too bad in myself, but like most people I find I tire quickly and have little real stamina, also 'black-outs' are prevalent.

SELERANG SPECIAL ORDER No. 3 dated 4 Sep 42.

1. On 30 Aug 42, I, together with my Area Commds was summoned to the Conference House, Changi Gaol, where I was informed by the representative of Maj General Shimpei Fukuye, GOC Prisoner of War Camps Malaya, that all Prisoners of War in Changi Camp were to be given forms of promise not to escape, and that all were to be given an opportunity to sign this form.

2. By the Laws and Usages of War a prisoner of war cannot be required by the Power holding him to give his parole, and in our Army those who have become prisoners of war are not permitted to give their parole. I pointed out this position to the Japanese Authorities.

3. I informed the representative of Maj General Shimpei Fukuye that I was not prepared to sign the form, and that I did not consider that any offrs or men in the Changi Camp would be prepared to sign the form. In accordance with the orders of the Japanese Authorities, all prisoners of war were given an opportunity to sign.

   The result of that opportunity is well known.

4. On the 31 Aug I was informed by the Japanese Authorities that those personnel who refused to sign the certificate would be subjected to "measures of severity" and that refusal to sign would be regarded as a direct refusal to obey a regulation which the Imperial Japanese Army considered it necessary to enforce.

5. Later, on the night of the 31 Aug/1 Sep I was warned that on the 1 Sep all prisoners of war persisting in refusal to sign were to move by 1800 hrs to Selerang Barrack Square. I confirmed, both on my own behalf and in the names of the prisoners of war, our refusal to sign.

6. The move to Selerang Barrack Square was sucessfully accomplished on the same afternoon.

7. I and the Area Commds have been in constant conference with the Imperial Japanese Army and have endeavoured by negotiation to have the form either abolished or at least modified. All that I have been able to obtain is that which was originally a demand, accompanied by threats of "measures of severity", has now been issued as an official order of the Imperial Japanese Government.

/ Over.

17. Special Order No. 3, Col. E B Holmes

8. During the period of the occupation of the Selerang Barrack Square the conditions in which we have been placed have been under my constant consideration. These may be briefly described as such that existence therein will result in a very few days in the outbreak of epidemic and the most serious consequences to those under my Command and inevitable death to many. Taking into account the low state of health in which many of us now are, and the need to preserve our force intact. as long as possible, and in the full conviction on that my action were the circumstances in which we are now living known to them, would meet with the approval of His Majesty's Government. I have felt it my duty to order all personnel to sign the certificate under the duress imposed by the Japanese Army.

9. I am fully convinced that His Majesty's Government only expects prisoners of war not to give parole when such parole is to be given voluntarily. This factor can in no circumstances be regarded as applicable to our present condition. The responsibility for this decision rests with me, and with me alone, and I fully accept it in ordering you to sign.

10. I wish to record in this order my deep appreciation of the excellent spirit and good discipline which all ranks have shewn during the trying period.

I look to all ranks to continue in good heart, discipline and morale.

Thank you all for your loyalty and co-operation.

Sgd: E.B.HOLMES. Colonel.
Commanding British and Australian
Troops.
CHANGI.

Selerang.
Sep: 4. 42.

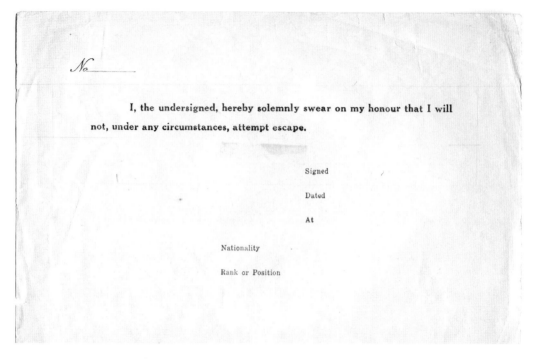

I, the undersigned, hereby solemnly swear on my honour that I will not, under any circumstances, attempt escape.

Signed

Dated

At

Nationality

Rank or Position

18. Submission (we had to sign this form 'under duress' after it was realised that there was a very real danger of widespread disease. Four men who breached the perimeter wire were shot and their execution had to be witnessed by Senior Officers)

17 September
Dress rehearsal of the show last night played to a full house – general opinion seems to be that it's better than *The Dover Road* – the REs have made some first class scenery; the flats are made of tent cloth distempered and modern furniture has either been made or old furniture altered. The general effect is of a modern flat at its best, with a cream-and-red colour scheme. A sapper called Searle whose drawings used to appear in *Lilliput* is their leading light.

My weight is still dropping, down now to 10st 6lbs – I thought I was in for an attack of dysentery as I had acute stomach pains, but these have passed – curse this blasted climate!

19 September
Our opening night of *I Killed the Count* played to a house of 50% officers and was a great success. In spite of a 'Sumatra' which made part of Act I inaudible half way down the hall. General Heath was guest of honour. My part, which is perhaps designed to provide most of the comic relief, went down even better than I could have hoped and the laughter was so prolonged sometimes as to hold up the show. Incidentally my moustache is now à la Charlie Chaplin to fit my part in the play. What a come-down from a pukka cavalry!

SPECIAL ORDER OF THE DAY

BY

LIEUTENANT-COLONEL S.W.HARRIS, O.B.E.,

Commanding 18 Div Area.

    I wish to record my deep appreciation of the splendid behaviour of all ranks during the past seventy-two hours. Your cheerfulness, self-restraint and discipline have been of the highest order. This has been the greatest assistance to me in the negotiations with the Japanese, throughout which I have been in constant touch with the Comd British and Australian troops and the other area comds. On Monday, I will give you personally an account of these negotiations.

    For your wholehearted support I thank you.

5th September, 1942.

Lt.Col.

19. Special Order from Lt Col. S W Harris

20. *I Killed the Count*

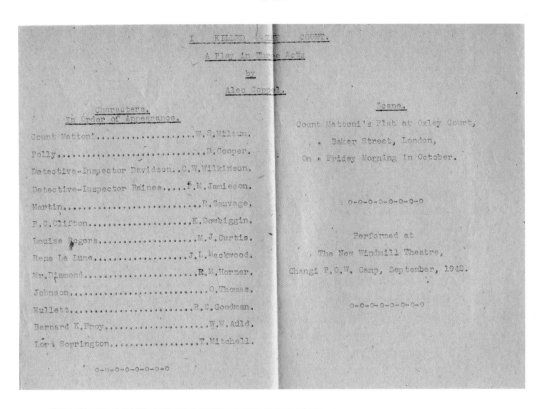

I KILLED THE COUNT.

A Play in Three Acts

by

Alec Coppel.

Characters.
In Order of Appearance.

Count Mattoni	W. S. Milsum.
Polly	D. Cooper.
Detective-Inspector Davidson	C. W. Wilkinson.
Detective-Inspector Raines	F. M. Jamieson.
Martin	R. Sauvage.
P. C. Clifton	K. Dowbiggin.
Louise Rogers	M. J. Curtis.
Rene La Lune	J. L. Meckwood.
Mr. Diamond	E. M. Horner.
Johnson	O. Thomas.
Mullett	R. C. Goodman.
Bernard K. Froy	W. W. Auld.
Lord Sorrington	T. Mitchell.

o-o-o-o-o-o-o-o-o

Scene.

Count Mattoni's Flat at Oxley Court,

Baker Street, London,

On a Friday Morning in October.

o-o-o-o-o-o-o-o

Performed at

The New Windmill Theatre,

Changi P. O. W. Camp, September, 1942.

o-o-o-o-o-o-o-o

As Samuel Diamond in "I Killed the Count"

20a. *I Killed the Count*

21. RMH in *I Killed the Count*

21 September

Have just returned from the South Padang where the 'Rest' beat the Australians by one run 107 to 106. Dick Vaughan behind the stumps got four good wickets. Three stumped and one magnificent catch low down on the off. Colonel Scott, CO of 11 Indian Division. Signals bowled beautifully and got nine wickets for forty. Barnett the Australian Test Match player got seven before being clean bowled by Colonel Scott.

1,000 RAF personnel have arrived in Changi from Java *en route* for Japan or Formosa. I have thirteen officers in this Mess. They've had a pretty lousy time and have all had to have their heads shaved – this is a rule for all the POWs in Java, but thank heavens hasn't been insisted on here.

We understand that all the Red + supplies mentioned on 19 August have been unloaded at Keppel Harbour – the ship was the *Tatuta Maru* and we are told that there may be some mail on the next one. Gosh, how I long for word from home, even a postcard. That is one of the hardest things we have to bear, this complete severance from home. If we were in Germany with parcels and three letters a month things would seem so much better, but not having received a word since we left England, I don't know if Ian is on the way. I shudder to think how many parcels and letters are awaiting collection either in India or the Middle East.

27 September

Harvest Festival Sunday, have just returned from morning service, the sermon was preached by the RAF padre. The church was excellently decorated, palm fronds covered all pillars, pulpit and prayer desk were entwined with flowers and creeper. There were many gifts of fruit, vegetable etc., which will be passed on to the Hospital. The pièce de résistance was a sheaf of wheat made in our Field Bakery. Incidentally, I don't think I've mentioned the Field Bakery before; using six 'Aldershot' ovens they produce bread from a sour dough giving us one slice every ten days.

2 October

Went to a very interesting lecture by Major Burgess, who before the war was a diet specialist in Malaya. Altho' there have been only thirty deaths from beri-beri, there are 1,000 hospital cases and many more being treated in the lines for scrotal dermatitis, sore eyes and tongues, swollen feet etc. He advocates rice polishings (usually used as cattle food and tasting like sawdust), peanuts, towgay, soya beans and whitebait.

3 October

Ration scale cut by Japs today as they say we will be getting extra supplies from the Red + issues, soon to be delivered (we hope!).

5 October

Am suffering from a lot of 'black-outs' these days – dizziness when you get up suddenly or do something quickly. I had this in the early days but it has only recently returned. My weight has gone up to 10st 8lb – I don't want to get a 'rice pod' but some extra flesh is desirable to help combat any disease one might get.

Am feeling homesick after reading several stories with a strong love interest – oh hell I'm fed up with this place! The continual heat and humidity and deficient diet, combine to make one fed to the teeth and a firm hold is necessary not to go downhill as a good many officers have done.

10 October

Red + rations have arrived and are as per list noted on 19 August. At a general Mess meeting of all eighty officers it was decided to hand them all into my keeping with the exception of the cigarettes. They were also very complimentary about my work as PMC which was heartening, altho' as I told them, it's the cooks who produce the food. I don't like scenes like this, they're highly embarrassing.

Owing to the increase in diphtheria we may not be allowed to play *I Killed the Count* to outside areas – incidentally they want me to compère the next show, a revue – won't that be an adventure!

11 October

We have been trying to catch a pet monkey belonging to one of the gunners, without success. Ken Charnock had one for a short time, but found it was too much of a handful to train with so many distractions. There aren't any wild ones here but beyond the Hospital Area there are quite a lot.

15 October

Pay folks has arrived $20, less $5 to messing, how affluent we feel, I'm smoking some Malayan tobacco, in flake form it's not too bad and at 44c per packet of just over 1 ounce I make it go a long way by mixing it with cheroot butts. There is also a fine cigarette tobacco from Java and this mixed in as well helps to swell the whole. One fairly pleasant combination when stocks (and funds) are low is this mixed with dried cherry leaves. In fact this latter was the only tobacco (?) we could get at one time until canteen stocks became available.

The Japanese are taking over control of all canteen purchases; this may mean an increase in prices and certainly no advantages are apparent over the previous method, whereby we went out with a Jap to the Kampongs in the vicinity and bought direct.

My first splash with my pay is as follows: four packets tobacco, thirty cheroots, a wrist-watch strap and a pound of peanuts – bring on the dancing girls!

18 October

I Killed the Count came off last night, Command deciding in their wisdom that we might spread diphtheria if the other areas (AIF, 11 Indian Division and Southern Area) came to our theatre. So now we're going ahead with the production of *Gentlemen Only*, our revue which is to open tomorrow fortnight. I'm not too happy about this compèring job, never having done it before, but my part in the last show having gone over so well, I'm going to have a crack at it.

19 October

Have met an Australian called Bush, who was an announcer in Australia. He knows Uncle Harold slightly.

20 October

Having bother with my eyes, due, the MO tells me, to vitamin deficiency. Several people have come down from Kuala Lumpur, where they were locked up in the gaol when taken prisoner. Padre Duckworth (the old Cambridge cox) is one and he is nearly blind, but this can be cured and a concentration of sources of vitamin B should effect a cure.

21 October

Had Barnett the Australian Test cricketer to supper last night; he had been lecturing to our troops.

24 October

Large party of Dutch and Javanese arrived here yesterday *en route* for Japan or Formosa. A large exodus of troops from Changi is also on the cards, 4,000-odd from 18 Division.

27 October

Some of the Dutch officers are grand fellows, we've had quite a few in the Mess and in fact are shortly moving all British officers to the top floor to give the bottom floor to the Dutch. They've had a pretty gruelling time and some of the stories of their treatment makes 'interesting' hearing.

30 October

Gentlemen Only opened last night; we've advanced the opening so as to play twice nightly to all the personnel going up-country from 18 Division. I'm told my compèring was a success – I felt a momentary qualm when first face to face with the audience but soon gained confidence. Sang my old favourite, Leonard Henry's 'Ah' song with suitable adjustments to conform with the surroundings.

22/23. *Gentlemen Only,*
plus inside programme

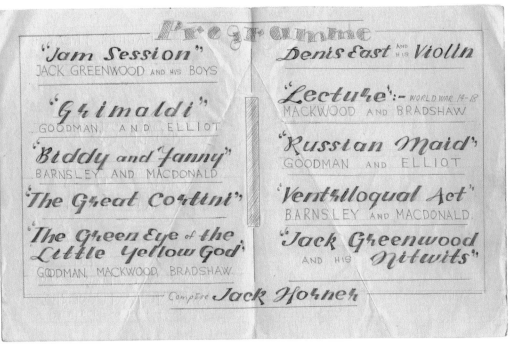

31 October

Bill Cowell is going up-country – he hasn't been 'yessing' well enough! Hell's bells these senior officers are bum, the whole bloody lot of them; the more I see of them the less respect I have.

4 November

Having played *Gentlemen Only* to all those going up-country twice nightly (including Sunday) we opened last night to the rest of the Division with a pukka 'first night'. Colonel Harris the Area Commander made an opening speech in appreciation of our efforts and the whole show went with a bang.

I don't think I've mentioned that we have a Dutch illusionist included in the programme; he has got together several illusions with the aid of our sappers and with material he brought with him he puts on an entertaining turn. Named Cortini, he's a nephew of Houdini.

8 November

Last night was great night at the show, General Heath, 'Black Jack' GOC, AIF and Major Horryin of the American Air Force were guests of honour. The latter is a charming fellow and after a series of misfortunes was taken prisoner in Java.

These birds of interest seen lately: the golden oriel, kingfisher and woodpeckers. There are always a lot of chattering Minahs around and also bee-catchers with their long bills.

An interesting caterpillar that later turns into a moth is the Cadis – it makes as it grows, from the bark of trees, a cone-shaped shell in which it lies – you see these cones, anything up to an inch in length, sticking out from palm trees. If you pull them sharply the grub is left on the tree and the crust comes away. I did this to one and, poor fellow, before you could say 'Knife' red ants that infest all palm trees, had set on him and settled his account in a matter of seconds.

Incidentally I'll always laugh at photos of Dorothy Lamour and Co., in their sarongs reclining amorously against palm trees – they contain far too many ants and bugs to make this possible and could only be done in a studio or on plantations that had been specially treated.

9 November

The New Windmill Theatre has been closed on medical grounds; it's a farce really as units who live and sleep in close proximity in their billets are no more likely to spread infection when in a theatre, but there it is, orders are orders and altho' Colonel Harris argued with Colonel Holmes for an hour, the latter was insistent. The great tragedy of this is that we had in this theatre, been able to reproduce a pukka theatre atmosphere and people could forget for a couple of hours that they were POWs – In open air shows or even in huts, the atmosphere cannot be obtained and altho' shows may not be any the worse, the psychological effect is not the same.

Some of the Dutch officers came in to see me about one of my jokes in the show – they were very perturbed. However I knew what I was risking and had everything well in hand. Some say! More anon. [*I spent the show wearing white shirt, black tie, long johns and a woman's négligé. I did a twirl and had the Jap flag sewn to the seat of my long johns. I called it 'My target for tonight'. To ensure no Nips were about I had someone posted at both entrances of the building.*]

12 November
Attended the funeral today of Colonel Welch, who, in the old Norfolk days of 1940 was Jack Feather's batman. He died after a bout of dysentery had pulled him down. I am very sad to see his passing, particularly as I know his wife and know that their first child was born either just before or after our embarkation.

14 November
I don't think I'll ever bother if I'm bitten by fleas in England – here, everything seems infested with bugs. Every chair, desk, form, table, has its quota, and it is literally impossible to sit in comfort for any length of time.

17 November
Spent a most enjoyable evening last night – two Dutchmen came in, one to do sleight of hand and conjuring tricks; the other, thought-reading. The latter was quite amazing. He'd go outside with one of us to see that there was no eavesdropping and those remaining would decide on something for him to do – for example one of the tests was to take a pack of cards from a shelf. Take out one of the black ones and give it to Colonel Hingston – he was then to go back to the pack, pick out the other black one, go to Colonel Rossall, pull off his left shoe, put the card in, replace and tie up the shoe. He did all this without much trouble. His method is to have a 'medium' from us who holds his right wrist with the right hand, placing each one's forefinger on the pulse. The 'medium' has to concentrate on what action the thought-reader is to do and the results were staggering. I acted as 'medium' on one occasion and obtained the correct result. It was quite amazing feeling him respond to your thoughts, just as if you'd spoken to him.

20 November
Watched a battle royal today between 500 termites and hundreds of 'garden' ants. The termites had found their way into a malarial drain and either due to their blindness, or because the sides were too steep and they were unable to scale them, they failed to find an outlet. The ants spotted them and came in their hundreds to do battle. The termites would be attacked by the ants, bowled over and carried up for transportation to the ants' nest. The 'worker' termites are at a complete disadvantage being blind and having no means of defence – the 'soldiers' however accounted for quite a lot of ants before succumbing, one nip of their pincers being enough to cut the ants in half. In just over an hour, there were no live termites, but

Compèreing "Gentlemen Only" – New Windmill Theatre Nov. '42

24. RMH 'Jap Flag'

perhaps it was poetic justice that just as this occurred a 'Sumatra' turned the dry drain into a raging torrent of water and certainly none of the decimated termites would reach their intended destination and in all probability lots of the ants would be drowned – such is the way of the world! I feel that this perfectly true story has a moral; certainly it can be likened to the nations of the world.

I'm producing a 'Road Show' to play to British and Dutch troops on alternate nights in a theatre that Cortini has fixed up in the Dutch lines – I will compère and a Dutch 'conferencier' their nights – as so few of the Divisions have heard the 'Ah' song, I'm doing that on British and Dutch nights. We open on Monday.

1810hrs: Have just been asked to compère a show got up in the Lines, a variety show of British and Dutch artistes – I'm going to have a job to think up gags in time! 1945hrs Word has just come through that our GOC Major General MB Beckwith-Smith, better known to us as 'Becky', has died at the POW camp Tai Wan (Formosa) of diphtheria. He was a loveable man and we all feel his death very deeply – he had a great capacity for understanding men and we all felt that in this campaign he had a pretty raw deal. We wonder whether to cancel this evening's show, but as it will disappoint so many and 'Becky' would be the last man to want any cancellation, we've decided to carry on.

21 November
Played to a packed and highly enthusiastic audience last night; it is estimated there were at least 1,500 there. I made a preliminary announcement regarding 'Becky's' death and how we felt it would have been his wish for the show to go on. The show went with a bang and I'm told my part was a success. I included *Sam's Medal* and *The Schoolhouse at Runcorn* amongst other things. I last did them in 1937.

22 November
Have just attended a memorial service to 'Becky', held on India Lines Padang; it was most impressive. We feel that we have all lost a loved friend in the passing of 'Becky'.

24 November
Road Show opened last night – the 'Ah' song went down well with the Dutch who were our first audience and having learned one or two Dutch 'gags' was able to get them to do what I wanted.

25 November
A few facts of interest ref. Japan, gleaned from several books I've been reading on the subject lately: Admiral Perry the American sowed the seeds of their revival in 1853 when he sailed into Tokyo Bay and brought the outside world home to them. Before that the penalty for anyone who built a boat over 100 tons, was death. The Meiji Restoration followed in 1868 when the Chosu clan formed the army and the Satsuma clan the navy, thereby starting a rivalry that has continued to this day.

On New Year's day rice straws and orange blossom are hung in the entrance to your house to denote purification – a lobster denotes long life, whilst cherry blossom is always associated with the soldier, as they die in full bloom! Kokutai – the body and spirit of the nation – Shakai Taishuto – Social Mass Party – Bushido – the way of the warrior. Most soldiers carry in their caps a piece of material with stitches in it, from as many friends and relations as possible – it's supposed to act as a talisman of protection.

Have been reading John Buchan's *Mr. Standfast* and in it that grand character of his Peter Pienaar, a prisoner of war in Germany is writing back to England to his friend Dick Hannay on the question of courage – I find that one paragraph could well serve as our guiding light here during the present time when freedom seems at times so very far away. 'But the big courage is the cold-blooded kind, the kind that never lets go even when you're empty inside, and your blood's thin, and there's no kind of fun or profit to be had, and the trouble's not over in an hour or two but lasts for months and years'.

One of the men here was speaking about that kind, and he called it 'Fortitude'. I reckon fortitude's the biggest thing a man can have – just to go on enduring when there's no guts or heart left in you.

29 November

Saw an interesting sight today; a body of red ants had killed a snake of about 2ft in length. They wanted to get it up a palm tree at the top of which was their nest. They carted it about four yards to the edge of a malarial drain and then realised that it was too steep, so they dragged it up a post that was nearby and which was attached to their tree by wire. By clinging to the wire with their back legs and holding on to the snake with pincers and fore-legs, they traversed the wire, very slowly, up the tree and so home.

Their team work was excellent, they even pushed it through a loop in the wire that was in their way and never once did they lose their grip.

The same 'family' of ants discovered and killed shortly afterwards a 5in long centipede; for some reason they decided not to carry this up – they gorged themselves sick and then carried chunks off to the nest. They really are most fascinating creatures to watch.

25. Drawing of ants

6 December

St Nicholas' Day – kept by the Dutch as a children's festival with Santa Claus etc. We had a combined service with them, attended by Santa Claus who had previously inspected their meals (extra special ones). After the service they had a social to the accompaniment of music by our band (arranged by me).

In the afternoon listened to a most interesting lecture by 'Ducky' on his boat racing experiences – as he coxed Cambridge to victory three years in succession. Funnily enough in 11 Indian Division Signals is Paul Burrows, who stroked Oxford to victory the two years following 'Ducky's' reign – he's a charming chap and is I believe, also going into the Church.

In the evening, put on a variety show at the hospital Sergeants' Mess; I acted as compère. Unfortunately torrential rain, which incidentally has been falling all day, rather spoiled the show as hearing was difficult.

10 December

The heavy rain mentioned in the last entry has persisted and we have now had five days' solid downpour. December is the heaviest rainfall in Malaya, but inhabitants say a continuous downpour like this is most unusual. Everything you touch is damp and humidity is terrific, altho' the temperature is comparatively low (about 70°).

13 December

Am putting on and compèring a variety show to open the new RASC open air theatre the 'Kokonut Grove'. Built out from their Mess room, it is an excellent stage with fair room in the flies and wings and with the Mess Room behind as dressing room.

14 December

Show went with a bang last night, about 1,500 people saw it and were most enthusiastic. I've written and composed a song called 'When We're Free' which I got them to sing. Ronald Searle wrote the words on stretched canvas so that they could be read and sung by the audience – it went down so well that I had to give it to them again. Another item that went down well was a poem I made up when at Felsted written after the style of Studdert Kennedy's *Rough Rhymes of a Padre*.

When we're free yes, when we're free
O how happy we shall be.
When we see the last of Changi tree
Oh what a wonderful day for you and me.
As we sail away o'er the ocean blue
The palm and rubber trees fade from view
Then give three cheers and one cheer more
For we'll have seen the last of Singapore

[This poem I composed when we were first all jammed into Changi Gaol. I produced the first show with combined Australian and British performers. I had many requests for copies – including 'Black Jack' CO of the Australians – and was told a padre used it as a basis for a sermon. What price fame?!! In 1942 the Allies had the tree referred to be cut down as they believed it would be a marker for the Japs. I still have an ashtray that was made out of the tree at the time. I have absolutely no recollection of the poem I made up at Felsted – rather odd really.]

16 December
My Road Show at the Cortini Theatre ends on Thursday. I won't be sorry, I've had quite a lot of bother with Cortini and also with one or two of our own fellows who had been trying a temperamental act.

20 December
We are putting on *Gentlemen Only* at the new Hospital Theatre 'The Palladium' for hospital walking patients and staff and later for British troops who are returning to Changi from Singapore camps in the near future. The theatre was a cinema that had been knocked about by bombs. It has an excellent stage and has now been completely re-decorated and rewired and is first class. The floor is sloping, so, whether sitting on the floor or forms, everyone will be able to see.

21 December
Have just been to see the 18 Division's Toy Exhibition, toys made in the camp for the sixty-odd children in Changi Gaol. It was an amazing assortment and some really first class toys have been produced.

There are 1,000-odd civilian internees in the gaol, separated by sexes and not even allowed to meet even tho' husband and wife. These toys are our contribution to try and brighten the Xmas for them, AIF and other areas have also made some. The AIF have produced a panto. And I had arranged to take the band up to play carols and nursery rhymes, but the Japs have refused permission for both of these, altho' they have allowed the toys. What a hellish start in life for these children whose ages range from a few months to the later teens.

22 December
The IJA have intimated that there will be no further issues of meat; fish is to be issued instead. Up till now we've been having about 6 ounces twice a week. Owing to the climate it will be impossible to keep the fish overnight, so messing looks like being a tricky job – who wants my job of Messing Officer?!

25 December
Xmas Day, yet another away from my loved ones, and a day when one's thoughts are nearer home than possibly on any other.

Last night there was a serious concert on the padang in front of the Mess with carols – this evening I have been asked to arrange a fun and games show with com-

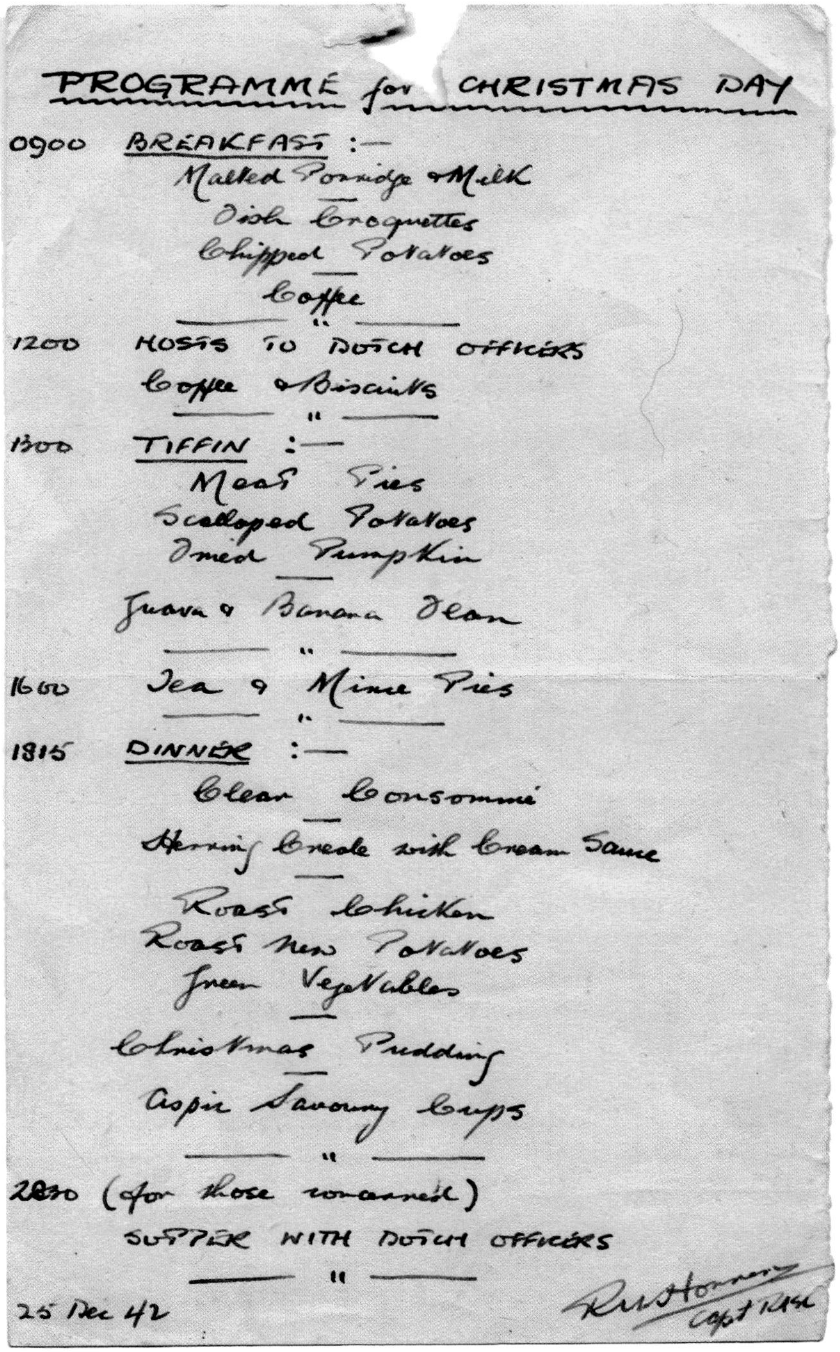

PROGRAMME *for* CHRISTMAS DAY

0900   BREAKFAST :—
          Malted Porridge & Milk
          Dish Croquettes
          Chipped Potatoes
          Coffee
          "
1200   HOSTS TO DUTCH OFFICERS
          Coffee & Biscuits
          "
1300   TIFFIN :—
          Meat Pies
          Scalloped Potatoes
          Dried Pumpkin

          Guava & Banana Flan
          ————— " —————
1600   Tea & Mince Pies
          "
1815   DINNER :—
          Clear Consommé

          Herring Creole with Cream Sauce

          Roast Chicken
          Roast New Potatoes
          Green Vegetables

          Christmas Pudding

          Aspic Savoury Cups
          ————— " —————
2030   (for those concerned)
          SUPPER WITH DUTCH OFFICERS
          ————— " —————
25 Dec 42   R.W.Honner
                                    Capt. R.A.S.C.

26. Programme for Christmas Day

munity singing to finish up with. There was a crowd of at least 2,000 last night. Our programme for the officers today is as follows (as PMC this is my job to arrange): 1200hrs we entertain the Dutch officers to coffee and biscuits (with the band to provide music). All our meals are extra special for the occasion and in the evening we join the Dutch officers downstairs in supper.

Our meals for the day are as follows:

Breakfast :	malted porridge with milk and sugar, fish croquettes and chips
Tiffin :	meat pies, scalloped sweet potatoes and fried pumpkin : guava and banana flan
Tea :	tea with milk and sugar, hot mince pies (made with white flour and mincemeat)
Dinner :	clear consomme, herring creole with cream sauce, roast chicken with roast new potatoes and greens, Xmas pudding and aspic savoury cups

With homemade wine as well. I don't think they'll be doing too badly for a POW camp, definitely a riceless day!

26 December

The meals went down well yesterday and have been much appreciated. The supper with the Dutch was a convivial affair, but hardly worth the 75c we all paid – soup, a bully sandwich and a sweet of coconut and pineapple juice. My show on the padang, seen by, it is reckoned, something like 3,500 was an immense success – the community singing, which I conducted, was terrific and left a lot of hoarse voices in its wake. I was quite exhausted at the end: it was some job controlling so many, but I couldn't have wished for a more enthusiastic audience.

Have just heard that Mike Kennan died this morning, he was OC over 55 Company. He had been in hospital for several months with diphtheric ulcers. His funeral is this afternoon; in the tropics they have to follow very quickly.

1800hrs: Have a very heavy cold that developed during the evening following last night's show on the padang and has not been helped by heavy rain falling during Mike Kennan's funeral after we had paraded in sunshine (and therefore no raincoats). Hope I get through tonight's performance of *Gentlemen Only* OK.

Denis Pearl has arrived back from Singapore, I've already mentioned that all working parties down there have had to return. I'm delighted to have him back; we spent a lot of time together during the battle and shared everything we had with one another in the early days up here when things were pretty bad.

31 December

The year 1942 is rapidly drawing to its close. In view of the fact that it clashes with some Jap festival, they have sent up some tinned pineapple and wog-made brandy. Three-and-a-half men to one tin of pineapple and ten to one bottle of brandy.

1943

2 January
GSO 2 (ops) at Command, GSO 2 AIF and the Red + representative have been arrested by the Japs. This latter is the most serious, as if he has been abusing such privileges as he had, he is our only contact with civilians for buying drugs and medical stores and that may now cease.

3 January
All Sikh Guards removed! Interesting lecture by Australian CSM who had been through first Libyan campaign and later our push into Syria.

4 January
Not feeling too good these days, have noticed the pinch since our Red + supplies ran out, a diet mainly consisting of fish and rice is hardly sustaining, particularly when the former is mostly dried, fresh coming in in very small quantities making a small issue of 2 ounces-odd every three or four days.

My weight is 10st 4lbs and my eyes and mouth are sore, both signs of vitamin deficiency. Doc. has put me on Palm oil and Rice Polishings! (lousy, both of them).

7 January
We get an amazing variety of fish in our issues these days, a cannibal fish that has sometimes as many as three smaller fish inside when cut open, blue nose and hammer head sharks (a shark's flesh is quite pleasant altho' rather strong), and sting rays of varying sizes and mud fish with fierce whiskers.

9 January
Sale of Mike Kennan's effects today, fetched £102 – payable by cheque on your home bank. I bought five pairs of socks for £2.6.0. payable at Cox's and King's after the war – seems a high price but my own are in a poor way and none are obtainable. One lot of four tins bully, one tin milk and one tin oval sardines went for £5.11.0. Such are values in a POW camp!

10 January
All the Dutch officers below here are leaving for overseas with the exception of four. These, together with nine Australians who arrived earlier this week, are coming to mess with us.

13 January
Saw the AIF panto *Cinderella* today that was intended for the children, for our troops returned from Singapore and the Australians who've just arrived from Java.

19 January
Heard a lecture today by Major Hunt AIF on diet – extremely good but not exactly heartening. He was speaking for the research departments of both British and Australian Medical Staffs, and stressed the need for rice polishings and various vitamin sources, all of which are now becoming hard to get.

In fact the food situation is extremely serious; we are definitely not getting sufficient to live on from the Japs and even with the supplements from the canteen with such items as dried prawns, and herring and whitebait, soya beans and towgay, peanuts and palm oil – our daily meals always have one feeling hungry. I used to revel in my new-found slimness, but am not very happy about my continued decrease (now below 10st 4lbs) in weight. It is not that I feel ill, but any real effort I find quickly tires me, and if I get up suddenly from a chair I get 'blackouts' – added to which I feel I ought to have more flesh on me in case of dysentery or malaria – however, there are troops much worse than I am; some are walking skeletons and many have deficiency diseases of the skin which make my own sore eyes and mouth paltry by comparison.

20 January
Concluded *Gentlemen Only* last night after fifty-odd performances, I wasn't sorry. On Monday I'm producing a Roadshow at the Kokonut Grove in India Lines, which is to run for a fortnight. After that I intend to give these shows a rest; I've been at it since the middle of September and feel that I need a rest.

22 January
Tomorrow from 0930–1300hrs we all have to be in our billets, all tent flaps have to be drawn and blankets put over any doors in the atap huts etc. – some high ranking personage of the IJA is inspecting the area. Some say! A request has been made to the Japs (i) that we should be allowed further facilities for writing home (ii) That the censorship of the letters from home that we understand have arrived in Singapore, should be accelerated (iii) that the rations should be increased so that a balanced ration that would obviate vitamin deficiencies could be arrived at, and (iv) that further Red + supplies should be allowed. We are told that all these have been answered in the negative, but hope that they may set the wheels moving! I am finding mess catering one helluva job these days; it's such a job to keep a varied menu day after day.

23 January
Am putting on a show for 'U' ward in the hospital this evening – they are all suffering from eye-trouble due to vitamin deficiency and consequently live all day under shaded blue lights.

26 January
First night of my new show at the Kokonut Grove last evening – the show went very well and it is reckoned by some as being the best show yet.

J A C K   H O R N E R

P r e s e n t s

"R O A D   S H O W   N O. 3".

1. Jack Greenwood & His Swingtette....
            "Jam Session".

2. Joe Bernstein (Tenor)...............
            "One Night of Love".
            "Rose Marie".

3. Sketch - "Happy Event"..............
                    Rich Goodman ,
            Hugh Eliot, Aubrey King.

4. Changi Carpentry...'Wimpy' Walpole,
                    and Partner.

5. Gypsy Trio............Gil Mitchell,
            Eric Fowler, Jack Jackson.

6. The Changi Nightingale.

7. Two Roving Reporters................,
            Rich Goodman, Hugh Eliot.

8. Jack Greenwood & His Nitwits.......
            "Sweet & Hot".

o-o-o-o-o-o-o-o-o

Performed at

The Kokonut Grove Theatre,

India Lines, Changi

P.O.W. Camp, Jan.1943.

o-o-o-o-o

Produced & Compered by........

J A C K   H O R N E R.

o-o-o-o-o

27/28. *Road Show*, plus inside programme

Subject.   Visit by "A certain High Officer" of the I.J.A.   No 1 Rln.

The following instructions are now issued in extension of those already issued verbally.

1.   The Comd No 1 POW Camp Changi calls upon all ranks to comply with the instructions strictly, so as to avoid all incidents in connection with this visit. It is most important at present that no incidents shall occur.

2.   An I.J.A. Officer will drive round the area at 0930 hrs by which time all personnel, including police, gate guards and cooks will be indoors out of sight. The sole exception to this order is the Comd Gardent party to which separate instructions have been given direct.

3.   All personnel will remain out of sight indoors from 0930 hrs until 1300 hrs

4.   All windows with a view of any roads however distant will be closed. There will be no peering out of windows or from verandahs or balconies, or from ground floor doorways and tents.

5.   Tent flaps will be secured so that the interior of the tent is invisible from any road however distant.

6.   No open cookhouse will be occupied or used during the period, only those cookhouses may be used which are properly built-in structures forming an intregal part of the quarters to which they are attached, and from xxxxxxxxx which movement cannot be seen from the outside.

7.   There will be no movement to and from latrines or urinals during the period.

8.   No movement whatever will take place on the roads or between buildings whithin the Camp area during the above period.

9.   RA Gp Only. Shops adjacent to the Singapore gate will be evacuated for the period.

10 . There are certain to be many Japanese Patrols in operation in the area, and it is again impressed on all ranks that at the present moment it is most important that all incidents should be avoided. As these patrols may be expectee to go through huts barracks and tents, all ranks are warned to be on the alert, as these patrols must be saluted in accordance with normal rules.

11. The I.J.A. have stressed the necessity for the adherance of the above instructions by recently arrived Java Parties, and mentioned in particular the Java Party 9B in its present camp which is clearly visible from the road.

sgd. F.J. DILLON

CHANGI
22 Jan 43.

29. Orders re. visit by Jap Official

I haven't mentioned before that my participation and production of shows as Jack Horner has got me known by this title all over the camp – it is embarrassing sometimes as troops sing out 'Morning Jack' when they see you in the distance and to keep discipline one has to pretend not to hear. In this show I introduce myself to the tune of Arthur Askey's 'Little Jack Horner they call me, little Jack Horner that's me' and so on to some words I've made up. What fun!

31 January
Didn't have a show last night as a Race Meeting was organised on the padang. A large course (made of bamboos) laid down, human horses etc., etc., a 'tote' very realistically made by the Sappers – very good fun.

3 February
Very excited, we are allowed to send wireless messages to Australia; I have cabled Uncle Harold at the Australian Broadcasting Commission 'Feathers and I both fit and well, don't worry, love to you, Frank and all at St Albans' – thereby overcoming the ban that no requests are to be made to forward information onto England.

5 February
Have a slight attack of dengue fever and find it hard to keep merry and bright in my Road Show each night, which as compère and producer keeps me on the go all evening. I've promised to take a modified version of it over to the AIF in the hospital to play to their staff and walking patients. Tomorrow we all have a dysentery test by the Japs which consists of having a glass rod shoved up your bottom and a slide made.

7 February
Successfully lost my virginity to the Japs yesterday – I was lucky in only having a small glass rod used – some were colossal!

8 February
My show to the hospital AIF last night was a terrific success. They crammed nearly a thousand in and around their Mess room (a former gym) and were tremendously enthusiastic.

My 'When we're Free' song has become quite a hit and it is a common occurrence to hear it being sung around the camp – such is fame!

11 February
Two rather amusing incidents that occurred in Singapore soon after our working parties went down there: The first, when an issue of peanuts was made to counteract vitamin B deficiency which was largely responsible for the prevalence of Singapore foot – one fellow complained that he found them most uncomfortable, he'd got them in his boots! And then there was the fellow who had ringworm on his chest and on being given a jar of marmite to take, spread it on the affected place!

30. Injection (From the sublime to the ridiculous! Just before the senior officers departed for Formosa, we had the first attack on our virginity! This drawing was copied from a mural done by an unknown artist which so impressed me that I felt I had to try to retain it for posterity or should I say 'posterior?!!)

13 February
After two false starts we today paraded, 15,000-strong for some propaganda film the Japs are making. I never was a lover of pantomimes and this five-hour effort in rain and mud did nothing to alter my views.

15 February
Went to 11 Indian Division last night as guest of the Gurkhas – they are moving to Southern Area and all wood-felling and gardening personnel are moving into theirs. Several members of the AIF Concert Party gave a show and altogether it was quite a jolly gathering.

We have now been POWs for twelve months – I wish I could feel that things had improved 100% – as long as we had Red + supplies we were OK, but now things are pretty desperate again and there seems no hope of extra supplies anyhow in the near future. It would appear that the Red + representative Roberts, who, as I mentioned on 2 January was arrested by the Japs, has, by his behaviour, not only prejudiced our chances in that direction, but also has cut off the only supply of drugs etc., for the hospital which is far more serious – still, while there's life there's hope, or does that sound too depressing?

I don't think that we'll die of starvation, altho' in all conscience the diet has little to provide real sustenance, but I do think that we'll gradually get lower in health and will have little or nothing with which to combat any serious disease.

W.C.WILDER. JAN 20 1943
P.O.W CAMP CHANGI SINGAPORE

31. RMH, by W C Wilder

17 February

Rice issue reduced from nineteen ounces per man per day to fifteen-and-a half ounces – of this we eat about half, boiled as 'padding' and the rest made into buns, rissoles, fried bases, pasties etc.

Met an officer last night in 21 Gurkhas called Skene, is marked No. 4 in world's polo players. We were all going to see the AIF's latest concert at Selerang.

20 February

A German raider has put in here with Greek, British and American prisoners on board, survivors from boats sunk by her. The Japs have refused to take off the first named as they say they're not at war with Greece, but the British and Americans are now up here – in fact the British skipper and company with the American officers are below us in the Mess here; they've been able to give us some idea of the conditions in England as late as last September, and their description of the Raider and its methods is very interesting.

Had another Race Meeting on the padang last night; I was roped in to do a running commentary, but found it uphill work with such comparatively slow action.

23 February

Amongst the prisoners from the German raider mentioned above is a twelve year old cabin boy. The Raider, called the *Michel* was a converted 10,000 ton cargo vessel with two seaplanes, two MTB and innumerable concealed guns, as well as torpedo tubes.

28 February

Have been very busy lately organising an 18 Divison Area Saw Mill where we intend to saw all the wood for the troops in our area into choppable sizes – this means something like forty five tons a week. Up till now we have issued small sizes by scale and roots and large tree trunks by guess-weight, this new method will mean that we will be able to weigh all the wood we issue and so save any waste.

1 March

Sawmill started in grand style and we are already ahead of schedule. I have asked to be relieved of the job of PMC of this Mess, I've held the job for ten months and feel that I've had enough, apart from the fact that this sawmill will not give me any time to spare on running the Mess as well.

6 March

5,000 British and AIF going up-country, 1,800 of which are to be found by 18 Division.

2215hrs Colonel Hingston has just come into the Mess and congratulated me on the birth of my son and heir Ian – what a delightful surprise and thrill when I didn't even know for certain that he was on the way. For the last two days Major Agnew and the postal unit staff have been sorting mail at the gaol and 'Aggie' spotted a postcard telling me the gladsome news. I hope my Flossie's OK, but rather gather he'd have told me had the postcard had anything on it to the contrary. Poor darling, what a worrying time; in July she wouldn't know definitely what my fate was.

In a way and purely from a selfish viewpoint, it was rather nice hearing of Ian's arrival without any worry or anxiety, but as that means I hadn't heard a word since leaving England, I think the scales tip in favour of the latter. Boy oh boy, am I excited! Paul Wadsley has also heard that there's a postcard for him with similar news, this is his first and he had been worrying about it as he knew it was on the way.

11 March
Joy oh joy, mail from home, letters from Flossie and Mother and postcard from Frank – this being presumably the one that had been spotted on the 6th. What a grand sensation and thrill these letters have given us – life takes on a different aspect. It is hard to realise that they have taken eight months to arrive, but never could they have a greater welcome than now. The letters were dated the 16th, the date of the publication of the official address and the postcard telling of Flossie's and Ian's return to 'Field House' the 21st. [*Frank was my father and Dot was my mother.*]

16 March
Saw an interesting demonstration this evening by a half-caste Dutch soldier of the art of hypnotism. With the AMS and our own MO to test the fellow who was 'under', there was no doubt of its authenticity.

17 March
Letters from Flossie and Frank dated 10th and 14th respectively, how I love getting them. Dick has had seven and several other officers five and six; Denis Pearl and Jack Feathers so far have been unlucky.

18 March
Adrian Hedley (Captain AE Hedley MBE, MC, and RNF) was badly beaten up by a Jap corporal today for the 'crime' of trying to interpret what the Jap was saying. I don't know whether I've mentioned that failure to salute any Jap private (altho' the orders state only armed patrols and cars flying flags must be saluted) is likely to earn face slapping, kicking etc., in return. I have seen some really bad beating ups for no reason at all and remembering that he's at the right end of the rifle, there's nothing we can do about it.

A newly appointed Red + representative has been able to get $40,000 for hospital supplies from the International Red +; those were sorely needed, as since Roberts was arrested, none have been obtainable.

19 March
Terrific thrill; five of us bought and shared a tin of M&V for $1.20, gosh how good the meat tasted! With it we had a slice of maize and sago flour bread that is now being turned out at the Field Bakery – a good time was had by all!

21 March

Brian Milnes who is officer in charge the up-country RASC party, left today with 150 men.

23 March

Started rehearsals today for the reproduction of *I Killed the Count* which opens at the Hospital Palladium on April 10th. I find I still remember all my part in spite of 'Singapore Memory'.

25 March

Dined last evening in the Gurkha Mess at Southern Area and afterwards saw the Temple Hill Players' presentation of *Androcles and the Lion*.

26 March

A letter from Frank written on July 6th giving news of Ian who was born that day. Gosh how I agree with his wish to be home again; it was grand seeing Bis' initials written by herself and her very own squiggle. That now gives me writing by all of them, always excepting of course wee Ian! This looks like being the last of the letters for the time being.

A board has been set up to receive items of general interest from letters received and a bulletin is issued which makes interesting reading, even tho' we know full well that it is eight months old.

28 March

The sappers in the Mess have made a still and concoct an excellent cocktail every Sunday of the pure alcohol flavoured with lime. An egg-cup full is quite enough to give you a warm glow inside.

Last night I went with the Gurkhas to see the AIF Concert Party. George Booker and I go with their party to each of their new shows and very good they are too.

29 March

Have just tasted some 'millionaire's breakfast' – so named, because it is the heart of the palm tree at its top and from which all the fronds and coconuts emanate – when cut off the tree dies and is therefore an expensive luxury. I found it very pleasant without having a particularly characteristic flavour.

2 April

A lot of cases of scabies, there is unfortunately not very much in the camp with which to cure this. My jolly old eyes are getting pretty groggy, altho' nowhere near as bad as some people's. I can still read for short spells at a time; quite a large number of both officers and men can't read at all. One thing that has been worrying me lately is a clicking in my head when I walk, so far the MO can't tell what is wrong, altho' I have traced it to a vein (?) at the base of the skull. Hey ho, the usual verdict of rice polishings and keep out of the sun! Still I don't like that sort of thing, you wonder just where it's going to end.

3 April
The Dutch have started a restaurant and several kinds of fried dishes for quite reasonable prices. This has fired the RASC canteen to do the same and it is now possible to get fried fish rissole, chips and fried bread for 13c. The food lately owing to lack of supplies has been very poor and a spot extra in the evening helps a lot.

4 April
As well as the restaurants mentioned above, two Dutch boys make daily an extract from soya beans. In the form of milk (it smells like paint and its taste is little better) it is said by the MOs to contain all the vitamins contained in the bean, so is well worth the 4c per cup that it costs.

Dick Vaughan and I are reading the lessons at church this evening; I have the parable of the prodigal son from St Luke for my little piece. This evening service is always very well attended and very popular. I will always associate the hymn 'The day Thou gavest Lord is ended' with this, as it always concluded the service as does 'God be in My Head' always follow the 'Blessing'. St George's has just had a new altar installed made by the sappers, it is in fact very well equipped with pulpit, prayer desk, altar rails all made in the area by first class craftsmen.

9 April
7,000-odd British and AIF going up-country. 18 Division's HQ are to go in an administrative capacity, 'They have seen the light!' I am left in charge here of 100-odd RASC personnel. Denis is staying; also Eric Poulter, Bill Ireland and George Booker. Actually this area is closing down and all remaining personnel are moving to the old 11 India Division area in Selerang – It'll make a change anyway! We're told there are twenty more mail bags arrived from England – Whacko!!

11 April
Opened *I Killed the Count* at the Palladium last night to a most enthusiastic audience.

13 April
We have killed all our Mess cockerels bar one and have just finished our evening meal. After a diet consisting of rice and vegetables with occasionally a little fish (even dried fish hasn't been available lately) issued, the roast chicken just consumed was a terrific thrill.

17 April
Killed all our drakes and had a grand feed last night. Have got a postcard from Frank dated 18 June '43, ten months for delivery! It seems difficult to believe that so long has elapsed between time of posting and time of delivery.

Great fun and games, Divisional HQ wanted to go on the early trains with the 18 Division Personnel on the up-country party – the Japs have said the AIF will go first and 18 Division last.

18 April

A letter from Frank last night dated 8 August '42. They still have no news of us. I only wish we were able to write more often ourselves, two postcards in fourteen months of captivity is almost the last word; that is what makes us all feel so very cut off from our loved ones, and they must feel us just as far away – a monthly letter service would keep one in touch and make you feel that you weren't so far away.

Later – Rumours of more mail bags, but so far only rumours.

20 April

A postcard from Dot last night – so Uncle Sidney has married again. As the Aussies would say 'Whacko, good on you son!'

The Dutch at the Restaurant do some excellent 'Sweet Balls' made of sago and maize flour with a filling gula malacca, they're like a small doughnut and at 3c each are grand.

23 April

Another postcard from Frank and a letter from my darling. There are disturbing stories going round that the postcard we wrote during the early part of March haven't yet left the gaol – oh hell I hope it's not true, altho' now that I know Uncle Harold is in touch with home I've great hopes of my wireless message getting back.

25 April

All the 18 Division's Personnel have now left for 'up-country', saw Jack Feathers and company off at 0400hrs this morning and am now sorting out the remains, actually three officers and 122 OR's including those in hospital. Had the unpleasant job of picking four men to proceed on a working party, destination believed to be Borneo, who had been reserves for the 'up-country' party and had therefore had inoculations and dysentery inspections etc. As their lot may be a hard one, I hated having to pick any particular men, but it had to be done. We move to the G & W Area on Friday.

2 May

Since the last entry I've been having a pretty hectic time. The G & W Area is on the opposite side of the Changi Road., to Selerang and is a mile from India Lines with a long hill to climb in the bargain.

All our kit and equipment had to be manhandled on trailers (the car and lorry chassis that I have mentioned previously) and it has been one helluva job. Still we're all in now. Denis and I have a small room about 14ft x 8ft and are quite comfortable. The hut has an attap roof that seems to be weatherproof (we hope!). The men are pretty crowded at the moment, but as there is to be a further party of 3,000 going away, of which I have to find 50, the few crocks remaining will have space to spare – that is if we still remain in this area.

3 May
The Japs loaned us a lorry to bring up certain heavy items from our old area – I was in charge and got up a good load of RE stores, the field bakery and we towed a water trailer – no' so bad!

Terrific rumours of forthcoming moves, one says 500 officers to Japan, another says 3,500 for up-country – the Command interpreter whom I saw this morning reckons that after this 3,000 there won't be any more for some time and this is rather borne out by a re-adjustment to the wiring which now takes in Selerang and this area, the command area around the Gun Park and the hospital – time will tell!

5 May
Big 'bore-hole' (rumour) that 700 officers and 300 men are to proceed overseas – it seems to bear the stamp of authenticity, but there are no definite orders. Actually, when this next party leaves this week there are not enough fit men left to carry on the essential details, wood-cutting, and sawing, trailer parties etc.

Without the extra food we buy, such as dried whitebait, herrings, towgay, soya beans, palm and coconut oil and eggs we couldn't live long on the Jap ration. This only provides rice, tea, sugar, pepper (tons of it for some unknown reason) and about twice a week 4oz gross weight of fresh fish. And as all these extras have to be manhandled on trailers, their delivery is essential to our very existence.

'All officer' trailer parties are going out and these look like increasing in number. Colonel Pratley CO 5 Norfolks, who is in command of the 18 Division's troops remaining here, has protested that it is against both Geneva and Hague conventions to make officer POWs work – and they'll all have to work damn hard to bring in enough wood with which to cook and enough food to keep us alive.

8 May
Our boys move off tonight or rather at 0330hrs tomorrow morning, so I look like losing my beauty sleep as I intend to see them off. Having been in here nearly a week a resumé may not be out of place.

Our bunk is quite OK. The only snag is that there are innumerable rats who live up in the rafters beneath the attap roof and invade by night (loss of banana last night and half a piece of soap!). There are few bugs thank heavens, but to make up for this there are ants – the two never go together, the ants see to that. We hope for electricity, a string wick in a pot of palm oil is our only means of illumination so far. Latrines are of the bore-hole pattern out of doors – actually nestling coyly in a banana grove. On the whole it's no' so bad!

9 May

The 'bore-hole' of 5 May has now crystallised into 320 including 240-odd officers to 'superintend' the making of a road or railway, returning at the end of four months maximum! Remembering that some of our Singapore working parties went down for ten days and stayed eight months I wonder.

Heavy baggage is to be left behind – I intend to lock non-essentials in my suitcase and hope for the best – this bringing me to the all-important point as far as I'm concerned that I'm one of the 320. 18 Division found forty including five of the Mercantile Marine wallahs. Denis is going as well and altogether the list looks quite a cheery party. Anyhow I'm not worrying, it'll make a change altho' I'll be sorry to leave all the men behind.

These seamen officers are a mixed bag, British, American, Mexican, Tahitian, Puerto Rican to name a few, but on the whole they're OK.

11 May

For the last two days have been on wood trailer parties, taking trailers out the odd 2 miles to the wood-felling area and bringing it back loaded.

We're off on Friday morning around 0400hrs. I'm doing 'Q' for our seventy officers from the G & W area.

Had dysentery and malaria inspections today. The former, the now familiar 'glass rod' and the latter, a blood smear on a slide (from a needle pricked finger).

13 May

Had a narrow squeak from a scorpion sting yesterday when lifting a log in the wood-felling area, found afterwards two of these jolly little fellows nestling coyly underneath.

We are now leaving for 'up-country' at 1200hrs on Monday 17 May. Great rumours of long marches the other end, only taking the kit you can carry – certainly we've had official notification that we must be able to carry all we take, but they so typically don't say how far!

22 May

I'm writing this at Bangpong, a small town about thirty miles N-N.W. of Bangkok in Thailand – the story of our journey so far is as follows:

On Monday the 17th we left in lorries from Selerang Square for the station. I took my web equipment, haversack, pack and valise containing, bed, mosquito net, flea-bag and odd towels etc. Altogether a helluva weight, but I reckoned I could make a mile with it, carrying the valise on top of the pack; if we had to go further, then the valise would have to be dumped.

We left Singapore Station at 1610hrs. twenty-six officers or ORs or, as we were, mixed with twelve officers and fourteen ORs to a closed goods truck! These were very smelly, measured 19ft x 8ft and had sliding doors in the centre which were left open, a table top being placed over the base of the opening to give space for people to sit and so giving us a little air and a sight of the passing countryside.

So began a journey that lasted until 0930hrs on Friday, three and a half days! The discomfort had to be experienced to be believed, for apart from the heat and overcrowding, the vibration was terrific, making reading impossible.

We had long stops in Malaya for feeding at Gemas, Kuala Lumpur, Ipoh, Krai (off Penang) and Padang Besar. We got a wash if we were lucky, the food which we supplemented with tinned stuff we had brought with us, was the inevitable rice and stew, usually vegetables with pork fat swimming in it.

There were occasional stops for relieving of nature and these in Malaya were fairly frequent. Also Chinese and Malay had pineapple, bananas, plantains, and biscuits for sale. In Thailand we were treated with less regard altho' the local populations were as friendly as in Malaya – the stops were less frequent (one of the big difficulties was one's personal functions. To go to the loo one hung onto the table top with the rest outside. Someone had to hold onto your wrists so you did not overbalance and also to keep a look out for on coming trains and approaching bridges that were very narrow and very liable to slice off a portion of one's bottom! It actually worked very well). The other places we stopped at in Thailand I don't know as the names weren't in English. The scenery all through was jungle, padi, rubber or pineapple.

It was a nightmarish journey and altho' we were told that we would have to carry all our kit from the station to this next camp, we were relieved to get out of that train for the last time.

The trip to this camp was hard work but both Denis and I made it with all our kit. The camp itself is appalling, attap huts with no floors and mud everywhere – the latrine situation is ghastly and the only water from a well smells putrid and looks dirty. We have been told that a valise per person will be transported by MT to our destination some 120 kilometers from here. We do two marches by night of 17 and 15 miles respectively – then a train journey and finally another march! Good clean fun one way and another. Last night it rained and we were flooded out, just to add a final touch!

The locals are very friendly and we can buy from them at specified times. We had some 'Mah Mee' a well-known eastern dish of fried food which is excellent consisting of suce-hoon, onions, eggs, meat, tomato and odds and ends.

The women folk and children as well as the men can see all that goes on in the camp. When washing they see all! and it is a usual thing to have a Siamese or Chinaman come up as you squat on the latrine and offer to buy your shirt, shorts, watch, ring or whatever takes his fancy. Even here you are in full view of the passing gentry. Such is our first glimpse of Thailand!

The Japs are friendly and the privates are buying up all they can in the way of clothes, watches, pens etc., for resale to the local population. The only way I've found so far to make them stop worrying you is to say 'Presento wifeo' and they, who are sentimentalists at heart, will then desist.

[*On one occasion an Australian and myself were doing a job for a local captain in charge of that stretch of the railway. During a rest period I got out my pipe – the tobacco I used looked rather like Shredded Wheat made from wog-weed. I filled my pipe and took out my Ronson lighter. The Jap called me over and took my Ronson throwing me a cheap tin lighter of Japanese manufacture. I said "Wifeo Presento", he said "Wifeo Presento Cur?" I said "yes". "Show me, come here" – luckily my wife had had my initials RMH engraved on the front. I pointed this out to him and he said "Buggeiro" (which means 'fool') threw the lighter on the ground and I gave him back his own lighter.*]

So now we await our long trek, it doesn't sound too good to me, but I'm travelling much lighter, just equipment and pack and hope my feet will make the grade. Our job seems to be to make a railway through the jungle joining Burma to Bangkok. As this project has been turned down by experts in the past as impossible, we look like having a gay time. We learned on arrival that Ken Charnock who came up in November had died of diphtheria.

Amusing interludes of this camp: When we were flooded out last night as we had sent our heavy baggage to go on by MT we were all sleeping on the floor and those unfortunates who were nearest the flooded drain were caught napping – two cracks from Ralph Sparks are worthy of repetition – the first that the only dry things he'd got left were those he'd washed and were now hanging out to dry and the second, when he was waking up a fellow called Ferguson in the Gordons who had for some time gone on sleeping although surrounded by water, said "Excuse me my friend, but you're under water!" – Hundreds of hard-boiled eggs are being sold by the wogs, to show how fresh boiled they were; one small girl pressed a boiling hot egg to a lad's belly and said "Velly good, all hot."

23 May

The first lap of our journey is over and there are many blistered feet and aching limbs this morning – I am no exception and am wondering how the devil I'll make fifteen more miles tonight. Of course this march is against all international law for POWs the maximum laid down is 20 kilometers (twelve and a half miles).

I don't know the name of this dump but there's a handy if muddy river in which I bathed my weary limbs this morning. Denis and I had a bad break as regards a billet, our first choice was taken over by the AIF and we are now under a wooden building with mud as a floor! All buildings are on props to prevent flooding and we're under these, so if it rains we're sunk. Hey ho, what a life – gosh for a hot bath and a nice soft bed!

25 May

I'm writing this from the Reception Camp at Kambhuri where we arrived at 0830hrs yesterday morning – on arrival we found that there was no accommodation available! The journey had been seventeen and not fifteen miles and we were all dead beat, so we just flopped down where we were and slept, then at mid-morning, set about putting tents up. My feet are in poor shape.

We've contacted quite a lot of 18 Division's folk here; the main 18 Division party that left three to four weeks before us have had to march all the way. Poor devils, actually they were so selfish taking practically every available item of any use from Changi, that most people aren't very sorry for them. I'm told that Hodge is in poor shape – as he rode a bike everywhere at Changi never walking anywhere, he must have found it hard going.

This camp is the worst we have struck yet, it's dirty, water is so scarce that there is no official issue with meals, you have to draw your own from a well, boil or chlorinate it and then drink it. Food consists of rice and 'jungle stew' (vegetable) and one way and another the thing is a shambles.

All POWs in Thailand are spread over the stretch of railway being built from Bangkok to Burma. Those the furthest away have to clear jungle and are having a bad time. The further away, the worse food and conditions. As far as we know, our camp is not too bad. There must be fifty or sixty thousand troops (POWs) here in Thailand and they are dying at the rate of six to eight per day – dysentery, malaria and, diphtheria being chief causes. I'm not surprised if other camps are run as this one is by the Japs.

Some of the Jap guards have been behaving very well on this journey. One in charge of the badly foot-sore on our second lap was most considerate and even helped to carry some of the fellows' kits. Another from whom I borrowed a pick and shovel to dig a trench around our tent, when I in fun suggested he should dig too, he promptly turned to and hacked away.

This morning we had our third malaria, dysentery inspections, with an injection and vaccination thrown in. This was the third time I had 'lost my virginity' and it was by far the most painful – very thorough these Japanese!

26 May

My valise has arrived here, intact but soaked through – I don't think it is rain, it looks rather as if it had been dumped in a pond! However a brief contact with the sun and everything is dry now. The sun is much hotter here than Singapore, but the humidity is less. I look forward to a sleep on my camp bed having slept on the earth or floor now for over a week.

The Japs are round here like flies buying kit – they are chiefly interested in fountain pens, pencils, rings, watches, pullovers, blankets. I have refused all offers for mine as most have sentimental value and unless I'm really starving I don't intend to part with anything.

I'm surprised how many people have sold articles given them as twenty first birthday presents or from their wives or relations. There is a lot of pilfering going on both by Thais and our own troops who sell their spoils to the Wogs. Consequently we have to have a night picquet and keep our eyes open by day. As I write this three more Japs have come in to buy kit. They are coming in droves, one is looking over my shoulder as I write, he has an eye on my pen, but "Presento wifeo" puts him off the track.

This would appear to be the main Jap supply route to the Burma front, and it is interesting to see and <u>quite enlightening</u>. The roads soon get very bad and many of the lorries have wheel chains. A convoy of troops passed us on our march in impressed civilian buses and these are far from trustworthy.

That reminds me of one aspect of our march that I haven't previously mentioned; we passed acres and acres of padi fields with their irrigation canals running parallel to the road; the noise of bull-frogs, cicadas, crickets etc., was terrific and quite deafening. On the second day after each rest (we marched three-quarters and rested one-quarter hour with one long halt of an hour where tea was available) we would get so stiff that for the next mile after each rest we would find movement difficult and just hobbled along. Also the thousands of fire flies and bugs made an attractive sight altho' we were hardly in the mood to appreciate them.

[*Because we had been warned about the locals, I wrapped myself inside a valise and had all my other goods and chattels inside with me.*(Editor's note: Sydney Humphries, ex-5th Regiment, RA, believes this to be a 4–5 foot long canvas bag approximately 2 feet deep with two zips which allowed the bag to open flat.) *A Padre who didn't believe that he would be done, slept with his head on his pack and his arms through the straps. When he woke, his head was on the ground and the pack had disappeared! The first working camp was at Tamarkan. Here two bridges were built near the start of the railway. First a wooden one and at the same time building a concrete and steel girder one alongside. We went up on the wooden bridge and came back 6 months later over the concrete and girder bridge, which is still standing to this day.*]

27 May

Late last night we were told that some of us were to move the following morning by 0730hrs. We had to march to the station and were then packed fifty to a railway truck and taken over the newly constructed railway. This is an extraordinary construction, very rough, but some of the feats of engineering are amazing. On some parts there is a sheer drop of 200 feet to the Kwai River and steep cliffs on the other and we held or breaths.

We arrived at Tarso at about 1430hrs and marched one and a half miles (with full kit) to a staging camp. We had machan and then moved off at 2100hrs for a 6 kilometer march to Tonchan where I'm writing this. I still have all my kit; the march, on a very rough road, was hellish and we were pretty done in at the end of it. We were dumped in a field, actually we learned afterwards in the wrong camp, and were shifted about 200yds away on the other side of the road about half an hour afterwards. Apparently the other side is run by the Jap guards and this by the Engineers and the two don't see eye to eye – all good fun! We dossed down in a clearing made in the jungle the same day and snakes, scorpions and ants failed to prevent me having a first class sleep.

28 May

Today we're told we're staying for the time being and are now in the process of clearing a space in the jungle to put up tents. I have never seen so many bugs, ants, insects, butterflies etc., as there are here. I'm now going to do some more jungle clearing.

31 May

We have been sent out on working fatigues, carting felled trees in the jungle – this in spite of the fact that at Changi we were assured that on no account would we do anything other than supervise – today is the third day we've been out and it has poured all the time. This is the rainy season and the monsoon should start at any time.

Accommodation is dreadful, eighteen of us in a small tent – no room between beds or bunking spaces. The road and camp are ankle deep in mud and under water in many places. It is impossible to keep dry and in fact it would appear that the only dry period will be at night – our daily routine is as follows: Breakfast 0730hrs – Parade 0800hrs working until 1230 or 1300hrs – 1300hrs tiffin – 1500hrs working parade until 1900 or 2000hrs – supper is at 1900hrs and roll call 2000hrs, so until after roll call at 2000hrs it's no good changing into dry clothes at all.

We've met quite a lot of fellows who preceded us up here: Bill Cowell, Andrews, Brian Milnes, Joe Clymer, Dickie Ritchie to name but a few. The early parties had a very rough time, the road was a jungle track last October and they've made it, such as it is.

The Colonel protested about sending officers out on working parties, but as in the case of previous occasions was told (a) situation had altered since the guarantee given in Changi (b) no work, no food or pay. This is assuredly our lowest ebb.

On the first day a tree fell on me and badly scraped my back and earlier I crushed a finger between a tree and a rock with a result that the nail is black and looks like coming off. Today, we, Jap troops, Chinese and Tamil coolies (imported from Malaya) carted felled trees through the jungle to the roadside. So here we are, with a prospect of eleven or twelve working hours a day, very nearly continuous rain, overcrowded accommodation and not very rain proof at that, and mud and slush everywhere. Not too rosy, but we're not letting it get us down; once you let that happen you go rapidly downhill.

The Dutch have given up very easily and their death rate is very high, the British death rate is reduced from the early figures, but as far as this camp is concerned, in the course of construction at the same time as we work, they've no system of evacuation of sick which is serious, particularly as there are a number of men walking around with dysentery. Still here's hoping!

1 June

Today we had to pull small trolleys one and a half miles through the slush and mud, and drag felled trees – there were two Shoko (officer) parties and two mixed coolie parties. A fine thing when you come to think of it, officers and coolies both working on the <u>same</u> trunk or log and then our cup of humiliation will be full. Still, as I've said before, it's no good letting it get you down, that is probably the idea anyhow.

2 June

I have a 'yasume' day today (day of rest) – actually it is not official, but we have so organised our parades that six officers stay in each day as well as the sick to do dhobying and in fact to generally have a free day for personal use. The continuous wet state of my clothes with no sun to dry them has brought on a heavy cold. Denis Pearl has a dose of jungle fever, a mild form of malaria that is very prevalent here.

Where we are working in the jungle there are quite a lot of snakes, but so far they haven't been offensive, being only too glad to slip away out of sight. There are also quite a lot of scorpions and centipedes – one of the former was found in my bed the other day but hadn't touched me – we're so crowded in the tent that it is impossible to put up a mosquito net.

[*I saw a scorpion that was the size of a lobster. On another occasion a number of us were waiting to take our turn to clear jungle and were watching some fellows cutting down large bamboo, suddenly out jumped a centipede about one and a half feet in length with thick orange legs, about twenty on each side. It went towards a Puerto Rican who didn't like work and had developed an 'agonising' back, so that any effort on his part would make him cry out in pain. You have never seen anyone move so fast as this Puerto Rican when he saw the centipede come towards him, he bent down, picked up an axe and cut the centipede in half. He got up with a look of triumph on his face which was quickly replaced with a look of utter dismay when he realised what he had done. If his back was that bad he would never have been able to be so agile. Needless to say after that he had to work as hard as the rest of us!*]

The food here is very bad, just rice, a little vegetable and salted fish, there is no issue of tea or sugar and we have tried to supplement by putting in all surplus Thai money we've got and buying coffee, sugar, dried pressed meat and pig oil.

<u>Later</u>. My remarks regarding a 'yasume' day were too previous – about half an hour after writing the last paragraph the Japs turned everyone out who was not actually bed down and made them work in the camp or cutting bamboo in the surrounding jungle. Hey ho, it's a luverly life!

5 June

Life is pretty hellish, unless anything untoward happens I won't write a daily diary – each day is very much like the next, either carrying or pulling trees from the jungle – usually six miles a day along the 'main' road ankle deep in mud and slush whilst going to and from our work.

Incidentally the appalling state of the roads makes one wonder how (a) our rations will arrive when the monsoon really breaks and (b) how the forward camps and railway itself will fare. Presumably as long as they have control of the Bay of Bengal, the Japs needn't depend on this road as a supply route – were it to be so, the forward troops would have a hectic time as the road, only constructed since last October is dreadful and will grow far worse as I've said before.

Washing is done in a small stream that runs through the camp; in view of the fact that the British POW allotment of space is down river of the coolies one has one's doubts about the purity of the water.

[*The Tamils have no idea of hygiene. I saw one squatting in a stream doing his natural functions and at the same time dip his finger into the water and clean his teeth!*]

The butterflies here are wonderful, of all shapes and sizes and with delightful colouring, some seem to have almost transparent wings.

6 June
Got quite excited today when three elephants passed through; they are used for carrying trees and also to a lesser degree, ploughing padi fields – a number of the camps further up the line have elephants to help them, whereas we have to do it all by sheer manpower – not so funny when you're part of the manpower! Unfortunately they passed straight through so our backs look like having some more bending. We're getting used to it now, but that doesn't alter the fact that by the end of the day we're absolutely whacked.

A rather better variety of vegetable has arrived and this evening we had a mixed vegetable stew with our rice – tiffin was rice and green vegetable, breakfast plain boiled rice – Changi with its fried whitebait rissoles etc, was the Ritz compared to this!

8 June
Had an excellent supper last night by invitation of Sergeant Towell of the 125 A/Tank Regiment who runs a battalion cookhouse in the other camp. Hearing I was here he asked me over and produced pork and beef rissoles and vegetable and onion stew. Haven't felt so full for days!

10 June
Have got a slight dose of dysentery – this is very rife in the camps and I am consequently bed-down. Everyone was made to go on working parades today who was not actually in bed.

Later. An outbreak of cholera has occurred, so far it is rumoured one Jap and three BORs are affected – we are not allowed to go over to the other camp either visiting or bathing. We have coolie camps on three sides of us here (the noise of the spitting and retching makes gay music as one rises each morning.)

11 June
Cholera or whatever it is has already claimed something like fifty Tamil coolies and a dozen odd BORs, it would appear that the water is to blame and we are now not

allowed to use water for any purpose whatsoever unless it has been boiled. Some of our officers had to carry away the dead and dying from the coolie camp – hell's bells it's a great prospect with the coolie camp alongside ours.

The Japs are in a great panic and are taking as many precautions as they can to stop it spreading. My dysentery is much better today, but thirty six hours with only liquid diet has left me very weak in our already weakened state.

I've had to remove my ring from my pinky as it is in danger of coming off (what a sign of the times!) and my eyes seem to have sunk a long way into my head with a result that the eye-lids seem much heavier. Still, keep smiling, this is probably the worst period and maybe the better times are round the corner.

13 June

Yet another wedding anniversary away from my Flossie – Oh God I hope we celebrate the next one together. My celebration today consisted in carrying on stretchers dead and dying Tamil coolies of whom about 150 have now died – filthy degrading jobs that we needn't have done with so many other coolies standing around just watching. When protestations have been made that it is disgraceful, we are told that it is disgraceful to be a POW, their shokos (officers) would have 'split-belly'!!! Oh for a day of reckoning!

Later. Was hit by a Nip Lance Corporal for refusing to lift a dead Chinaman on to a stretcher. I have put in a strong protest but don't expect any results owing to the lack of forcefulness of our CO – In view of the fact that the Nip eventually did the job, consider I won the round!

2000hrs: Have just heard the tragic news that Sergeant Towell mentioned in the entry of 8 June has died of cholera. Such a kind-hearted fellow, it is hard that he should be singled out to die when there are so many unworthy souls that one meets every day.

It is the fact that the Japanese have gone ahead with this railroad project without regard for human life or the necessities for existence that makes it such a crime against civilisation.

We are still only getting rice, vegetables and occasionally an infinitesimal piece of dried fish – the vegetable is mostly marrow with a little sweet potato and onion and can have little if any vitamin content. We all feel weaker and it is an unpleasant fact to have to face that our resistance to any disease must of necessity be slight.

14 June

Have been working today with elephants; a team of five arrived the other day. They pull the heavier logs on small sleighs, which travel over the mud quite easily. About fifty travelled through on their way up the line.

[*On 31 May I was working with Tamil coolies, humping teak trees and carrying them down to a clearing where they were to be shaped ready to make the bridges. It was my job to follow behind the elephant so that if a tree got stuck I could lever it out using a crow bar. It was while I was following one of the elephants that I heard a rumbling noise, not realising what it was I carried on. Suffice to say that no one would come near me until I'd had an opportunity to go down to the river and wash myself and my clothes!]*

A lot of Japs with bullock-drawn transport have been passing through each day, Burma-wards! My jaw is pretty sore today where the Nip socked me yesterday, happy days! The Jap doctor says that the cholera deaths were on the decrease – it doesn't take long, Sergeant Towell went to bed OK., woke vomiting etc., and was dead by the evening – certainly a good many of those that we carried yesterday who were alive in the morning, were dead and buried by the later afternoon – thereby hangs a tale. There have been some heart-rending sights during these last few days.

19 June

A relapse of my dysentery, brought on I think by the fact of having to carry with one other, a sack of rice from Tarso, six kilometers away along the road that is now in a helluva state.

Actually my helpmate on the journey was Kellehar of the US Merchant Navy, not a bad fellow altho' by nature loud of mouth – The cholera seems to be dying down altho' another fellow was taken from this camp this morning. I don't know the figures now, but it's something like thirty British and 350 coolies (at least).

Random Shots

I have come to the conclusion that after death, hunger must be the greatest leveller, no-one who has not experienced real hunger without the wherewithal to appease it, can truly appreciate what I mean.

It is difficult to imagine fourteen British officers receiving with real delight plain boiled rice and quaffing it down with relish, the same fourteen receiving with equal rapture two small pieces of pork crackling as a 'presento' (both these from a Japanese Lance Corporal named Osawa who speaks a little English and who has shown kindness to us in many small actions).

A king cobra killed on our working party the other day measured over 4ft in length; some Chinese slit it open and removed certain portions of its anatomy which they apparently find appetising. A centipede killed near our tent measured nearly a foot in length. Scorpions vary in size from two inches to over a foot with tail extended.

It is a wise precaution to shake your boots and shoes before putting them on as scorpions have a nasty habit of getting inside.

It would appear that Party H, of which we're a part, are 'on loan' to the Jap Thai Administration, still being part of the Malayan Administration (all guards etc., are ex-Changi), that is why the food is so bloody, the others say we're not part of them, altho' they asked for extra help to complete this damned railway, and won't help. Generally speaking their food is quite good with meat or eggs every day.

We've had one pig (for 900) since we came and eggs (hard-boiled) twice, which we bought ourselves. The coolies' food is far better than ours. Our guards still say we'll go back to Changi when the railway is completed – gosh the food there with the extra buying facilities available (not the Jap issue on which one couldn't exist) seems wonderful to this.

21 June

Have just been re-reading my letters from home for the umpteenth time, they make me very homesick and I only hope and pray that our suspicions that news home has been held up is not true in actual fact. Even two postcards and a wireless message are something, but I wonder whether they all, if any, got through. The canaries rarely sing up here which is maddening!

['Canaries singing' is news received from hidden wireless sets.]

24 June

The maddening round goes on, today it was unloading elephants. One of the mahoots (elephant drivers) is a boy of six or seven; he has his beast as well trained as any of them. Some of their more natural noises and functions are quite fearsome!

The cholera death rate of British is now around the seventy mark, that of the coolies is not known officially, but must be near 500; we see dead and dying going down each day, but the numbers seem definitely on the decrease. We now learn that they also have cholera further up the line – there is no doubt that it is brought in by the coolies – and we have to work and lie side by side with them!

It is regrettable to have to state that our CO here is more concerned with a quiet life and appeasing the Japs, than taking a strong line of resistance.

26 June

We have been able to buy a few extras, soya beans, whitebait, eggs, pig oil etc., and these have helped our messing during the last few days – we haven't been paid yet since we left Changi, but have been able to change some of our Malayan currency, so this, together with an advance from a fund brought up from Changi, has helped a lot.

27 June

We are standing by (thirty of us) to move further up the line, probable day of departure, tomorrow. They say it's a fifty mile trek altogether so doubt if I'll be able to get my bed that far; I'll leave it and hope it will follow with some of our sick. This should take us to the Burma frontier at Three Pagoda Pass or darned near it.

30 June

The move eventually concerned 110 of us, 18 Division, Australia, 11 India Division, and I am writing this from a camp overlooking the river near Hintock – the situation sounds and is ideal, but there it rests and we all wish we were back at Tonchan South, imagine it!

We left at 1010hrs on Monday 28 June; I had full kit plus a valise balanced on my pack containing mosquito net, mac., sleeping bag, shoes and gym shoes – the total weight not far short of a hundred-weight, we had two rests with hot water laid on for drinking and arrived at Colonel Humphrey's camp (he is CO of our group) at 1600hrs. The Japs insisted on our staying there until 2200hrs when we set off for this place ten miles distant, pitch dark and roads (?) in an impossible condition, with ruts two foot deep and mud, slush and water everywhere.

Having fallen over twice in the mud I eventually packed up at 2330hrs with eight others and dossed down in a clearing waiting for daylight. I have never had a more appalling night, hundreds of ants and midges, with quite a few mosquito as well. We left at 0740hrs and arrived at the Main Camp at 1130hrs, had a meal and then set off for here up a difficult face that included a ladder ascent of fifteen feet and very rough going for five miles.

[*On the 28 June we were on the move again and marched from 10.00am – 4.00pm. They then decided that we should wait until 11.00pm before going on. It was the monsoon season and the conditions were appalling with great two foot ruts and mud, it was also very dark. I got fed up and persuaded eight other chaps to join me to slip off to one side, lay up for the night and rejoin the party at day break. The only thing one chap* (editor's note: Tony Chenevix Trench, afterwards Headmaster of Eton) *had to cover himself was the Union Jack that was used to cover the dead before they were interred. There we were lying in a row when we heard the clinking of horses' harnesses. Peeping out with one eye, I saw a number of Japs with mountain ponies going up to the Burma front. We didn't know what they would do when they saw us, but suddenly we heard the words, 'cholera, cholera', and realised that they thought we were dead and waiting for burial – needless to say they didn't come near!*]

On arrival we had hardly got our equipment off before we had to set to clearing the jungle and erecting tents. (This after 22 miles with a heavy load on appalling roads!) – today we have been on a working party from 0830–1600hrs – the Jap engineers in charge were charming (!?) and kept us at it hard. In fact all our captors up here seem to take a delight in making life as unpleasant for you as they can – more can be said at another time.

The food is as bad as when we first arrived at Tonchan and all in all the prospect is not too rosy with cholera rife, no washing allowed in the river, hard work, altho' the hours aren't bad and damn all food. Hey ho says Rolly!

3 July

That item ref. hours of working being not too bad, can be cancelled as there are invariably fatigues to be done on return to camp. Life is really pretty hellish, every day sees someone getting a beating up, usually for their failure to understand some

8.

INSTRUCTIONS GIVEN TO P.O.W. ON MY ASSUMING COMMAND.

I have the pleasure to lead you on the charge of last stretch of Railway Construction Wardoom. In examination of various reports as well as to the result of my partial inspection of the present conditions, I am pleased to find that you in general keeping discipline and working diligently. At the same time I regret to find seriousness in health matters, it is evident that there are various causes inevitable for this and but to my opinion, due mainly to the fact of absence of firm belief as Japanese.

Health follows will and Cease only when the enemy is annihilated.

Those who fail to reach objective in charge by lack of health or spirit is considered in the Japanese Army most shameful deed. Devotion to death is good. Yet still we have the Spirit? Devotion to the Imperial Cause even to the 7th of life in reincarnation the spirit which cannot become void by death.

You are in act of charge in colleague with I.J.A. You are expected to charge to the last stage of this work in good spirit by taking good care of your health. Besides you are to remember that your welfare is guaranteed only by obedience to the order of the I.J.A.

I.J.A. will not be unfair to those who are honest and obey them, but protect such.

You are to understand that this fundamental Japanese Spirit and carry out the task given you with perfect ease of mind under protection to the Japanese Army.

Given in Kanchanburi June 26th, 1943 by Col. Siguo Nakamura, Commanding P.O.W. Camps in Thailand.

32. Instructions to POWs

33. RMH with pickaxe (clearing limestone cutting, drawn by Ken Archer in Sept. '44)

order in Japanese, and really I begin to understand why Dutch troops decided that life was hardly worth living. I don't mean by this that that is the way I feel, we are all determined not to allow this treatment to get us down – but you need all the guts you can muster together to keep your chin up and keep smiling. I obviously cannot say all I want to at this stage, but look forward to the time when I can!

I would hardly be recognisable to the folks at home, with hair cropped (not a convict crop but only about one inch off it for cleanliness) my beard, seen days old, and body burned deep brown in the sun to say nothing of my girth!

We are working at clearing a limestone cutting for the railway and the sun from 1030hrs until we break off at 1600hrs beats down the whole time – the heat and glare are terrific. We heard (a) that we'll move 100km in five days and (b) 80km in a month (?!!) we also hear that pay is on the way – whacko! This at least is authentic altho' we have no knowledge as to when.

[*I lost count of the number of times we were beaten up, but I do remember that there was a little chap, we called him 'Rosebud' (they all had nick names), three of us had got protection from the rain by standing under some trees, and didn't hear them telling us to go back to work until we heard Rosebud screaming. We set off back, but he lined us up deciding he was going to punch us. The first fellow was a 6 foot 2 Indian army major who had a beard. Rosebud, who was quite small, took a swing at him but his wrist whizzed through the beard and didn't hit anything solid, with the result that he fell flat on his face in the mud. Well of course we couldn't contain our laughter, but managed to straighten our faces before he got up. Unluckily I was the second one (he didn't go back to the major) and got double the whack.*]

6 July

My wee Ian's birthday, one whole year and I've never even seen him – maybe next year I'll be able to help him blow out the candles!

I'm qualifying to take my place with any Dartmoor convict, chipping away day after day at the railway cutting that is our 8-hour daily task. Pay has arrived and we are putting most of it to help both ours and the men's messing – that is if facilities are made available for buying local produce, eggs, soya beans, pig oil etc.

Reports from other camps up and down the line make grim hearing; cholera, malaria, dysentery, beri-beri and general malnutrition and the death rate is slowly mounting. By the time the railway is completed, the casualties amongst British, Australian and Dutch troops must surely amount to several thousand, to say nothing of the coolies.

9 July

Terrific 'speedo speedo' on the railway, the Nips say that the rail is to come through in five days' time. Even the sick are made to work and it's been hell today even more than usual. Was there ever such a monotonous, back-breaking job as this everlasting picking and shovelling. 'Dynamite Dan,' the Nip who is in charge of the actual dynamiting has taken a dislike to me and endeavours to do everything he can to make life bloody – hey ho, however much he hits me and slaps me, I don't intend to let him get me down, altho' I was furious today when, after an afternoon of persecution he threw quite a large stone at me and hit me on the chest.

Like the elephant, I won't forget and only hope for a chance to hit back some day – am suffering from pellagra of the mouth (sore tongue and lips) this is very prevalent and is due to vitamin deficiency.

Some fellows have appalling tropical ulcers, these have mostly emanated from bamboo scratches, altho' any scratch festers as a matter of course. I have just had two that are now OK, and am watching with some care several cuts and scratches on my hands and legs done at the cutting.

13 July

Still the daily grind continues, have a dose of jungle fever and also several tropical ulcers on my left leg – both these would have kept me off parade at Changi, but here they mean full work. However, there are signs that the visit of a lieutenant-colonel of the Jap administrative staff has improved or started to improve both conditions and food.

We hear we've got five bullocks and one pig and a more lenient view is being taken about illness – of course the fact that our job is now nearly completed may have some bearing, but we don't know and only hope for the best. I hope that attention will be drawn to the footwear question, as those without boots or shoes have to work barefooted. Grand fun on limestone and granite chips!

16 July

My left leg has swelled up like a balloon; this is quite common as a natural effect of standing and walking whilst you have tropical ulcers – it doesn't alter the fact that it's damned painful, but is just one of the many jolly old crosses we have to bear. These ulcers together with painful swelling are apt to get people down, this state of despondency is most dangerous. Both Colonel Cobley and young Huxtable of the 88th Field Regiment who have died at Tonchan since we left, altho' dying of dysentery, had put up little or no fight, due to their depressed and underfed condition.

It is a marked fact how rarely one hears troops singing or whistling, they're just too tired. Last night we had the first meat meal for months, the first of our 5 bullocks was duly despatched and altho' as tough as leather was grand. This morning we had some more and it was more tender, Oh what a thrill!

[I nearly lost the diary. A wireless was found at base hospital camp and word went up the whole line that a search was to be made of all our kit etc., so when we were lined up on parade, except for those who were too sick, a search was made of our things. I was later told by one of the fellows who had remained in the hut, that a Jap took the diary up, extracted a picture of a German raider that an American officer had drawn and which I had copied, and put the diary back again! A Padre who was with us was taken and eventually called for

and given a very rough time as he had stupidly referred to wireless news in his diary. Now whenever news came through, I very rarely mentioned it in my diary, but if I did I simply said that the 'canaries were singing'.]

28 July

A long gap since my last entry, but as each day is almost identical with another, it doesn't matter. The facts of the case are that I just haven't had the time; this may sound far fetched, but we are now on parade at 0730hrs each day and don't get back until between 1930 and 2000hrs at night – we have roughly an hour and a half of daylight in which to queue up for our evening meal and again for the canteen and wash if possible.

[When we went to Thailand the entries in my diary were less frequent as we had little leisure time.]

Several evenings a week there are fatigues awaiting us, carrying rations up from the river or stores. In fact with the Nip guards in the camp endeavouring to be as unpleasant as possible and those on the job taking the same attitude, life is pretty hellish.

[The River Kwai was a vital lifeline for the railway which ran parallel wherever possible to the river. The worst fatigue for us was when we had to collect supplies from the barges. We had to climb down steps cut into the mud of the river bank and hump sacks of rice back to our camp. It was soon apparent that we were getting too weak to carry them up the steps. The first step was alright, but when we had to balance on one leg to put the other on the next step the leg would collapse. So what the Japs did was to get the walking wounded to line up on each side so that when you got your leg on the next step they would give you a 'hump' up by the bottom so that the other leg could then join the firm leg.]

I've lost count of the number of times I've been beaten up, varying from solid punches to the jaw with clenched fist, to slaps and blows from a bamboo cane – oh what a jolly life we lead!

[When you were getting beaten up by the Japs the only thing you could do to keep your self respect was to simply take it, stand to attention and they would then punch you about the face and stomach and sometimes would kick you. I was always afraid that if I got a kick on an ulcer, it would have been quite impossible not to show pain as they were very painful and I might lash out and hit them which would be a short circuit to suicide.]

Cholera has claimed a lot of people in the camp, Digby Gates has died and from our tent (which now has twelve BORs in it) we've had four cases, two of which have died. Altogether the original party that left Changi have had eight officer deaths and many who are seriously ill.

I've had another recurrence of mild dysentery, but here you have to work, dysentery or not, in fact you've got to be pretty bad to be bed down. The morning parade, when men suffering from malaria, dysentery and beri-beri have to go out to work, is one of the most heart-rending sights I have seen and one that never should be allowed by any civilised nation.

I find I'm beginning to feel the strain of little sleep and hard work, but will not let it get me down, that's fatal as I've said before. Digby Gates died through lack of the will to live and I've no intention to go the same way.

So the days roll by, two days to my thirty second birthday, hey ho we do see life – if one were in a fit state to appreciate it, there's some grand scenery around, wild and rugged – but trudging to and from work down a track, slimy with mud and slime and usually wet through, one has hardly the attitude to admire Mother Nature. Had such a vivid dream of my Flossie last night that awoke terribly depressed.

31 July

Thirty two today, an uneventful day being identical with those previous. I haven't mentioned previously that owing to the lack of time I have let my beard grow.

I very much doubt whether my weight is over 10st now, my bones seem awfully prominent – we're all suffering from aching limbs, due it is believed, to mild rheumatism brought on by the continuous wettings we get with our clothes drying on us as many as three times in a day and getting up to put on wet clothes in the morning. Willie Nash has died of cholera; he was dead eighteen hours after admission to hospital, and we hear Jack Jordan has died back at Tonchan. Our strength goes up to 700 with the addition of all the main Hintock camp personnel.

7 August

The continuous strain of lack of food, dysentery and work caused me to collapse on parade this morning, so I've been given a day off and tomorrow will do light duties around the camp. The rations apart from meat which we've had for our evening meal three days out of the last four consist of rice, tea and dehydrated potatoes sliced, all available vegetables seem to miss us, altho' the Japs, coolies and Aussies across the way have a good supply – the same old story of different administration.

Actually this dysentery is more of a diarrhoea brought on by the continuous strain on the stomach muscles caused by our work, picking, shovelling, lifting heavy weights and so on, combined with lack of anything solid in the diet. The complete lack of any fruit as well is bad, I shared a pomelo (kind of large grapefruit) with four others the other day and it seemed grand.

Great rumours about our return to Changi, I wonder! On the credit side, purchases via barges can be made of eggs and sometimes tinned fish, jam and milk which help to swell the frugal fare – I have an egg to fry for my tiffin today, the official meal is rice and potato stew! The amount of emaciated men that have come down from Hintock is dreadful, many are nothing more than walking skeletons. They lost 150lbs in twenty eight days!

9 August
Spent four hours lost in the jungle last night, trying to find my way home (?) from Hintock Railway Station, where I'd been guarding some rice – this in spite of the fact that I was a hospital out-patient.

[*After I had finished one of the shifts, I had to find my own way back to the camp which was about a quarter of a mile away. I got totally lost and believe you me it is a very frightening experience to be lost in the jungle. It was very dark and eventually took me four hours to get back. Luckily when I was completely lost and didn't know which way to go I heard a train and knew that it should be on my right hand side if I was headed in the right direction for camp. Eventually I saw a light and went into a tent. A broad Australian voice said 'I should get the hell out of here Cobber, this is the cholera area'. I subsequently heard of a fellow who was lost in the jungle for almost three days and he was never the same again, his hair went white and he was a complete nervous wreck.*]

13 August
Have been on twelve hour night shift for last two nights.

15 August
Don Glazer has died and I'm attending his funeral this evening – he had dysentery and had little fight to recover – I've never seen such a walking skeleton as he was just before the end. Willie Williams, a volunteer, has also died here. Total of officers who have died is now fifteen I think.

17 August
Have a 'yasume' day today at long last, that is provided we don't get called out to unload any barges or some similar fatigue. We've been working thirteen and fourteen hour stretches to get certain portions of the line finished.

Things are looking up, we're getting meat every day and some vegetables came in the other day. I'm on liquids at the moment owing to my dysentery but the meat stock and various canteen purchases one can make, eggs, tinned milk, pomelos etc. all help to keep up one's strength, which is so necessary. I'm now quite an expert cook; we have our own fire each night and we cook omelettes etc., to go with our evening meal or have late suppers with a brew of tea at 11 or 12 o'clock. I prefer earlier meals however as I like to get to bed by 2300hrs if possible.

No signs of our going back to Changi altho' we've now done three months up here and all the important jobs are finished.

21 August
200 of us going either up or down country within next few days. Saw a silver

gibbon (species of ape) – we've heard them in the jungle but they rarely come close enough to see them.

24 August

Standing-by to move, our number reduced to 170, we are told that we go two days journey to the end of the rail and then have a 20 kilometer (?!) march the other end. An advance party goes on the 26th at 0600hrs and we go on the following day at the same time and as we are taking tents etc., we look like having a pretty bloody time for some days until we get settled. Still hey ho and hi-de-ho, it's a great life if you don't weaken, so as it can't last forever, one day we'll be able to sit back and laugh at it all.

We're told we go for two months, no pay while we're there, so prospects aren't too rosy. My next entry will probably be at our destination or *en route*, so perhaps we'll have more information then.

Total of all ranks of our force (H force) who have died since we left Changi 3,320 strong is 800, a very high percentage considering that is only since the end of April of this year.

The meat we are getting is usually very tough as it has to be eaten so soon after killing – consequently it has made our teeth and gums very sore, being so unaccustomed to chewing – not a very happy omen for normal food again. They've been killing an extra bullock a day and issuing everyone with a raw steak; I parboiled mine then fried it with onions – boy oh boy!

[*The night of the 26th spent at Tameron Park and on the 27th at Kurna Kri surrounded by Coolie corpses.*]

31 August

As I anticipated, my next entry is being written from our new camp up-country, we duly moved on the 25th at 0600hrs. Had a helluva struggle up the rocky slope to the railway in the dark, I was carrying my valise on my pack again and found it hard going.

We went to the extent of the rail-laying by train packed 60–70 in an open truck; the journey was about 50 kilometers. We had a march of 10 kilometers to our first night's halt, where we bivouacked (Takanoon) in the open and of course it rained, kits got wet and consequently twice as heavy. We had a further two and a half days march ahead of us, altho' we didn't know it and for absolute hell it would be hard to beat it.

[*During the two and a half day march we had to wade through two rivers, climb over a mountain with low creepers and to cross thick bamboo bridges by walking on a tree trunk rather like a tightrope with a 50 – 60 foot drop below.*]

Had they tried to put obstacles in our way they couldn't have made the going harder. Mud slime, low creepers, thick bamboo, boggy padi fields, two rivers to wade through and mountains to cross – I have never been through such hell, but was determined not to dump any kit. On arrival here we found that it was virgin jungle 200ft from the river and adjoining the site for the rail which area hasn't been cleared (our first job?) – incidentally we passed a number of skeletons on the way, presumably coolies who had developed cholera or something like it *en route* for up-country – there are 150,000-odd up and down the line.

Our new home is now getting ship-shape with jungle cleared, tents up and barges bringing rations and stores in. There are millions of ants and at night mosquitoes and midges to make us frantic, the latter can penetrate a mosquito net. So far we haven't done any work on the railway concentrating on ours and the Nips' camps erections.

Dicky Burn has found the strain too much and is mentally deranged, we hope only temporarily. Fever and dysentery are on the increase; tomorrow we have another cholera injection and after that plague. I failed to mention that on the march here one fellow died of cholera.

14 September

A long gap, but once more hard work is the cause with all spare time taken up with messing queues, washing and sleeping.

Work has been pretty bloody, my party is on felling trees, from mighty jungle giants to the smaller varieties, all will go to make up the various bridges required in the sector. The hellish part is not so much the felling but the trekking and hacking through the jungle to get to the trees, with a trip up and down the mountainside twice a day over fallen creepers, trees, bamboos etc.

[*When felling trees to make three bridges we were split into groups. A Japanese in charge, two Tamil coolies and one white coolie i.e. one POW. What a grand bunch of chaps the Tamils were, it was a privilege to work with them and as they felt sorry for us, would try and take our jobs when the Japs weren't looking to ease the strain.*]

In all conscience the jungle is bad enough to get through, but add dozens of huge fallen trees which not only spread their branches and leaves everywhere, but bring down in their wake other trees, bamboos and creepers to make passage difficult. Whether it was the march or this infernal jungle, but we all are feeling the strain – certainly we haven't had a break since we got here and long for even a 'yasume' afternoon.

We saw some samba (wild deer) on the other side of the river so we expect big game there; they usually follow samba and wild pig.

There are some turtles that dig their way into the sand on the river bank, but we haven't had a chance of trying for any. Mosquitoes and insects are here in their thousands, there are some grand varieties of butterflies of all hues and sizes and in the felling of the trees some snakes that presumably come down with the trees. One coolie was bitten the other day but not fatally.

I fell in a Koringa (red ant) nest and got bitten all over. Hey ho, it's a helluva life, but we're trying to keep our peckers up.

[*On one occasion when we were about to join some others in clearing a clump of bushes we couldn't understand why the fellows working there kept rushing out; we soon did. The only way was to go in in small groups, work for two or three minutes and then come out and take off your boots as the ants bit like mad.*]

19 September
Rain almost continuous these last few days. Consequently we're wet from head to foot from the time we go out to the time we crawl into bed. Trench feet are rife and I fear everyone is getting to the state of wondering how long the human frame can endure such treatment.

20 September
Was allowed to stay in after tiffin today (a) owing to a fall from a tree trunk on to a bough bruising my ribs and (b) owing to an attack of trench foot. The latter is very painful, a rest however is acceptable even if only for a couple of days, and trench feet respond readily to a daily application of powder (which I still have) and of oil (which I've scrounged).

I haven't mentioned the food here, for the first two weeks we had only rice, salt fish and dried potatoes; we have had recently a few fresh vegetables and a little dried meat and tinned fish – the cookhouse have actually worked wonders with the little material available and are due considerable credit.

4 October
Another day in camp after a particularly severe bout of this dysentery-cum-diarrhoea I passed out while working yesterday.

We have been having a terrific 'speedo' which continues for another six days we're told – my job is now on bridge building, our party doing the pile-driving and we're at it all day long. We take a meal out with us and have breakfast at 0645hrs in the dark too.

[*To make a bridge you have to shape the felled tree like a pencil. Bore a hole where the piles are going to be put, and this is then driven in by hand. It's difficult to describe, but they had a big weight on a pole which fitted into the hole i.e. where the lead of a pencil would go. Rather like a cat o'nine tails with a rope that went over a pulley with 20 or 30 smaller ropes with either a POW or coolie on the end. To get the rhythm they had a chant 'ichi ni san yon' (you would pull arm over arm as the numbers were called out and then let the rope drop). I was on with a number of Japs and I decided that it was no good killing yourself, but just do enough, keep the rope taut so that it looked as if I was putting all my energy into it, because the combined energy of the others was enough to get the job done. Unfortunately, there was a Jap that had taken a dislike to me, by this time I had grown a beard as I had no opportunity*] to shave. When the corporal realised what I was doing and was not putting as much effort into it as I could, he knocked me to the ground and kicked me, then made me get up and shook my head from side to side by my beard – that night I cut it off with a pair of nail scissors.]

The strain is colossal and I must confess that this short break is most acceptable. Saw Keith Bailey passing through yesterday on his way to the camp above ours, he's been at Nom Paduk near Bangpong for months and has had a pretty 'cushy' time.

The railway is due through here in seven to ten days, thus the 'speedo', we believe this is near or is to be the actual meeting place of the line from Burma and the Thai line, very few canaries round here which is maddening.

[On another occasion two of us were sent back to the quarter master's stores to get some bolts which were put into a basket (this resembled a dustbin with handles at both ends) some 100 in all. To get them all in we carefully packed them nose to tail. On the way back to the bridge we saw a female elephant with a mahout on its neck coming down the jungle with a baby elephant. Suddenly we heard pounding and saw the baby elephant running towards us. We put the basket down carefully and waved our arms and eventually the elephant turned away. Now a baby elephant may be very sweet to another elephant, but to us it's still a very big thing and if it charged could do a lot of damage. We set off again but once more heard pounding and this time the elephant was on top of us. We put down the basket and dived for cover. The elephant saw the basket, picked it up by a handle, and of course the bolts went all over the place. We managed to get rid of the elephant and then had to try and find 100 bolts which were by then strewn all over the jungle floor. We found as many as we could and arrived back at the camp having taken three or four times longer than we should have done. Because we had held up the job the Jap screamed in fury at us, we got an interpreter and tried to tell him what had happened, but the Jap didn't believe us and made the next few minutes very unpleasant for us.]

Altogether 106 sick have been evacuated to Kambhuri from here and we're expecting reinforcements. With luck we haven't much longer up here as all indications are that we re-assemble as a party at Kambhuri and then go back to Changi or some other destination – we couldn't endure this present life for much longer, the food is mostly vegetables and rice, even the fish is now short and on four occasions we've had a bullock which has given us two meat stews, and the work is not only hard, but of such long hours.

The general state of health of the camp is not good; everyone has one or more ailments in varying degrees of severity. One man has gone mad and died due to beri-beri and another is on the way.

Incidentally Dicky Burn has only partially recovered and is still very simple. I have two ulcers, septic sweat rash, slight beri-beri in the legs, trench feet and a sore mouth – a gay life all in all!

5 October

Have shaved off my beard, it had developed into a thick flourishing growth, but I never felt really clean with it on.

11 October

A 'yasume' day after an even greater 'speedo' than hitherto; we completed our three bridges yesterday.

Food is very bad; we now only have rice and dried potatoes and greens and a little gula malacca that we managed to buy. This is having a very bad effect on everyone with the long working hours.

Reinforcements have arrived, seventy of our own 'H' force from Kanburi and 125 including Keith Bailey from the next camp up. It is said that 1,700 of 'F' force, which took a larger number of 18 Division have died – I hope the figure is exaggerated, but their strength was 7,000 and our own 800 deaths out of 3,400 is a similar proportion.

Reason given for the bad food is that the weather which suddenly dried up after the monsoon, has caused the river the Kwa Noi to be nearly dry further down and no barges can get up! This camp Konkoita is 257 kilometers from Nom Paduk where the rail starts, so heaven knows when the rations arrive.

15 October

The rail passed over our bridges yesterday and joy oh joy we've got another 'yasume' day – so hey ho for a wash and swim in the river.

Another thirty five sick are to be evacuated – the latest reports say we leave for Kambhuri around the end of the month – hell I hope so, we're mostly very nearly at the end of our powers of endurance – I have beri-beri in both legs and it's a helluva effort to walk uphill or even very far, but I'm not half as bad as many others; I only hope if we do go down we don't have to march – those days march up here were absolute hell and I don't think I could make it again.

24 October

'Yasume' day today and tomorrow, the latter being the official opening ceremony for the railway. Since my last entry, altho' the 'speedo' was reduced to a day with knocking-off at 1900hrs and a rest in the morning and afternoon, we were still kept pretty busy.

At the time of writing we are confined to our camp; we are not to be allowed within sight of the big-shot who is opening the railway.

We are hoping to be allowed to bathe as it is infernally hot (it has been for days now) and the sweat is pouring from us – Peter Pickersgill has died of cerebral malaria and jaundice, he is our first officer casualty up here, altho' we hear from Kambhuri that Peter Ram has died.

We are due to go down any day now and are only awaiting the starting gun. Oh gosh how we long to get away from this jungle and the constant 'curra, speedo,

34. RMH in Thailand (Drawing of me done by some chap when we were at Konkoita)

buggeiro' of our employers which becomes very wearing on one's nerves.

Rations have gradually deteriorated and for several days we had only rice, dried greens and potatoes, in fact for about a fortnight. We have recently had an issue of towgay (a sort of lentil), soya beans and half sack of sugar, but no fish or meat. We have no cooking fat or oil left so everything has to be boiled or stewed. White ants have invaded my pack. One of the cow elephants used for hauling timber for our bridges had its offspring with it and altho' small it was heavy enough to play havoc with you when in a playful mood, which it often was to the consternation of all concerned.

Have three new ulcers, all are small and I think I've checked their growth.

There are hundreds of thousands of flies to plague us by day; even on the job they are legion and any cut or open sore soon has a cluster on it. How I long for home, it is the constant memory of all waiting there that keeps one going.

25 October
First entry of yesterday was a trifle too previous as today we have had to work around the Nip camp – not a very congenial task after they had been celebrating the night before.

1 November
Still not yet gone down to Kambhuri altho' rumour is rife. Thirty five sick have been evacuated and we hope to follow soon.

I'm gradually going rotten, have now five ulcers on the go and septic sores in all sweaty parts of the body. Vitamin deficiency has also given us all very irritating skins that give us hell at night. 'I wanna go home!' Food improved, some towgay and soya beans, fish and oil to give us a spot more variety.

4 November
We are told we go south in the near future, gosh I hope so. I'm feeling pretty down these days and the sores and rash due to a form of scabies are maddening.

6 November
Standing by to move. Forty two sick went yesterday, roll on that magic moment. The Japs have done a lot of blasting in the river for fish and the other day got one of at least 80lb.

9 November
We are now at Kambhuri taking two-and-a-half days to do the odd 200 kilometers down, having a steam train for two-thirds of the journey.

The track is much smoother than when we travelled up and is now looking like the real thing – seeing parts grow from rough rock and jungle to cuttings and embankments has been interesting.

Here everyone looks very fit, work is light and of the nature of camp fatigues – I'm second in charge to our party. I hope we stay long enough to get benefit from the fresh fruit and vegetables and pork that they have as regular fare here, 'what a contrast!!'

Later. Joy oh joy, six letters dated September and October over a year ago! One from my Flossie, two from Dot and three from Frank.

[*What magnificent work was done by an Australian doctor at base camp called Dr. Fagan. If you've had tropical ulcers which were so bad that they took the whole of your leg, the only way to cure it was to amputate your leg. At that time we had some ether, and he devised a way, by sharpening a table spoon, putting people out, scraping the whole of the ulcer out, and wrapping it up with M & B tablets. This saved a lot of lives, because very often when a leg has been amputated the shock sets in after about ten days and the patient dies.*]

11 November
Food has been grand, fresh vegetables and pork each day. Tonight I'm putting on a concert.

13 November
Food continues good in quality but 200 extra men are now in the camp, the quantity is poor.

White ants are the bane of our lives. We have to move our kits every day to prevent them being eaten through.

The concert on the night of the 11th was very successful, there were about thirty Japs there and they allowed us an extension over lights out.

We expect to be going to Singapore on the 21st, rumour has it to Bukit Timah and not Changi, but who knows?! Have met a lot of ORs who came up here just before us, they all say they hardly recognise me I've lost so much weight – as I was only 10st 2lb when I left Changi, I must be around the 9st mark now, in fact that is the general estimate. Another concert tomorrow night.

[*Extract from 'Clink Chronicles' No. 8 dated 19.11.43 – 'Ronnie Horner is back on the road they tell me, touring the Hospital Wards with Robin Welby, Slim de Grey, 'Max Miller', Frank Woods and other variety turns. I understand they are being well received.'*]

18 November
500 more to Nom Paduk tomorrow and we follow on the 21st – unfortunately I haven't been able to get the full advantage of the fresh vegetables as I've had fever and the consequential quinine lost my appetite for me. I've also got scabies which is now clearing up slowly so that one way and another things haven't been so good. We've been able to buy a limited quantity of eggs and also plantains and pomelos.

26 November
I'm writing this at Sime Road Camp Singapore – our journey took us four-and-a-half days and, packed twenty five to a closed goods truck, we're mighty relieved to be free from the cramped accommodation, heat and bumping.

By old standards we're crowded, but after what we've had to undergo these last six months in Thailand we're living in the lap of luxury. I've got myself a charpoy and am hoping it's not too full of bugs! My scabies is clearing up slowly but made travelling in the train very uncomfortable.

27 November
Bugs not too bad last night, the joy of sleeping on a charpoy after months of chungs made of bamboo slats or bare earth! Officers are segregated from men here and look like doing jobs around the camp – gardening, chicken and pig farming etc. There is a canteen run by Chinese contractors.

30 November

Have got a dose of Malaria, since my arrival at Kambhuri I've had several small doses of fever, but this is the first time I've had Malaria – this after six months in the jungle! I don't like it much it's so sudden, from feeling perfectly fit to a raging fever with temperature of 105 within the hour, some going! I'm now deaf due to the quinine: Twenty one grains yesterday, twenty seven today and eighteen for five more days.

Canteens closed due to a BOR found by the Japs talking to the contractor behind the counter, we hope to open our own shortly. I'm running the theatre here, but this fever has prevented me making a start. A number of Wop internees are in a camp adjoining this.

2 December

More letters! Two from Flossie, three from Dot and two from Frank and maybe more to come! The greatest relief of all and the most joyous news that on December 18 they had been officially informed that I was a POW – now it only remains for my postcard to get home and all will be well – that's hardly correct as two postcards in twenty two months is so paltry even if the wireless message got home as well. Why oh why can't *we* write once a fortnight as well. (hardly possible on second consideration in Thailand).

Weighed myself on Avery Scales today. 9st 5lb – allowing for a gain of a few pounds since arriving at Kambhuri the figure of 9st. I should think the last time I was that weight was when I was fourteen or fifteen. Ye Gods, no wonder every bone in my body seems to protrude something 'orrible.

We are now settling down here, our hut is attap roofed but well constructed wooden floor and a ceiling etc., and tonight we get one x fifteen watt bulb to light our room! We have one batman to seven officers. I share a leading Aircraftsman named Edwards with Brown and Pullen of the Gurkhas, Brochi of the Leicesters, Kirkwood of the IAOC, Ferguson of the Gordons, and English, an Australian, a mixed bag! In fact we have now got back our officers status at last and are no longer white coolies. This hut contains British, Australian and Dutch officers.

I do not intend to write a summing up of my impressions of Thailand. Our force of 3,320 had lost 817 when we left Kambhuri, there were 100 hospital cases who were not expected to survive and many who, altho' passed fit, had, owing to amoebic dysentery an expectation of life of less than five years. I have lost many friends amongst officers and ORs, but the saddest blow of all was the news that Jack Feathers had died in an unsuccessful attempt to escape – they were actually in Burma and so on the western side of the mountain range that separated us from the Burma frontier.

4 December

All letters sorted now with still more for me – so far since our first mail bag arrived I've had eleven letters from my Flossie, twelve and three postcards from Frank, eight and one postcard from Dot and one from Winifred Horner. I consider myself

35. Map of Thailand
showing camps

36. Telegram

37. Three Christmas cards

very lucky when some have had none or only one or two whereas others have had forty or fifty with photos as well. However it's grand to know everything's OK. I'd love a photo but most of all wish my own postcards would get through.

9 December

Have read postcards to be sent home, I do hope they get home quickly. Am in charge of entertainments here, so far can't get hold of a piano, but we have an open-air theatre that needs patching up, but has a natural auditorium of a grass bank that will hold 3,000 or 4,000. The Wops here are interned from two Subs. Three officers; Fergie of the Gordons, Bob Hughes of AIF and Avelink of the Dutch Navy have set up a snack-bar and sell coffee and cakes each evening. Prices are very high, eggs at 40c are prohibitive, I buy bananas at 35c a pound for sheer food value.

14 December

The remainder of 'H' Force have now come down from Thailand – the total death rate of our force of 3,320 is now 823. 'F' Force are also on their way down either to Bangkok or possibly another camp in Singapore. Their casualties are over 3,000 already and they are dying at a rate of eight to twelve a day. They lost a lot from cholera and pure starvation. As 18 Division had a large number of this force I fear I'll have lost many friends. I've so far heard of no officers, but twelve ORs all of whom I knew well are I'm told only scratching at the surface of the RASC casualties. The 18 Division Provost Company sent seventy odd on 'F' and 'H' parties and of these only six have survived. 'F' Force went up 7,000 strong, were the other side of the Burma border and apparently their only means of supply at one stage was by elephant who brought beans and rice in very small quantities.

'Fergie' of the Gordons and I have formed a combine – we buy such things as whitebait, blachang mee, tamaran onions, coconut and palm oil and 'Fergie' who is one of our Snack Bar Cooks concocts sambals, pies, stews etc., to go with our tiffin, very good and a good boost to what is usually a smallish meal.

19 December

Concert I arranged for tonight cancelled owing to rain. This being the rainy season we get rain every afternoon and most evenings thus putting on a show presents some difficulties as the audience are in the open.

Barber has been left up in Burma by 'F' Force with cardiac beri-beri, 'Jamie' is also there with the same complaint. Had another ten names of RASC personnel who had died up-country.

Our food these days is pretty good with the extra we can buy with our $10 Mess subs. The actual Jap issue is fresh fish (usually very small and bony) twice a week, fresh vegetables in the form of sweet potatoes, tallus, chinese cabbage, bayam, whilst from our own gardens here we get sweet potato tops, ladies fingers, brinjals and chillies – so that we get anyhow one vegetable meal a day. Soya beans are an issue, also palm oil and sugar – to these we add further oil, whitebait, blachang, coconuts, gula malacca, root ginger, pineapples – quantity is governed by prices which are all high.

We hear that in future the monthly sub that we make to men's messing from our pay is to come out of the sum that is being banked for us in the Yokohama Specie Bank, so we will see more money each month! Nips have agreed to lend us their piano over Christmas.

24 December

Officially announced there's a Red + ship in, whacko! Hard at work rehearsing a show I'm putting on tomorrow afternoon.

25 December

Show was great success, audience of about 1,500, weather was kind all day. The meals were: Breakfast - papped rice with milk and sugar, whitebait rissole - Tiffin – sambal oudang and nase goreng, – Dinner - towgay soup, fish champal, meat pies, fried chips and onion sauce, pineapple and banana trifle, Xmas cake and savoury biscuits and coffee. Pretty good for nearly two years' POW.

26 December

Down with malaria again – Doc. Dixon is going to put me on a course of plasmaquin to try and get the bug out of my system. The quinine (27 grains per day) is making me very deaf and muzzy and has to be endured for a week before the plasmaquin starts.

1944

1 January

Had durian today and toasted the seeds; eaten with salt they're excellent. Got a concert on tonight but am feeling lousy.

2 January

Concert great success – am ordered to hospital with jaundice.

13 January

Returned from hospital, jaundice now quite OK., but have a sweat rash all over my body and septic sores on hands and feet due to some deficiency or other.

Bought a lot of fresh pineapples when in hospital, found they tempted one's appetite when all else failed.

17 January

Ref. to septic sores in last entry now confirmed as scabies which I had hoped was cleared up. Hands very sore – the rash is still present and gives great irritation at nights. Concerts are now improving, heavy kits of officers have arrived from Changi (I have my suitcase and mattress) and props on loan are forthcoming, making shows more presentable.

We have got a piano from Changi but still need a curtain. I'm producing *Cinderella and the Magic Soya Bean* we also have Shaw's *Man of Destiny* and Shakespeare's *Othello* in rehearsal as well as ideas for a Ragbag Revue. Having this damned scabies on the feet as well I have to clip-clop around on Chinese clogs, OK by day but on rough paths by night *très difficile*. Jap interpreter has asked for words and music of my *When we're free* song – as I haven't yet sung it here, I wonder how he's got to hear of it.

Had a search yesterday in which a one-inch map of Singapore was taken from my case. Food not as good these days, rice ration down and vegetable issue scanty with little or no green vegetables.

29 January

The Saturday night variety shows are going with a great bang, we have about 2,000 each time. Sang 'When we're Free' tonight and got the audience to join in. Am taking part of King in *Cinderella* and Trotter in *Journey's End* – Hector McLean of 17th Dogras has written the latter from memory and made a fine job of it. Had two lots of meat in, tastes rather like veal.

7 February

Japs having ordered a permanent 'black-out', we're moving our theatre to a hut. My feet are very bad with septic sores making walking absolute hell – I'm lying up for a few days.

10 February

Have been laid up with my feet for two days, they're very sore. Rehearsed *Cinderella* this morning. Had lecture last night by P/O Fowler USN on 'Last Cruise of USS Houston' – next Wednesday I've arranged for Ken Luke to talk on his experiences when torpedoed in the North Atlantic, he had a very rough passage.

Food pretty lousy, altho' still getting meat occasionally – prices have rocketed sky-high, pipe tobacco is unobtainable. I smoke cut up cheroots! Sugar now $2 per pound.

13 February

Have been ordered to write an essay for IJA on certain subjects. I chose 'My First Impressions of the Japs,' which I wrote unexpurgated. Some were very clever!

15 February

Some more letters in, have got one from the Hinkleys dated 1 March 1943.

23 February

Opening night of *Cinderella and the Magic Soya Bean* last night, played to packed house of very enthusiastic audience. Jon Mackwood and Hector McLean have re-written *Rope* by Patrick Hamilton, am taking the part of Harry – very Bohemian! The Barn Theatre looks very good and is able to create a very intimate atmosphere – Ron Searle has done our decorations and scenic effects.

27 February

Bis' birthday – can she really be six, seems impossible; surely she'll have grown out of all recognition.

Cinderella etc. has been a howling success – On Tuesday we start GBS's *Man of Destiny*. Am not in this.

I've been resting each day as my legs and feet have been covered with sores, thank heavens they're now drying up. I had over forty on legs and feet and a dozen or so on my hands.

29 February

Am basking in the fragrant aroma of 'Camel' cigarettes – a number of American Red + parcels have come in, some items are going into the cookhouse and others such as soap, chocolate etc., are being given to individuals. The tinned goods include bully, pork and beans, butter etc. So the mystery of the Red + ship continues. Individual parcels have been received by American POWs, medical stores marked Bombay

38. Sprod's *Cinderella*

39/39a. Searle's scenery

September 1943 have been received and now these, which are single parcels, altho' not addressed to anyone, only for distribution by International Red +. We were told at Xmas that there were tinned goods, tobacco, and cigarettes awaiting distribution, so far this is all we've seen and the quantities are roughly seven people to one individual parcel.

9 March
We are showing a non-stop variety *Bats in the Barn* this week which Alan Roberts and I are producing. Going very well, I do two front-tab items with Hector McLean and also a solo 'Goalkeeping' act that's gone down well.

16 March
Been down with food-poisoning but have managed to make the theatre each night where I'm playing Trotter in *Journey's End* – my legs and feet have improved with the rest. There's no doubt a complete 'lie-up' would clear them but the shows have to take first place.

17 March
Inspection this morning by new Jap Guard in charge POW Malaya, one Major General Saito – on parade from 0900–1215hrs all for an address of two minutes – the sun of course was beating down on our backs with no shade available.

24 March
Show this week *Ragbag Revue* going very well – am not in this as I'm trying to rest my feet which continue to break out in septic sores. A lot of us having stomach trouble, acute pains and diarrhoea.

29 March
First night last evening of *Rope* in which I take the part of Harry, a Bohemian play-boy – a very enthusiastic audience.

General Saito has forbidden officers to contribute any pay to ORs' rations. Owing to high price of tobacco, pipe in particular – we're experimenting with making our own – dried papaya leaves cut up fine, boiled in tea and then with a drop of Worcester Sauce added is said to make quite a reasonable smoke. The Chinese contractor has said that the tobacco we buy is banana leaves and gula malacca – hey nonny no!

31 March
No more tobacco coming in – our manufactured stuff is out for its last drying. The Wops who were here during our first few weeks and then left here returned only this time we're allowed to talk to them. Rations being altered – less vegetable (is this possible?!) more rice (half an ounce per man) and more beans – less meat (again this seems difficult unless it's cut out altogether).

5 April

Went to a birthday party on Saturday night – the home-brewed 'hooch' was pretty good. The Italians are a pleasant crowd, no animosity has been shown towards them – were they pro-Mussolini, they wouldn't have been here and they're certainly very anti. Most of them are off two subs that came here and which were going back filled with rubber.

The show this week *Music Thru' the Years* is the most popular yet. Got up by Bill Williams it runs for two hours and has tunes from 1910–1944 interspersed with news items of the period, which I do, which necessitates my presence on the stage all the time. The news items get a lot of noisy comment which is most amusing – references to Hitler etc, gets boos and catcalls – to Test Matches, boos or cheers according to whether the audience is mainly Australian or British and so on.

9 April

Easter Sunday – we couldn't help being amused (?) comparing our mid-day meal with that of even a war-time England. Potato-tops, a little papaya and soya beans, with boiled rice in addition. And yet such is one's point of view after two-and-a-quarter years of captivity, that by and large it seemed an adequate meal!

15 April

Last night tonight of *Nuts and Wine* this week's show at the Barn, a revue that is reckoned by most as our best ever. I appear four times, the two main items being in a burlesque on *Rope* and some of our other shows that's been very popular – actually the idea emanated from Robert Edwards and myself – and then as recitateur in *The Green Eye of the Little Yellow God*. Had a fruit called soursap looking rather like a durian, they have a very pleasant taste.

20 April

This week we've *Bird in the Hand* by John Drinkwater at the Barn – I take the part of Blanquet an enjoyable character part of a middle-aged apologetic commercial traveller. The show is very popular and maintains our run of successes. 'Fergie' of the Gordons is producer.

The IJA have taken over the detention barracks – prisoners only are allowed to take with them, one hat, one shirt, one pair shorts, one pair boots, mess tin and spoon. They do no work, from 0600–2000hrs they spend varying periods in various positions either standing, sitting or kneeling, positions that have to be maintained all the time. At nights they are awakened every hour. Last night according to a released OR today they spent from 2200–0300hrs kneeling! Should put a stop to crime in the camp but is not too good really.

23 April

Have not mentioned before that for the last two months we have been able to get a voluntary subscription to the gaol for the children still interned there, poor wee souls, what a start in life they are getting.

40. *Journey's End*

41. RMH as Blanquet (George Sprod, the Australian artist who drew the caricature of me as Blanquet in *Bird in the Hand* later became a regular contributor to 'Punch')

As Blanquet in "Bird in Hand" [Act II]

"Goodnight's been said so often in this house its become a mockery"

George Sprod
Sime Rd P.OW
Camp
April 18-44

42/43. *Bird in the Hand,*
plus inside programme

"BIRD in HAND"

Characters in Order of Appearance.

JOAN.................JON MACKWOOD.
ALICE.................BOB BOWMAN.
THOMAS...............ROBIN WELBURY.
GERRY................RONALD SEARLE.
BEVERLEY............ROBERT EDWARDS.
BLANQUET.............JACK HORNER.
GODOLPHIN...............KEN LUKE.
SIR ROBERT.........DUGGIE FORBES.

P R O D U C E D
B Y
W. H O G G   F E R G U S O N.

Synopsis of Scenery.

ACT 1 ... ... The Bar Sitting Room - Evening

ACT 2 ... ... A Bedroom - Later.

ACT 3 ... ... The Bar Sitting Room - At
Breakfast the Next Day.

MUSIC BY BILL WILLIAMS.

SETTINGS BY SEARLE AND SPROD.

STAGE MANAGER .. JACK WOOD.

STAGE LIGHTING ... DAVID EASTHAM.

STAGE CARPENTER .. NEVILLE CHADWICK.

Our new camp commandant has made us give all orders and numbering on roll call in Japanese! By paying $2.50, we have been able to buy some books and have got quite a good subscription library going. Previous to this we had one that was run by a Dutch officer and which was joined by putting a book in. I got a shocker up in Kambhuri and put that in, but it was a book!

I still have *Pickwick Papers* that I bought in Worcester and which has accompanied me all the time I have been a POW – up-country it was a god-send to read at odd moments (and weren't they odd!!!)) taking you out of yourself.

[I still have the book, one of the corners of which was eaten by white ants when they got into my pack whilst up-country]

Soya beans not coming in any more, maize, with practically no food value, being substituted. Not so good. 700 of our fittest men went to Changi yesterday and 700 of their unfit have come here – their standards of unfit are not far from our fit. There almost everyone is working on a huge fighter strip which means considerable levelling of ground. One man bashed to death (shades of Thailand?). all maps and atlases having been stamped on by the IJA a few weeks ago and returned – have now been called in and will not be returned.

[The Japanese disapproved of diaries and said that if anyone was found with a map or a diary they would be shot. I had a false bottom made to my suitcase and spread the diary at the bottom and this survived a number of searches; both are now in the Imperial War Museum. (Sally McQuaid recalls : Many years later, my father retrieved the case from the Rugby Club Jumble Sale. My mother had inadvertently handed it over for the sale and my father had to pay 1/6d to buy it back!)]

25 April

Big changes in near future. All civilian internees from Changi Gaol coming here, women in the area we are in and men at opposite end of camp. The space in between will hold the troops now housed in the whole camp for a week or so, before we move to the gaol. Anyhow that's how matters stand at the moment.

The crowding will be reminiscent of Thailand with over 200 to a hut that is crowded with 100 in, dear little playmates! Oh for a day of reckoning. It will be grand seeing white women and children again after over two years. And so we lose the Barn Theatre, our last show of the season *Scotch Broth* in which I don't appear goes on for three nights only and then we close down.

30 April

Just recovering from very heavy dose of fever, blood test slide shows 'B.T.++' which is the most violent form of recurrent malaria – am feeling as weak as a kitten and haven't eaten for thirty six hours.

44. Diary and suitcase showing false bottom (Photograph taken for the *Liverpool Echo*)

On Friday our playmates excelled themselves moving us and all paraphernalia to our new area and then telling us the move was postponed for five days. I'm very glad now, as yesterday I had a helluva day and was glad of a bed and comparative comfort which I wouldn't have had there.

Have a bees' nest in wall of our room. They swarm every afternoon, causes Jim Pullen much annoyance and Sammy the Spider – who lives in the roof – much joy.

1 May
General Saito has visited camp – male internees start to arrive. We're told to be prepared to move to Kurran Camp near the gaol any moment, possibly a prelude to trip to Japan!!!

My fever has caused me to lose a lot of weight and I have no strength at all – damnable with a move in the offing. Oh yes, and my voice has gone as well!!

2 May
Move to new area prior to leaving camp very cramped quarters, packed like sardines. Food Lousy.

4 May
Had party last night of Barnstormers, good line in 'hooch' – sang numbers from all old shows.

Move day after tomorrow, believed to be precincts of gaol for officers. Weighed myself – 9st 5lb – have lost half a stone during last bout of fever and am now only half a pound above my weight when I arrived in this camp.

5 May
Moved to Changi Gaol, all Sime Road Camp in one half, internees still in other half, did one good in one way to see white women again altho' heartbreaking to see them behind bars, particularly the children.

7 May
Food very short, 'pap' for breakfast and rice and stew for other two meals.

Ran a sing-song last night, we have all our 'props' from The Barn including the piano. Huts are being erected outside and all officers and something like 5,000 ORs will be living there with 5,000 in here. Don't like my first experience of 'behind bars', altho' I'm able to get outside as I'm helping the Supply Depot.

9 May
Five letters arrived: three from my Flossie and two from Frank, whacko! I hear from other sources that the postcards we wrote in June '42 arrived twelve months later, so hope mine was OK. – it's funny how homesick we have been lately, it wasn't until I spoke to others one evening that I discovered it was general. I suppose two-and-a-quarter years with so little contact with home is responsible – gosh how I long to be home and these letters have increased the longing.

12 May
Colonel Galleghan the redoubtable 'Black Jack' of the AIF has asked me to organise entertainments in the Gaol, we have had four concerts so far and several gramo-phone recitals (gramaphone ex-American Red +).

14 May
Had concert last night by members of the official AIF Concert Party – am trying amalgamation of them with British artists, but so far don't know how successful it will be, as they've been a separate unit for over two years.

Am now in third 'billet' since arriving here. First we were in the observation cell for mental suspects, then a punishment cell in the Refractory Block and now a ward in the hospital. In all case, latrines (Asiatic pattern) are in the cell and, even hardened as we are after Thailand, we feel some embarrassment when using them. In this ward we have a shower as well, which is most convenient.

16 May
First combined show of British and AIF concert group went very well last night – I compèred.

18 May

Another show last night; a sentimental poem I composed went over very well. BJ has asked for a copy to send to his unit. Forgot to mention am now in his HQ Mess!!!

" A THOUGHT FOR THE MOMENT "

Now that we're together here, together in the clink,
It gives you time to figure things; it gives you time to think,
Of all the folks we left behind who keep the home fires bright,
Who think of us and pray for us by day, yes, and by night.

It is'nt very difficult, behind this prison wall,
To let it sap your spirit, so It's up to one and all,
When things seem pretty bloody and everything goes wrong,
To grit your teeth and carry on, although the road seems long.

We've all of us got loved ones, mother, sweetheart, wife,
Waiting there to help us, enjoy the freer life,
With tender loving kindness and pr'haps a few shed tears,
They'll help us to forget the Hell that's been these last
                                                few years.

So isn't it worth trying, worth the effort made,
To make ourselves more fit for them with laws to be obeyed,
Not only laws of discipline but laws of right and wrong,
Of cleanliness and decency and where they both belong.

And when we do rejoin them, as free men once again,
We can hold our heads up high because we tried to Play the
                                                Game.

.....0000......

Changi Gaol.
17 May 1944.   R.M.H.

45. 'Thoughts for the Moment'

19 May
Am having a lot of requests for copies of my poem, is this fame?!

21 May
Six more letters, four from my Flossie (one with paragraph about Dobs billeting officers censored) one from Frank. Our combined AIF and British concerts are going with a terrific bang – around 3,000 at each show – the experiment of mixing the two has been successful and BJ is very pleased about it.

24 May
Show still going well, did my 'Goalkeeper' act last night which went down well. A senior US Air Force officer has arrived and is housed in the Tower and is not allowed to be spoken to. He looks quite young. Three pro-fascist Italians are now loose amongst us following a trip in a German sub from Bordeaux – not much love lost between the two!!! Moving out shortly to accommodation outside the walls. I'm in Coolie-quarters.

25 May
Gosh I'm hungry these days. Oh I hope when all this is over I never have to feel the real pangs of hunger again. Rations seem very short, no vegetables except greens from our own gardens. Bananas (unripe and fried) make a potato-like substitute for veg. and are used in nase gorengs.

28 May
Made my fourth move yesterday, this time to the Coolie lines outside the prison walls, am sharing a room with Denis Pearl, an RAF Flight Lieutenant named Sturrock and an RNR Lieutenant named Knight. Until tomorrow evening I'm feeding in BJ's Mess still.

1 June
Quite settled in our new quarters, unfortunately they're very hot at nights as they have the sun on the roof all day, but we have our meals out on the verandah and it's not too bad. In this block are 18 Division, RN, RAF and a number of US pilots etc., who have been shot down in Burma or SW Pacific. Wilf Wooler the Welsh 'Rugger' International is here from Java (one of the 77th Heavy AA Regiment) looking very convict-like with his close-cropped hair.

5 June
The following lines – ASM Hutchison's 'As once you were' could well be memorised by many here, where after two and a quarter years of POW life including for many of us six-to-eight months of hell up in Thailand, petty annoyances assume large proportions and tempers and nerves are frayed and taught: 'The hurtful word, the hate-full thought, cast from me Lord as Christ once wrought. The self-same miracle when He freed men possessed in Galilee.'

9 June

Down with another bout of Malaria, a nuisance as we've just started Road-shows (four inside and three outside the Gaol) which I am running. Blood test show B.T. + again.

11 June

Reading a book by Hamilton Gilles called 'Chances', talking of 'Good-byes' he says 'To say good-bye is to die a little' – many years ago some part of me died on a bleak Birmingham platform and won't be brought to life until I'm with my Flossie again.

13 June

Yet another of 'our days' comes and goes with a divide of many thousands of miles – surely the next one will see us together – my fever much better, hope today will be better than twelve months ago when I spent most of the day carrying dead and dying Tamils with cholera to the death pit – N.B.G.

23 June

Have mentioned before that I'm running the Road Shows here, four shows inside and four outside the Gaol. Our first which was by the AIF Concert Party finished on Friday 16th – our second which is all-British and which, owing to sickness and so-called artistic temperament has given me many headaches, started last night. Our next will be amalgamated British, Dutch and Australian talent.

26 June

A lot of dysentery about, those who haven't got that have stomach pains and diar-rhoea, myself included. Cause not certain, the latter believed due to quantity of tapioca root being consumed, our stomachs are not used to heavy digesting these days and the tapioca is too much for it.

Jap GOC Southern Regions (?!) inspecting us tomorrow – General Saito gave us the once-over today. Most of the building outside the gaol wall is now completed – there are roughly 10,000 – including 1,000 officers in and outside the gaol – almost all accommodation outside the gaol is attap huts.

[*On one occasion we had a search by the Kempi Tei (the equivalent of the German Gestapo). Knowing that they disapproved of diaries, I pushed my diary between the fronds of the Attap roof of the hut. It was only after, when I had gone outside and was returning to the hut, that I realised that the more I pushed the diary from the inside the more visible it was on the outside! Luckily it hadn't been spotted.*]

UP THE SPURS!

46. RMH – Goalkeeping

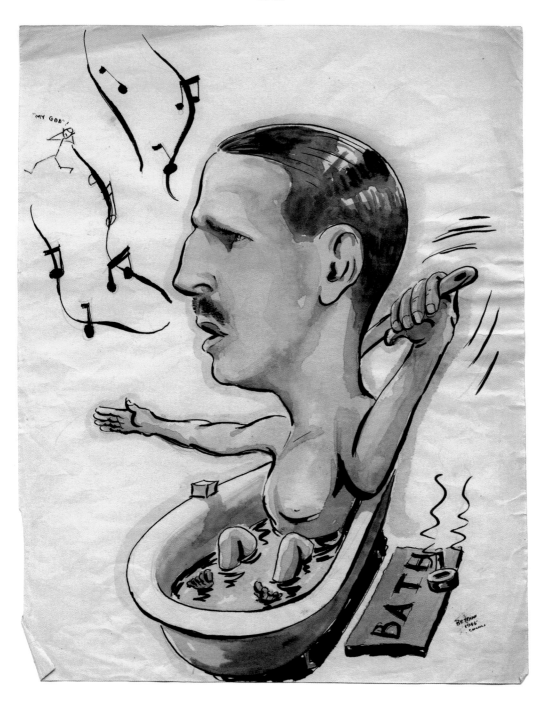

47. RMH in the bath (The significance of the bath was that I sang a song in a bath after a build up of having scoured the Camp to find a new outstanding singer, I always sang better in my bath!)

28 June

Sixty Dutch and Australian (only three of the latter) survivors from two ships torpedoed in the Malacca Straits off Medon arrived here today – out of 700 who left Sumatra some 300 were drowned, two so far have died and four more not expected to live.

Story told by Padre Duckworth of hospital at Tambya in Burma where 'F' Force sent their sick. One fellow who, like so many others, had no inclination to, and therefore refused to, eat – medical orderly trying to persuade him to take something said 'Did you come here to die?' – 'no', came the reply, 'yester-die!'

30 June

Paid visit to dentist, am trying to save a tooth, part of which broke off up-country, was stopped temporarily in Sime Road and which broke off with an extra bit the other day.

6 July

Me wee Iain's second birthday. I must surely be home for his third – like so many others am finding these days that I'm mortally fed up with this POW life with so little contact with home (we hear there are eighty-five bags of mail in by the way) time seems twice as long.

Last night dined with Robert Edwards of the Manchesters; afterwards he, Ken Archer (a grand chap with whom I'm very friendly in the Volunteer Armoured Car Company out here) and I sat listening to some excellent music from a portable gramophone. With a full moon shining, silhouettes of the palm trees, cheroots aglow and the haunting melodies of Delius to soothe our thoughts, life seemed quite good – if only!!!!! Ken, Ralph Sparks and I have a pact within six months of our arriving in England, we meet for lunch in town, next to 'The Feathers' at Ludlow, where we spend the night having, it is expected, had a pretty hilarious party together.

7 July

A letter from my Flossie, Frank and Dot, respective dates 30 May '43, 15 June '43 and 1 June '43, I only hope in this batch to hear that my first postcard has arrived home.

10 July

Amongst industries being done here are the following: Book-binding, rubber factory, complete workshops including welding apparatus, clothing and boot repairs, cotton from old Jap-issue, socks unravelled, brush factory including repair of tooth-brushes, soap manufacturing when there is a sufficiency of palm oil, watch repairs.

13 July

Compèred a show in officers' area last night; terrific crowd, just before the end 'Lights Out' was ordered and the air-raid alarm sounded. At 2330 a plane (? whose) dropped a flare and several were heard around for some time afterwards.

Heard today that the poem I made up (mentioned on 18 May) was read in the Australian Chapel at Selerang and formed the text of a sermon. Ahem! It's been tremendously hot these days, at nights I lie under my mosquito net and sweat and sweat – I have great difficulty in sleeping.

These Coolie quarters catch the sun all the day long and when you go into them at nights it's like entering a hot house. My Rolex has packed up and is now awaiting repair – it stood me in good stead under very adverse conditions.

14 July

Five more letters, one from Dot, three from Frank and one from Bess O'Kenton.

17 July

Three more letters; one from Frank, one from Betty le Mare and one dated August 1942 from my own. There is a great deal of vitamin deficiency about, mostly in the form of skin complaints. I feel fitter than I have done for ages and now have no septic sores on my feet. My weight is around the 10st mark.

21 July

Colonel Newey to take over representative officer from BJ, reasons given are finding of one Mountford trying to locate his wife in Singapore – all very amusing.

29 July

Having a mild recurrent Malaria, every other day and not enough to keep me in, but very annoying.

Have had my Rolex cleaned and overhauled by an Australian officer, very interesting watching him strip the whole thing. Another Aussie officer has repaired my Flossie's photo, the back of which was falling apart, boy oh boy nothing must happen to that.

Later. Going into hospital with B.T + Malaria.

31 July

Some way to spend one's birthday, in hospital. Received a most amusing birthday card from the lads of the Concert Party, drawn by Ronald Searle and with a verse made up by Bernard Campion. Rec'd two letters one from my Flossie and the other from Dot dated February and April respectively.

5 August

Discharged from hospital – have been compèring the Road Show which started on Thursday – Some think it's our best yet but I cannot tell myself.

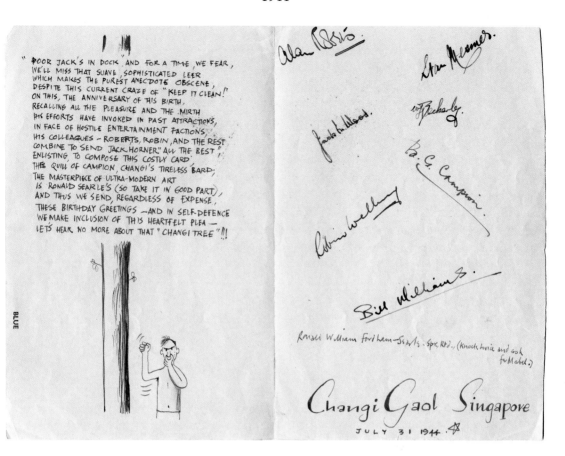

50/51. Searle's birthday card, plus inside (the card was, with verse inside, given to me when I was down with Malaria. I had kept a tin of Capstan Navy Cut which I said I would open when Germany capitulated – on the assumption that the Japs would follow soon afterwards. In fact, I opened it when news came through our hidden wireless set of the attempt on Hitler's life – thus all the cadging pipes!)

8 August

Have moved from Coolie quarters to a hut, am now next to Ken Archer which is 'very goodenar!' The hut is attap-roofed and airy. Actually I have much more room than I had before and the atmosphere won't be too stuffy at night. The only real advantages in the Coolie-quarter was the inclusion of a flush WC and tong for holding water with tap above it. Three letters two from Flossie and one from Dot. One of Flossie's was Feb '44 and contained a note from Bis!

Later. Received a letter from Frank – if only I could get some dated late July and August I might hear that my postcard had arrived home.

9 August

Allowed to write a postcard home – only hope we get there first! Weighed myself today, still under 10st; in only shorts I'm 9st 10lb – have gained only 5lb since leaving Thailand.

10 August

Letters received from Flossie (April '43) and Frank (January '44) – in the latter I hear that my second postcard arrived home on Christmas eve – rather sounds as if my first failed to make the grade.

12 August

Three more letters received: two from Flossie one April '43 and other January '44 and one of December '43 from Frank. Rather looks as if my first one went astray but can't yet be sure – hope my Flossie gets on OK at Torquay. My Flossie's birthday bless her. I hope I'll be with her next year.

14 August

Letter from Frank today March '43, the Apostolic Delegation whoever they may be, say I'm in Tai-Wan – they've missed the bus somewhere! Probably as 'Becky' died there and our Brigadiers are there they thought that all 18 Division were there also. Vitamin deficiency is on the increase; some 5,000 have skin trouble and 2,000 or more really bad eye troubles.

Later. Received another letter from Frank also of March '43 – I'm being very lucky this lot altho' there is a big gap for everyone from July – December.

Have not previously mentioned, I don't think, the weekly concerts by the Military Band composed of British and Australians numbering around thirty – they give a very good performance and make a pleasing contrast to my Road Shows.

17 August

I'm feeling 'browned-off' with this bloody POW life, just one of those waves of depression I suppose – two and a half years on a rice diet is apt to get one down, food seems so tasteless altho' the cooks work wonders in trying to disguise the beastly stuff. I long for the decent amenities of life and a varied diet, not rice and salt fish day after day with a little, a very little vegetable – mostly casava root (tapioca).

20 August
Injections for anti-dysentery and TAB have brought on a fever – not serious but depressing.

22 August
Some new 'Penal Laws' with regard to POWs have just been promulgated – for any of the following crimes against one's guards the punishment is – capital punishment, imprisonment or confined for an indefinite period of not less than one year – violence or threat – killing or causing the death, or of preparing or causing any plot or conspiracy to do this – inflicting injury, committing any violence or making any threat – anyone resisting any order or command or disobeying any order or command, anyone insulting one's guards etc., liable to imprisonment or confined not exceeding five years. RIP!!!!

Later. Letters received from Frank and Dot, one each dated June 1 and February 23 respectively.

Eye-sight trouble continues to take its toll due to vitamin deficiency, so far apart from occasional trouble and of course with the ever-present 'black-outs' if one stands up too suddenly. I've kept free (touch wood) – the tragedy is that the harm is permanent and will not heal on a proper diet in many cases, thus many fellows will lose their peace-time jobs or be unable to hold them down.

23 August
Our present Road Show, the sixth in the series, concludes on Saturday and will be the last for the moment anyway of band and variety turns. The 7th edition is all musical with two pianos, xylophone, violin solos, singing and accordion duets. The theatre we are building in the gaol should be ready in a few weeks (it's a mammoth construction) and rehearsals start next week for the opening show.

24 August
Have made a concoction of Soya Sauce 50c per quarter pint, vinegar 68c per quarter pint, onions 37c per ounce and chillis 'presento' from Dick Conway the Australian – its coming on well and will gain flavour as the onions get well and truly soaked.

27 August
Played in darts match RASC v Wales – we won 24-18; I won one of my three matches. When de-bugging my bed today caught a small scorpion – good thing it didn't get me first!!

48/49. Sprod's birthday card, plus inside

Wishing you all the
Best for the Coming Year
and a speedy Departure
from this wretched hole —

George Sproed

Changi Gaol
31 - 7 - 44

28 August

Amazing how filthy dirty some fellows are, some have a shower about once a week, this in a humid climate where personally I find the two showers a day we're allowed is hardly enough. An American merchant service radio-operator has just finished his evening toilet before supper – a bit of water on his hair from his water-bottle, out with his comb – finis!

One Indian army captain hasn't bathed for days – when first captured and put in Kuala Lumpur gaol, the same officer and gentleman (?!) didn't remove his socks for three weeks!!

Letter from Dot dated December '43 – goodo!

29 August

Have just returned from hearing a most interesting lecture by Captain Crapallo of the Royal Italian Navy on submarine tactics since the outbreak of the war, showing how anti-submarine measures have gradually, with the co-operation of aircraft, overcome the menace.

31 August

Letter from Dot today dated 28 May '43 – heartbreaking to hear that Vernon and Rodney get letters home regularly and I'll be lucky if I've got two postcards home in two and a half years!

3 September

Five years at war – went to evening service; 'Ducky' and an Australian padre called Jones pack their 'church' each Sunday. Ken Archer and I sit up after lights out until sometimes one o'clock yarning – thank God for him and Tony Gardener to keep me sane in this hellish life which at times seems almost unbearable.

10 September

Took part last night in *Wide World Magazine* organised by Major Bartram in the officers' area – I did ten minutes humour – seemed to go down alright.

12 September

Apparently they think that 'Horner's Corner' in last Saturday's *Wide World* programme was so successful that they want me to do one each month. Not so good – probably flop next time.

15 September

An issue of loz tobacco – the leaf in its natural state came in some time ago and some Dutch have been processing it. Not bad at all as local weed goes. Have compromised with Major Bartram ref. 'Horner's Corner'; I will organise the 'page' but need not appear myself.

16 September

My skin diseases are on the increase, scrotal dermatitis being extremely trying and now I fear the beginnings of a pile! Wot a bleedin' life!! We get an extract made from lalang and other green leaves that is said to contain vitamin B – tastes lousy but what the hell if it does one good. Food short these days, few vegetables coming in except from our own gardens and only occasional issues of whitebait, prawns.

24 September

Opening show of our new theatre built in the gaol on the same site where I first put on shows when we first arrived here – this was a 'command performance' for General Saito and staff military band and sundry solo items. The first night of our first show, a revue *All this and Heaven too* is tomorrow night, produced by John Wood the Australian, it includes all the foremost British and Australian artists – I am taking the part of a 'bobby' in a court-scene sketch. Getting in a few fish these days – mostly sting-ray and shark – we had ray last night (about 1oz); pathetic but good!

Later. Letters from Flossie and Dot dated 5 July and 7 May respectively – good-o! They've started on a new batch that came in recently and we hear there are photos – how grand to get one.

29 September

Weighed myself today 9st 9lb – should have thought I was more.

The Japs have furnished figures said to be up to April '44 of casualties on the Thailand Railway: British 3,612, American 127, Dutch 2,616, Australian 1,268, total 7,704; 15.1% of total troops up there. These figures exclude A, F & H Forces the total deaths of which are within the region of 4,500 making a grand total of somewhere about 12,000 dead. This excludes any killed in air action and we know of 90-odd killed in a recent bombing of Non Paduk and suspect many drowned off Saigon and Formosa.

Letter late last night from my Flossie – whooping cough!!! Silly peter at her age too!

30 September

Red letter day!! Ken, Tony and I have indulged in a concoction of blachang and soya sauce to have with our tiffins which are usually a form (rather vague) of nase goreng – smells the hut out by day and night the blachang being a paste of 'decomposed' prawns – but it adds a flavour if it is unique!

3 October

Funny story told by Ken Archer of a Chinese towkay (man of property) in Malacca who threw a party, his first mixed party – when the European ladies retired to their cloakroom they found a 'jerry' for each of them round the wall, with their name printed on a card above each!

52. Jalet, the American radio-operator who didn't like washing.

Vo-do-deo-Roe!

53. Roe, if I remember correctly, a bookie in Kuala Lumpur or Singapore

11 October

Took part last night in a one-night show to the Admin. Group in their admirable little theatre in the gaol – did my 'shaggy-dog' act which so far only the officers' area have seen.

13 October

My turn on Tuesday last has resulted in a request to compère a show there on Tuesday night and also to do one in another OR area the following day. A week later I'm putting on a small show in the officers' area, a sort of 'supplement' to the *Wide World Magazine* Horner's Corner.

Have just heard that Takahashi, the Camp Commandant, has cancelled all entertainment owing to 'the ribald singing of 'God Save the King' in the Hospital Area' – we are to be allowed two shows a week in the main theatre but nothing else. We are hopeful that the ban will be lifted again altho' there is nothing on which to base this hope unless it is the fact that Takahashi has always showed himself sympathetic and helpful.

ITEM	Oct '41	Oct.'44
Sugar	5c	$11.00
Onions	4c	$20.00 (Unprocurable)
Towgay	24c	$5.00 (Unprocurable)
Salt	6c	$2.00
Coffee	15c	$2.60
Curry Powder	25c	$2.40
Peanuts	5c	$5.40
Coconuts	4c	. 86 cents each

So much for the Greater East Asia Co-prosperity Sphere!

14 October

Singing of 'God Save the King' now traced to Indian sentries. Takahashi has approached General Saito with the view to the lifting the ban, but it must be kept on until the 21st. Saving face?!!

15 October

Funny how small things make you homesick. Wind prior to rain this afternoon made some telephone wires whistle. Extraordinary how this climate makes one forget names, forgot my own son's.

16 October

ARP exercises, ever so exciting! Roll on peace.

17 October

Bathed today, first bathe in sea since 1939 at Torquay – or did I have one at Ramsgate? Anyhow it's an awful long time ago!

18 October

Bought some cucumber today ($1.50 per lb), one of the few vegetables that are similar in the tropics to the home product.

Long talk with RSM Bruce who believes himself mediumistic and forecasts freedom by end of November with 19th the date. True story of the Nip sentry who showed Major Clarke, the Australian skin specialist, his trouble (usual one), Major Clarke said "itchy"? – "No buggeiro, ni" came the reply. Explanations needed and company chosen for this joke to be appreciated to the full.
(usual trouble = Scrotal Dermatitis "ichi" = one, "ni = two).

An OR named Bettanay has presented me with an excellent caricature of myself, feeding a biscuit to a shaggy dog! Very hot these days, even for Singapore – sweat simply pours off you without any effort.

21 October

Theatrical activities to be curtailed – two shows a week in the theatre only and lectures outside not more than twenty five. Representations being made. Alert last night and alarm this morning. Wot's the matter chum? Wind up?!!

22 October

In spite of theatrical restrictions which have been confirmed by IJA a Command Performance of *Autumn Crocus*, our next show, to be played to General Saito and staff tomorrow. Audience properly dressed (!!) allowed to fill the house.

24 October

Had letter from Maitland Jacob this evening. There is an odd bag of mail now.

26 October

Left England, or rather Droitwich, three years ago today. Ho hum, seems like three centuries. Postcard from my Flossie dated 19 May '44, whacko! Gathering of all 18 Division's RASC officers today to commemorate (commiserate?!) on yet one more anniversary from our loved ones. Hear there are seventy more mail bags. The recent letters are from three odd bags.

28 October

Getting a good deal of greens these days from our gardens. Bayam is the best as you can eat the stalk as well. Down with malaria again, a nuisance, I only hope it's only a slight bout.

<u>Later</u>. Fever confirmed B.T.+

54. Playhouse (this was given to me by an Australian on the first night at the theatre we built in one of the courtyards of Changi Gaol)

55. Shaggy Dog (the significance of this caricature is my predication to tell 'Shaggy Dog' stories)

30 October

Fever progressing well, damned quinine knocks you to blazes as well as making you deaf. Had a good buy of pair of wooden pattens with rubber soles and heels for 40c.

Canteen prices still soaring, pipe tobacco $2.00 per three-quarter ounce packet. Coconuts (some no larger than a cricket ball) 95c.

A Dutchman has just died here. He escaped in Thailand with another Dutchman, got up to Mandalay where his friend died and was caught just further north. Sentenced to twenty years' solitary confinement in Outram Road gaol, he was brought here suffering from advanced beri-beri. Being half Javanese he was able to look like a Burmese but even so his journey was an amazing feat of endurance.

5 November

Guy Fawkes' day and what a day to remember! For the first time since the capitulation in February '42 Allied planes are, even as I write, over Singapore. So far we've counted over thirty four-engined bombers; we are, needless to say, very excited. Is this the beginning of the month of our release? I don't think I'll ever forget the feeling when watching the ack-ack bursts and then spotting a plane, one of <u>ours</u> and realising that at last, it was not just another practice. Fireworks by Lord Louis!!

6 November

Apropos of yesterday's raid, Takahashi has ordered that anyone found picking up anything dropped from an aeroplane will be SHOT. (? Afraid of leaflets or that they may drop us Red + Supplies that the IJA want for themselves)

8 November

Another alarm due to a single raider flying at about 25,000ft – so far no bombs dropped near altho' some elsewhere we think. Plane came in from east this time. The 'Shonan Sinbun' reports that in last Sunday's raid fifty one planes were employed, bombs dropped on Seletar and naval base causing 1,500 casualties to innocent civilians, sinking two ships, one containing rice. The intrepid War Eagles brought down four over the Island and the remainder were chased out to sea where <u>all the rest</u> were shot down.

9 November

Took part last night in November issue of *Wide World Magazine* where I did another 'Horner's Corner' – went down well in spite of fact that whole show had to be done in daylight (no entertainment after 2000hrs outside the Gaol). Am organising some ward shows for the Hospital on Wednesdays and Saturdays. Report made above dated 8 November ref 'Sinbun' report proved incorrect, the true facts were thirty planes, one damaged, civilian casualties unspecified. Yesterday's raid was by two planes (twin-engined) and as far as can be ascertained no bombs dropped. My informant ref. fifty one is a bloody liar!

11 November

New orders ref. air-raid alarms: anyone found outside huts during an alarm will be shot, you are not even allowed to visit the latrine, so heaven help us if we have a twenty four or forty eight hours continuous alarm no food either as the orderlies couldn't bring it to us. Windy! Have started Ward-shows for the Hospital, produced and compèred the first today.

12 November

Heard from Jimmy Pearce, who is on the letter-sorting staff, that there are seven or eight for me so far – whacko! Am taking part in the next show in the Gaol, a panto *Twinkletoes,* feel these days even more than usual that we're sitting on the edge of a volcano. Had a long talk with 'Andy' Dillon about things in general – things rather complicated.

15 November

Am reading a *Strand Magazine* dated August 1940. Very tattered and torn but still intact. How homesick it makes one feel, so English!

16 November

Six letters, one from my Flossie, three from Frank, one from Dot and one from Bess O'Kenton. All old, dates from 26 July '43 to 13 November '43 – as Frank says in this one that no word had been received from me it looks as if my first card failed to make the grade. Hell!

18 November

Reliable information from Working Party in Singapore that Nips wounded at Alexandra Hospital all smoking American cigarettes and feeding on tinned goods – obviously source is parcels similar to those we had earlier this year. So the story of there being a Gondola full is probably true, altho' we won't see any of it.

19 November

Alert at 1015hrs, no general alarm followed and 'all clear' came three-quarters of an hour later. No planes seen.

20 November

Single B 29 came over at 1845hrs just as we were finishing our evening meal, very clear, the four engines were plainly visible – he came right overhead – the alarm went <u>after</u> he had turned on his way home.

22 November

'Sinbun' report that there was one plane over on the 19th and one on the 20th.

56. POW Life as per R Searle

The WIDE WORLD MAGAZINE
NOVEMBER ISSUE
WEDNESDAY 8TH NOV.
"COCONUT GROVE" THEATRE
at 1845 hrs.

EDITOR: Maj. V. BARTRUM , R.A.V.C.

Contributors:

Lt-Col. F.J. DILLON, Lt-Col. S.C. D'AUBUZ, Capt. C. WILKINSON, Capt. E.W.H. FILLMORE, Capt R.M. HORNER, Lieut. F.C. COOKE, Pte. S. GARLAND

Please do not place seats in position until after Melbourne Cup Broadcast at 1600hrs.

57. *Wide World Magazine*

24 November
No letters out for a week, they've been sorted and censored but are held up in Takahashi's office.

27 November
'Alert' sounded at 1230hrs, 'alarm' at 1330hrs, 'all-clear' at 1520hrs – as far as we could tell there were no bombers over this part of the Island altho' Nip aircraft up all the time. Tobacco so expensive these days ($2.80 per three-quarter ounce) am trying dried brinjal leaves, not too bad.

29 November
Four more letters, two from Flossie dated 13 Sepember and 6 October '43, one from Dot dated 1 November and one from Frank dated 25 October. Should imagine that that is the last full length letter to be written by my Flossie. Hell I'm fed up! Panto opens on Saturday, should go well I think, good tunes and crazy stuff.

1 December
Opening night of *Twinkletoes* last night – very enthusiastic audience. Harwood Harrison tells me there's a June or July postcard for me awaiting censoring.

6 December
Saw the exhibition of toys for children in Sime Road, very good indeed. Black-out tonight and tomorrow, postpones Panto until Friday so that we play two nights running.
   Windy about 7/8 December anniversary of attacks on Pearl Harbour [sic] and Singapore? Come on Sir Louis! I've mentioned already, I think, that we make voluntary contributions to the women and children each month – the special Christmas effort has realised $3,570, which should help quite a bit.

10 December
Another 'Command Performance.' On Tuesday next an hour's variety followed by the Panto M & B 693 made of chalk! No good for VD. Received three cards two from my darling dated 21 April and 15 July and one from Frank dated 5 June. In Flossie's later card hear my third card arrived, i.e. Actually third written altho' only second to be received.

11 December
More mail, two from Flossie one from Dot. and a photo from Frank of the wee Iain aged five months. Cheeky looking rascal. Bless him. Yanks at Osborne.

13 December
Command show went off OK last night. Afterwards we had <u>real</u> soup and sweet cocoa. Whacko! A taste of civilization. Amazing sense of values. Ken, Tony, and I

have just finished a baked tapioca root (very like baked potato) very filling and a taste of home side. Cost 1 x lb root $1.10.

Later. 'Alert' sounded at 1720hrs – 'all clear' an hour later.

14 December

Letter dated 10 May from Dot. I wonder whether Uncle Stanley's son turned up. We are to do a broadcast programme I'm doing a short 'Shaggy dog' turn in one of the two we're putting over. Pressed labour from Java (Men only film) – The CMF have been buying quite a lot of ragi and adzuka bean (both usually used as covert crops) very small ragi and the latter about the same size as soya bean. Weather very unsettled these days – 'Sumatras', strong wind and cooler nights.

20 December

Consider last entry gross understatement, now, finding it necessary to wear a pullover. Seems daft really when one considers that this here is 'damned cold' whilst at home it's a normal summer's day temperature. Rehearsing for *Red Peppers*, in which I play the Manager.

24 December

Broadcast not taken place yet – all British personnel are allowed to send wireless message (twenty five words) home. Whacko!

26 December

Christmas day has come and gone – Where will the next be spent? Starting with midnight communion and a sermon by 'Ducky' – after breakfast paid a round of calls, RASC personnel in the gaol, concert parties, officers took me to tiffin. From then until 1600hrs 'bashed' my bed. At 1630hrs paid round of visits to HQ personnel in Hospital. Dinner at 1815hrs after which took part in *Twinkletoes* which was quite hilarious and had a most responsive audience. Back in the lines by 1015hrs. Joined a sing-song until lights out at 2300hrs.

Couldn't sleep and from 0200–0330hrs sat talking to Chas Brunton (old Felstedian) smoking and so to bed. Unpleasantly full but conscious of having passed surely my last Christmas away from my loved ones. The cookhouse did us very well – starting with tea and a doughnut ring at 0800hrs, breakfast at 0900hrs consisted of porridge, fried whitebait with fried vegetables, fried bread and lime marmalade. 1100hrs coffee and shortbread. 1300hrs Tiffin – bayan soup, vegetable curry, mock apple tart, bread and cheese. 1600hrs – tea and Xmas cake. Dinner – hors d'oeuvres, towgay soup, pork pie, fried vegetables, Xmas pudding, cheese and biscuits, coffee. At 2100hrs – tea with mince pie.

The pork was from the Canteen at $20 per pound – we bought 7lb – and it made quite a good flavour. The cheese was some cartons of gorgonzola that were discovered in a 'go-down' at the docks and had been there since the capitulation. Too rancid for Nip consumption we got it and smeared on bread and on biscuits it

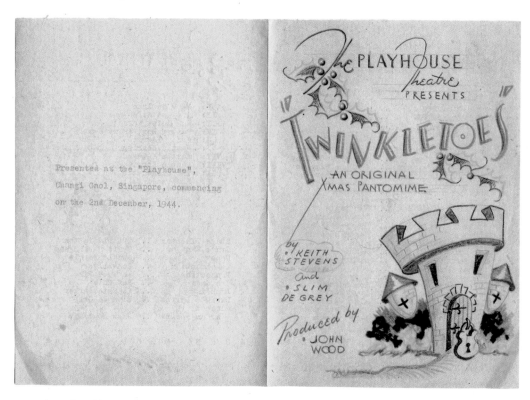

Presented at the "Playhouse",
Changi Gaol, Singapore, commencing
on the 2nd December, 1944.

The PLAYHOUSE Theatre PRESENTS

TWINKLETOES

AN ORIGINAL Xmas PANTOMIME

by KEITH STEVENS and SLIM DE GREY

Produced by JOHN WOOD

58/59. *Twinkletoes*, plus inside programme

PROGRAMME — "TWINKLETOES"

CHARACTERS:

John Truelove	.. Jack Geoghegan
Lengthy Leonard	.. Slim de Grey
Reckless Reggie	.. Jacky Smith
Nasty Norman	.. Jack Hibbs
Sir Bertram Butt	.. Frank Wood
Mrs Broadbottom	.. Bert Galbraith
Ben Broadbottom	.. Benney McCaffrey
Bertha Broadbottom	.. Charlie Wiggins
Wizard of Iz	.. Stan Kesmer
The Witch	.. Osmond Daltry
Mark I	.. Rex Cole
Mark II	.. Ginger Baines
The King	.. Ron Caple
The Queen	.. Harry Smith
Nutsy	.. Robin Wellbury
Princess Dizzy	.. Keith Stevens
Princess Twinkletoes	.. Stan Garland
Sjt Grinn	.. Bennie Barton
Sjt Bearit	.. Barney Bolton
Mashma Gandish	.. Jack Horner
Prince Bumblefoot	.. Joey the Doll
His Nurse	.. Ron Massey
The Duke	.. Doug Peart
Peg Leg	.. Alec Ogilvie
Ladies of Leisure	.. Reg Baker and Harry Wise

Act I:	Ye Olde Inne
II:	Road outside Inne
III:	Enchanted Forest
IV:	Sentry Box, Krazy Kastle
V:	Krazy Kastle
VI:	Kastle Korridor
VII:	Kastle Kitchen
VIII:	Kastle Korridor
IX:	The Dungeons
X:	Kondemned Cell
XI:	The Terrace

Stage Director	.. Syd Piddington
Stage Manager	.. Chris Buckingham
Decor	.. Ronald Searle
Construction	.. Joe Silver
Properties	.. Terence Pike
Costumes	.. Rex Cole
Lighting	.. Clarrie Barker
Music & Lyrics	.. Slim de Grey
Musical Arrangements	.. Jack Boardman

PRODUCED BY JOHN WOOD

1944

60. Four Christmas cards

155

made a nice change. Limes and spices such as ginger, cinnamon, clove etc., helped with the flavours. The hors d'oeuvres were boiled whitebait, fried coconut, brinjal, mashed artichoke, salt fish, shredded Ceylon spinach, blachang ball and boiled rice and tapioca root with a sweet sauce on it. All good stuff, but with weeks and weeks of lean meals, a day like this naturally finds one's belly blown out afterwards. Weather all day was excellent.

27 December

Did our recording for the Broadcast programme this afternoon. The show I was in goes on the air tomorrow morning, we understand that GB has been advised that it is coming over. The first Australian programme follows in the afternoon and then the two further shows the following day. Managed to get through mine without mishap, so can only hope those at home will be listening in – gosh I hope they are.

1945

1 January '45

I've got so tired of writing '… surely the next one will see me with my loved ones again' that a repetition seems superfluous.

There were no special celebrations, George Booker and I sat talking and suddenly George remembered he had a tin of Thai condensed milk in his pack, so at 2.30am this morning we solemnly sat down and celebrated the new year's advent with a 45c cheroot each and half a tin of milk – what fun!

Perhaps a quick survey of myself and conditions might not be out of place here – roughly 'My day' consists of: Rising at 0830hrs, shave and shower before breakfast at 0900hrs. Usually spend morning rehearsing or on some job connected with the theatre or Ward shows. Tiffin at 1300hrs, afternoon either lie on my bed or if there is a call, rehearsing. Shower and change between five and six. Supper at 1800hrs. Evening spent either with a show or visiting friends or reading. Lights out at 2300hrs. George Booker comes round at 2230hrs or thereabouts and we usually sit outside talking or smoking until midnight or later. Clothes – at night I wear a sarong and, according to how chilly it is, a shirt of white flannelette as a top. By day, shorts only: By night, shirt and either shorts or slacks. Food – Breakfast: rice 'pap', a 'doover', in other words a rissole or biscuit with a spread of blachang – Tiffin: stew and rice or a form of 'nase goreng' and a 'doover'– Supper: green stew and rice and four 'doovers'. Wednesday and Saturday is curry tiffin and five 'doovers' at night.

5 January

Not feeling too fit these days, can't make it out yet, it isn't fever, but as a sore mouth is one of the symptoms and a general lassitude, think it must be general deficiency trouble. My weight varies between 9st 12lb and 10st. Hey nonny no!

Going through a period of 'low' – it has been so long and the end seems so far off and try as they will, the cookhouse cannot alter the fact that greens and rice are 75% of the diet with fish in one form or another as the other flavouring. We're mortally sick of 'green' stew, but what have you?!

8 January

1330hrs single plane overhead, alarm coincides with ack ack – this was more plentiful than heretofore but was woefully inaccurate – good-o.

10 January

Single plane overhead at 1200hrs, ack ack and alarm not in evidence until it had cruised right overhead and was going away, four engines well in evidence. The increase in ack ack noted on Monday was not repeated and I think this was due to the presence of naval craft in the Naval Base who added their armament to the normal Island defences. Brown out 1245hrs.

11 January
Big raid on the Island this morning, alert went at 1010hrs, alarm at 1040hrs, there were many planes, how many it is difficult to say as they came in ones and twos from all directions. We fear one bomber was brought down, it looked like it, although we were not near enough to tell for certain. One fighter was shot down for certain and possibly another. It was the biggest thing yet with fighters up before the arrival of the bombers and many dog-fights. There may be more news later – 1830hrs – Krangi party just in confirm one bomber down, five or six crew bailed out, one fighter came down immediately afterwards in same area, so that makes two certain.

12 January
Still not feeling 100%, think it is my spleen which seems unhappy after several bouts of malaria. No planes today, feeling neglected!

13 January
'Drome working party who were sent home four hours early yesterday not working again today. Much shouting and 'ado' all night – wot fun!

14 January
Very little air activity yesterday, an ominous calm, same today. Compèred a new Ward Show yesterday and later took part in No. 1 of a new series of *Wide World Magazine* for the Hospital Area.

Alarm went, bombs dropped in Singapore area, saw only one plane. Have bought half a pint of Palm Oil ($1) put some on my hair, or rather rubbed it into my scalp which, with daily showers and no oil for two and a half years was woefully dry. Doesn't smell so good but what the hell?! The rest I put in my breakfast pap and such stews as seem to need it.

<u>Later</u>. I hear that three bombers were seen this morning.

19 January
Dress Rehearsal of *Tonight at 8.30* this evening. We open tomorrow.

Two full size sharks and one ray have just gone by on a trailer *en route* for the Hospital Kitchen. They smelt pretty high, but hope it means fresh fish issues are starting again – small as they were they made a pleasant change from salt fish and whitebait.

Very windy these days, rather like autumn in England. I find that I feel the slightest variation in temperature and shudder (both literally and figuratively) to think of winter in England.

Later. Hopes realised, had small portion of boiled minced shark this evening. From a large fish it smelt and tasted strong but was very good.

21 January
First night of *Tonight at 8.30* went off well last night, have been complimented on my own effort which is pleasing as it's not a big part.

22 January
Alert went at 1145hrs, 'all clear' half an hour later.

25 January
Alert went just before midnight last night, no development. Canteen expenditure $100,000 over camp income – verb sap! Takahashi takes poor view and clamps down on incoming supplies so it looks like brinjal leaf for a bit. Gosh I'm getting awfully sick of greens – true they're good for one, but they're so tasteless compared with the home-side cabbage. Surely 'Man shall not live by greens alone' – but it looks damn like it with greens and rice as 90% of our diet. Hey nonny no and carry six!! Maybe it won't be long now, I hope so as three years on this diet has begun to pall, apart from the many other considerations.

Latest news ref. Canteen is that Takahashi wants an explanation as to why the expenditure over the last three months exceeds the Camp income by $259,000!!! Weight today 9st 9lb.

26 January
An alert at 0300hrs this morning followed by an alarm at 1200hrs – a single B29 cruised over at about 25000 feet, saw one ack ack burst and that was all.

Later. There were two planes over, one going S to N and one W to E.

29 January
Plane over at 1245hrs; same old B29, no opposition, no alarm until after it was over.

30 January
1200hrs another plane over, no 'ack ack' – no fighters, no nuffin! 'Command' show for General Saito this evening of *Tonight at 8.30*.

1 February
Alert at 1025hrs, alarm 1030hrs. Have just called out 'Kurra' and all the folk on the hospital balcony disappeared by magic. Dirty dog! Soon after 1100hrs the raid began, concentrated on the Naval Base area, we counted eighty three, altho' the number may well be less as they may have done two circuits. The alert had gone when three more appeared and off went the alarm again. Attaboy!

2 February
Recce plane over at 1045hrs, nay bother! Sounded as if he dropped a load over Singapore and was met with ack ack, but nothing over here. All clear at 1100hrs.

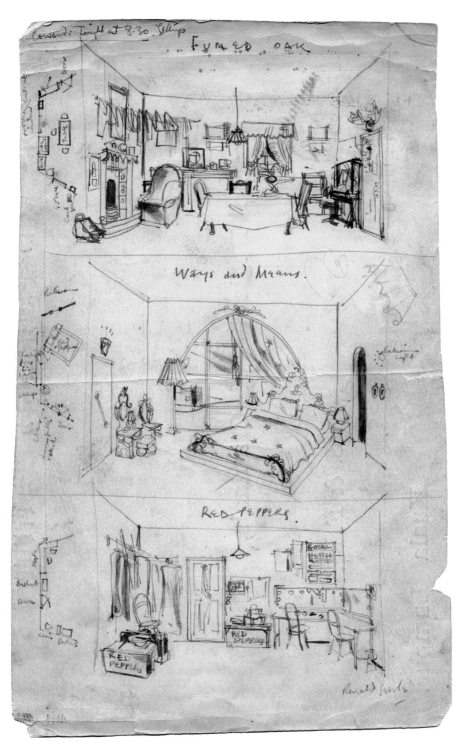

61. *Tonight at 8.30* (original sketches for the three sets from Noel Coward's *Tonight at 8.30* put on in the Playhouse)

Takahashi has stated that rations are likely to deteriorate in quantity and quality – canteen supplies are already almost nil (at present you can buy soap, tea or boot polish!) and are likely to become more difficult. Cheroots and tobacco come in occasionally – the last issue worked out at half an ounce of Perah tobacco (horrible stuff) and 3 x 15c cheroots per head. Tobacco $1.25 per half ounce. Oh to get out of here!

3 February
1100hrs – B29 over on its own, so high that each engine left a vapour trail, seemed to drop a few eggs on the Naval Base, otherwise the usual recce.

5 February
1245hrs saw B29 overhead, no ack ack or alert sounded. Fighters went into a dive. Another plane came over S to N and was attacked by several fighters without avail on either side. Weather has turned very hot again, humidity very high, in fact typical steamy Singapore weather.

6 February
Latest manufactured articles in the camp. Rubber shoes made from sheet rubber brought in from outside and tooth powder made of wood ash and something or other, but quite effective. There is also an IJA sawmill, nail factory and paper factory.

8 February
Story told of the Dutch officer who found that during the night he'd used soya sauce instead of water at the latrine.

10 February
Cut in rations, rice reduced by one third to 300 grams per head per day. My tummy all haywire these days, spleen upset. Went to funeral yesterday of one of the Australian Concert Party who had died of TB. A B29 was over I'm told, but didn't see it. 1215hrs B29 is over again, met with hot reception from fighters, but was last seen going for home apparently OK. More gunfire than we've heard before, thought we heard a plane coming down, but didn't see anything.

11 February
1040hrs alarm has just started; we're expecting big things today. Ken and I fixed up a 'Grand Stand' seat looking North, which is usually the best view; we have two windows in our corner of the hut, seats are eagerly sought after.

Busy day yesterday Ward Show at 1830hrs until 1915hrs, *Wide World Magazine* also in Hospital Area 1945–2030hrs and then *Red Peppers* at the Playhouse after that. 1115hrs B29 came over, turned and came right overhead. Looks as if we've 'had' our raid – pity.

Later. Have just seen two self-respecting officers making 'sparrow stew'.

13 February
My recent tummy upset now over thank heavens. After twenty four hours of starving, my voice had almost gone and I felt really weak, doesn't say much for our stamina. Weight 9st 6lb – not so hot!

14 February
Alert at 1215hrs, plane over very high leaving vapour trail, with much cloud about, didn't see anything. A large convoy came into Naval Base yesterday, so maybe they'll receive some attention soon.

15 February
Threee years ago today, Singapore capitulated, does this herald a raid?! Prospects generally, food etc., not good, but we've been through pretty bloody times since 1942 and mean to get back home. Now 1245hrs alarm just gone followed shortly afterwards by seven B29s in extended 'V' formation. Re-read for the umpteenth time all my letters today – how I long for home. Ken Archer got Jalet the Yank on the 'One-Man Jazz Band' last night, I haven't laughed so much for ages! The Star Venus visible at mid-day an unusual sight. Have got a lousy cold. I wanna go home Lord Louis!

17 February
Alert gone at 1115hrs. Alarm at 1145hrs – no raid materialised. Two AIF have beaten a Tamil to death – hope they swing for it.

19 February
Down with Malaria again, damn nuisance as it's the last night of *Tonight at 8.30* and I don't feel like going out one little bit.
   Later. Did the show OK, but felt lousy and had to concentrate like hell.

20 February
Party of Dutch in from Damar Laut, all in a bad way, one died on way up from Singapore another on admission to hospital. They were all kept in a lorry in the pouring rain outside the gaol main gate while the Nips reported in etc. I wonder what our ultimate fate is to be, it would be bloody if, after all this time 'events' prevented us from rejoining our loved ones. On the 'drome', when the 'alarm' is sounded, all the POWs are herded into a corner, their guard is doubled and a machine gun is trained on them. Hey ho, one way and another it makes a feller fink a bit, it don't 'arf!

21 February
We hear that there was a raid on Seletar aerodrome yesterday with considerable damage and casualties, so Indian drivers say. Attaboy! Weight today 9st 2lb, not so hot. The quinine is playing hell with me and I feel so sick I can't eat anything. 1215hrs. Just seen a B29 only by chance, no sirens went and no 'ack ack'. Where

are those 'Wild Eagles'? Am going to stop mentioning planes over unless anything startling happens as they're over nearly every day, sometimes only seen by a few.

24 February

First night of *Music Thru' the Years* tonight at the Playhouse. I'm singing 'Bull and Bush' and 'It's a great big Shame' on my own. 'The Lambeth Walk' with Stan Mesmer and a sketch in mime with Keith Stevens and Reg Baker in 'Paris', a new Bill Williams and Rawle Knox number.

0950hrs alert followed by 'alarm' at 1015hrs – planes started coming over at 1330hrs and we counted 105, the biggest B29 raid yet. Huge fires in the direction of Singapore, at least one of which is oil. Attaboy! Planes fired some form of explosive rocket when attacked by fighters.

25 February

According to returned working parties the raid was mostly incendiaries yesterday and the whole waterfront was ablaze. Go-downs, station, dumps etc., the parties themselves had narrow escape. The first night of *Music thru' the Years* went off well and would appear to be very popular.

28 February

Alarm last night or this morning. Mine-laying tomorrow?

A further cut in rations, another 10% off rice – the last one has left us permanently hungry so now what? I vow that when I get home I will never allow myself to feel the pangs of hunger again, even if it means munching biscuits between meals.

Have been put on an iron tonic as my blood-count is down. Strong rumour that the 'Mercy' ship is in with Red + supplies. Owing to transport restrictions, we wonder whether it will have to be manhandled up here on trailers.

1 March

Red + ship now more than a rumour, party to go down today to unload the ship (said to hold 1,200 tons), supplies then to go to a camp in Singapore from whence it will be distributed to POW internees in Malaya.

2 March

Latest news of Red + ship very conflicting, some say that it is in, others that it is expected. 1030hrs – 'Alert' went followed by 'alarm' at 1100hrs. B29s came over about 20 minutes later, altogether there were fifty-odd and the main objective seemed to be the Naval Base or Johore. A lot of light 'ack ack' and fighter opposition. No casualties on either side as far as we could see.

Have definitely proved to our own satisfaction that the 'explosive rocket' I mentioned on February 24 is actually a bomb dropped by fighters of some phosphorescent content that would catch fire to any plane that it hit or that passed through it. So far they've been used without any success whatsoever.

We buy tapioca root when we can ('we' being Ken Archer, Tony Gardner and myself) – 1 lb costs $1.70 – helps to fill a corner, we have it baked.

3 March
I fear that nerves these days on all sides are very frayed. It's sometimes extremely difficult to control oneself and altho' we've had few actual scrapes a number of times they've only been prevented by outside interference.

The half-caste Yanks are a damned nuisance, but I find myself, that people and little things annoy me and only strict self control prevents an outburst.

6 March
Parties in Singapore starting Red + supplies (including of all things puffed RICE and stew and rice in a tin!!) Nuffsaid!!!! Story told of Colonel Bano who had a swarm of bees hived by one of our bee keepers – the following day down came the Korean 'toban' with a jug to collect the honey!

7 March
Official notification ref. Red + ship – the stores are now all unloaded and are for white POWs, in Burma, Malaya, Sumatra and Borneo! That leaves some loopholes!! All individual parcels with some clothes, books, boots, medical stores in bulk, but as far as we know no mail. I suppose it will be another case of seven to a parcel with a good proportion falling into 'other' hands.

8 March
General Saito has ordered cessation of activities at the Playhouse as the present show has 'bad thoughts'! – First the order was that the whole theatre should be pulled down tomorrow, but this order has now been countermanded and we await further details. Cut in rice ration from tomorrow down to eight and a half ounces – and we are warned not to be too optimistic about the Red + supplies which are not expected to make a very great difference to the bulk of rations. Verb sap!!

[*For the finale, Ronald Searle had evolved a liner moving across the back-cloth belching smoke (oily rag) with cast singing 'On my return', composed by Bill Williams.*]

11 March
These rations – very trying, today our meals are as follows : Breakfast – half a pint Hash and a 'doover' – Tiffin – three-quarters of a pint of green water – Supper – three-quarters of a pint of vegetable pap and two 'doovers'. Had a 'command' performance this morning of certain parts of *Music thru' the Years*, apparently the chief bone of contention is a Ballet 'La Laniere' with an Australian and a Javanese. There's a spot of bother over Colonel Newey wanting me to run the theatre instead of Ossy Daltry.

13 March

Will probably run the theatre when the ban is lifted. We're all damned hungry these days and another cut is rumoured! Roll on the Red + supplies!

14 March

Went to the funeral this morning of Stewart Ludman. A lean day today, total Jap rations including rice, vegetables, tea etc., 9½oz.

16 March

Nip guards and Indian drivers smoking Red + cigarettes – I hope there'll be a few left for us, for whom they're meant. There is becoming more and more evidence that commodities other than cigarettes are being consumed by those not entitled to them. Gowd 'ow I 'ates 'em!

17 March

Our three monthly weighing today – everyone 'down' – my weight 9st 2lb. New Nip order – bore-hole lids will be lowered gently – windy? Red + supplies, some 80,000 parcels and food, clothes, medical stores in bulk – also some cases of theatrical stuff and gramophone.

Our sorting party has now returned and now we await our captors for delivery.

18 March

Roll on Red + supplies – today, Sunday our menu as a matter of interest:

Breakfast – half a pint Hash (rice and whitebait). Tiffin – one pint green stew – Supper – one pint goulash (mixed greens, tapioca root and rice) one round fried rice and blachang rissole, one pasty (rice and mixture of greens and salt fish) and a cup of baked rice filled with a coffee concoction.

At midday the 'HAG [*Horner, Archer, Gardner*] Kongsi' shared one pound of baked tapioca root – a Sunday treat! Three 'doovers' is one extra from weekdays. As there is actually rice in the gaol to last us until July on the old scale, this underfeeding would appear to be a deliberate attempt to weaken us – there is no doubt that they are succeeding.

20 March

Weather continues wet with little sun. Have had no B29s over for a fortnight – ominous lull or just not interested?!!!!

21 March

Postcards issued to send home. Hope we get there first.

22 March

The daily postman over again today and yesterday (B29).

23 March

Very much looking forward to a party we are having tonight. Costing $3 a head it will consist of a green stew and a savoury rissole of roughly half a pound! Ingredients: Chinese spinach, sweet potato tops, soya, tomatoes, onions, blachang, brinjal, coconut and tapioca root. Amazing what a kick we're getting out of it. There'll be seven there, our three selves, Eric Oram and Dick Turner, Australians – Paul Hartman, a Dutchman, who is OC cooking and Denis Lowe, a gunner. Whacko! Little things!!

24 March

Party a great success – the stew was excellent, the addition of a grated coconut and santan made a huge difference and the 'doover' was 100%.

   Later. 'Leggie' hash and doover made evening meal No. 1. Add to this <u>things!</u>

25 March

Weight now 9st dead, surely I can't go much lower. It is very noticeable these days that fellows you haven't seen for a few days have gone visibly thinner, hollow cheeks and very 'ribby'.

   Hear General Saito is endeavouring to get cigarettes. At least a token issue of Red + supplies for delivery at Easter next Sunday. Thank heavens these days for our own gardens, if we had to rely entirely on Nip supplies it would be a poor lookout.

   Party of 3,000 going to Singapore – am trying to arrange for a nucleus of the Concert Party to remain behind. Did *Wide World Magazine* and Ward Show in Hospital Area.

26 March

Latest news of 3,000 party is that they are to be split up into parties of 100, each with an officer in charge – it is also stated that the area south of the gaol is to be wired off and will serve as base camp and hospital for Singapore and working parties. They will be on heavy duty rations of 500g – we will continue at 230g. Not so hot.

   What contrasts one sees visiting in hospital – in adjoining beds you will find a man blown up like the 'Michelin' tyre advert only smooth instead of ribbed, and another fellow with all his bones showing, his stomach as concave as the other is convex, and so it has gone on month after month and yet actually deaths these days are comparatively few and far between.

27 March

What a glorious noise Cassurina trees make with the wind blowing through them. There are some on the south side of the gaol and one of our evening walks is round there – looks as if we'll lose this walk if that area is to be wired off. Pity, as it's the only one worth while and even there you're never away from your fellow prisoners. Oh for freedom! How glorious to be able to go where you like and get away from one's fellow man.

62/63. *Music thru the Years*

THE PLAYHOUSE

presents

"MUSIC THRU' THE YEARS".

PRODUCED BY
BILL WILLIAMS.

THE PLAYHOUSE THEATRE ORCHESTRA
UNDER THE DIRECTION OF HAP KELLY.

ANNOUNCER - OSMOND DALTRY.

STAGE MANAGER - SYD PIDDINGTON.
STAGE MANAGER - CHRIS BUCKINGHAM.
STAGE LIGHTING - CLARRIE BARKER.
STAGE CARPENTER - JOE SILVER.
SETTINGS & COSTUMES BY RONALD SEARLE.
COSTUMES EXECUTED BY REX COLE.
ORCHESTRATIONS BY 'HAP' KELLY.
o-o-o-o-o-o-o-o-o

CHANGI GAOL PRISONER OF WAR CAMP,

SINGAPORE.
o-o-o-o-o-o-o-o-o

"M U S I C T H R U T H E Y E A R S".

Overture - "Music Maestro Please".
Opening Number - "Music Thru' The Years".

1910 to 1914. "The Man Who Broke the
Bank at Monte Carlo" "Daisy" "Little
Grey Home in the West" "Daddy Wouldn't
Buy Me a Bow Wow" "Down at the Old Bull
& Bush" "It's a Great Big Shame".

1915 to 1918. "Pack Up Your Troubles"
"Keep the Home Fires Burning" "Sweet
Adeline" "Alexander's Ragtime Band"
"If You Were the Only Girl" "There's a
Long, Long Trail" "Tipperary".

1919 to 1922. "The Sheik of Araby"
"Memories" "Night Time in Italy" "Who"
"Love Will Find a Way" "L'Estralalita"

1923 to 1926. "Tea for Two" "Stardust"
"Rose Marie" "Ain't She Sweet"
"Tabu" - Specialty Dance Number".

1927 to 1930. "Lover Come Back To Me"
"Adios Muchacha" "Can I Forget You" "No,
No, a Thousand Times No" "Underneath the
Arches" "Trees" - Gil Mitchell - Violin.

1931 to 1934. "Sonny Boy" "Wedding of
the Painted Doll" "Breakaway" "Body and
Soul".

1935 to 1938. "The Way You Look Tonight"
"The Lambeth Walk" "The Continental"
"These Foolish Things" "The Music Goes
Round"

1938 to 1942. "The Breeze and I" "Boo Hoo"
"Deep Purple" "Franklin D.R.Jones"
"Big Red Apple" - Bill Williams.

1942 to 1945. Songs by Bill Williams and
Rawle Knox specially written for the show
"Sunday in London" "At the First
Opportunity" "The Sky is Too Clear"
"In Paris a Lifetime Ago".

This Year of Grace 1945.
The Ballet -"La Laniere"Dains & Ecoma.

Finale - "On My Return" - Full Cast.
o-o-o-o-o-o-o
THE CAST.
Bill Williams, Stan Mesmer, Keith Stevens,
Taffy Daniels, Ronnie Horner, Bernie
McCaffrey, Doug Peart, Harry Nibbs, Alan
Roberts, Hal Reid, Hap Kelly, Ron Caple, Jack
Geoghegan, Ernie Wearne, Les Jacques, Fred
Stringer, Frank Wood, Berkley Quill, Henri
Ecoma, Van Swem, Wray Gibson, Dutchy Holland,
Bill Willsden, Bob McDonald, Gil Mitchell,
Barney Bolton, Benny Barton, Charles Dolman,
Harry Wise, Charlie Wiggins, Robin Welbury,
and Stan Garland.

o-o-o-o-o-o-o-o

o-o-o-o-o-o-o

Put the Piddington-Braddon thought transference on in the TB Ward this evening, much appreciated.

[Piddington had a 'mind reading' act. On one occasion he knew that my father had the diary out and learned that the Japs were making spot checks. As there was no time to go and warn him he decided to warn him by thought transference and kept repeating "the Japs are coming, the Japs are coming". At exactly the same time my father decided he ought to put the diary back in the case; moments later the Japs entered the hut! –story told by Elizabeth Hurbas, daughter.]

The IJA have changed their minds seven times in the last twenty four hours about the 3,000 party! 350 Australians leave tomorrow for Singapore.

28 March

1,000 British and Australian troops leave tomorrow – the 350 party today were told they were going to Johore after Takahashi's assurance of yesterday that they wouldn't be leaving the Island.

Did a 'Horner's Corner' in the *Wide World Magazine* No. 7 in the Coconut Grove this evening – mainly comprising gentle 'digs' at previous contributions, it seemed to go down OK.

29 March

'Alert' went at about 0130hrs followed shortly by 'Alarm' and then later by planes. Sounded like twin-engined bombers and they appeared to be laying mines off the East coast here. Saw a couple of them momentarily against cloud and a spot of light ack-ack, sounded like Bofors.

The 1,000 move postponed for twenty four hours. Yesterday 300 were due in from Kranji according to the Nips – they never turned up. Such for their administration.

Later. Have just sampled an excellent stew made up of tapioca root, spinach and hermit crabs. These are easily crunched up in the mouth and have the true crab flavour. Given to me by Hans van Praag who, as his name suggests, is Dutch. There is no doubt that these Dutchmen are streaks ahead of us in obtaining flavours out of nothing at all. It's not surprising really I suppose, considering that they're all ex-Java and are using materials that they are used to.

30 March

Instead of the 600 British and 400 Australian troops, 700 British only go today and 400 come in from Krangi instead of 300 – damned clever these people! The token Red + issue for Easter Day is one parcel to twenty!! Rumour has it that there is to be an extra issue of 3oz of rice, Whacko!

Two blackouts last night, bombs dropped in Singapore area, fires started. Things are looking up! I am getting many 'black-outs' these days, consequently have to get up very slowly if sitting or lying down. Padre Duckworth collapsed during early service today and is now in hospital.

Ref. next Sunday's Red + issue. General Saito has ordered that all supplies must be consumed on the one day – empty tins to be noted by 0900 hrs Monday!

Later. Fire on Pulan Sambam started last night, still burning well this evening. Leaflets dropped on Singapore this morning, believed to be dropped from three carrier-borne planes. Leaflets in Japanese, Chinese, Tamil and possibly English apparently say that Singapore will be attacked next month following heavy bombardment. Whacko! Only 400-odd of the 700 left today, the remainder with 100 Aussies go tomorrow.

31 March

Human nature is amazing, some people more fortunate than others will sit down and solemnly eat half a chicken in front of friends who are taking green stew. Our Red + issue for tomorrow is as follows: to be divided amongst twenty two the following – (some packages vary including luncheon sausage, pilchards, soap and one packet of salt, at any rate they are obviously the normal fortnightly parcel for one) 16oz dried milk, 16oz jam, 16oz butter, 12oz bully, 8oz chocolate, 7oz raisins, 6oz prunes, 6oz sugar, 4oz cheese, one packet coffee, one packet biscuits C'est tout!

Ken stung by a centipede, hand very sore. Gala tiffin, mashed tapioca root, salt and palm oil, mixed with the greens of our green stew. Bubble and squeak.

Four stories of the Singapore working parties – The Nip demonstrating to Aussies how they stole tins from the Go-downs only to have his demonstration tin stolen while his back was turned. The Aussies who carried out of the Ford works, a radiogram in full view and when a Nip officer tapped it questioningly with his sword was told "Don't do that or you will break the valves", and they then continued on their way back to camp. The Aussie who drove away a lorry full of petrol and sold both lorry and petrol to a Chinaman. And the party, also of Aussies who consistently drew petrol to keep a steam roller rolling, needless to say they sold the petrol.

A Dutch and British batman have been pulled in by orders of Takahashi, they are charged with endeavouring to sell a revolver. This was not found and has to be produced tomorrow or we are threatened with reprisals.

1 April

Easter Sunday – Ken and I went to Communion. We had dried milk with our 'pap' and coffee, at midday we had green stew with a fresh fish rissole and for supper a thick soup, meat pie, fish rissole, cheese sandwich and 'duff' made of mashed biscuits with prunes, sultanas, coconut, jam and a chocolate sauce. I now feel pretty good – how galling to think that instead of a flash in the pan, we should have been having decent tasting food regularly.

4 April

Great comings and goings, following the 'revolver' scare, Takahashi has got on to other 'black market' sources in officers' area and has had quite a round-up, although he doesn't seem to be worrying unduly.

6 April
Three lorry loads of Red + supplies in, Whacko!

Later. Two loads of sacked tinned goods arrived.

7 April
We get an issue tomorrow of Red + supplies (less milk and soap) twenty to a parcel. Takahashi has forbidden anyone in officers' area to go bathing and also all entertainment in officers' area. Presumably punishment for the recent revelations ref. officers selling watches etc. The Cads!

8 April
Extra food absolutely grand. Gosh what a difference even this little amount makes. Roughly 3d per head the pre-war price works out. These fellows working on the 'drome have a hard time on normal rations, they get a half pint of rice extra but what is that if you've hard work to do all day in the sun. We feel weak enough as it is.

9 April
We hear that conditions now in Thailand are much improved, the camps are run by Red Cross; officers segregated from men. Meat and pork in rations. One pound of meat costs $1, eggs 10c or 15c fried, fresh vegetables plentiful etc. Here the no-duty personnel are reduced to 108g of rice and maize; however there is another lash-out of Red + supplies for consumption on Wednesday, and for three weeks we'll get an issue from two lorry loads of 'sacked' loose tins; and on Sunday we again have twenty to a parcel. And to think that there are thousands, nay millions of people in this world who turn up their noses at this sort of food, we daren't even clean our teeth after Sunday feeding for fear of losing some of the good things!

Later. Have just got the figures for HEAVY, LIGHT and NO-DUTY rations

Duty		Breakfast		Tiffin		Supper	
		Rice		Rice	Veg	Rice	
Heavy		80g		45g	180g	143g	
Light		80g			45g	143g	
No		35g			45g	143g	

10 April
Lorry load containing some 500 individual Red + parcels in.

Later. Theatrical stores arrive in two crates, all very Concert Partyish, nigger minstrel, pierrots etc., but make-up would be useful if all plays etc., hadn't been stopped in the two theatres.

11 April

B29 over, first time for days. Have Ward Show this afternoon followed by *Wide World Magazine* in gaol for other ranks. Following that am invited to supper party of fried rubber seed cakes – as the other three concerned are rubber planters and these seeds are usually eaten by pigs, dogs and rats the humour of the situation is obvious.

So far there are no signs of medical Red + stores arriving yet. Several recent deaths could have been prevented if the drugs had been available.

Exeunt 'screamers' in a hurry around 0300hrs. Some officers are eating rats, this seems to go a bit far I think, I have tasted unknowingly a cat stew and dog rissole and knowingly a snail, prawn and green concoction, iguana, cobra and hermit crab, but rats – no! A certain kind of seaweed has proved palatable and should contain some beneficial vitamins I should imagine – now with our bathing stopped it is impossible to collect this anymore.

13 April

Feeling depressed, largely I think because of the hopeless position some of our fellows are in hospital. On small rations they have no chance of regaining lost strength and there are not enough supplementary diets to go round. If this goes on much longer the cemetery will see many new graves I fear.

Tonight 'HAG Kongsi' celebrates Peg Archer's birthday with a cake – 2lb tapioca root, a coconut and a quarter pound of sugar, $5.10 worth!!).

Colonel Newey has, with the agreement of the medical authorities, refused to sign for the Red + medical stores which haven't arrived, so an order from Takahashi states that no further Red + supplies are to be issued – oh God! Some tobacco stalks have come in for sale to the canteen at 15c per oz – cheap! Cut into small chunks it's not bad in a pipe.

14 April

Film party in Singapore yesterday – had to swim about the Swimming Club baths singing 'Pack up your troubles' – happy POW!

Big upheaval in gaol kitchen due to pilfering of Red + rations. H. back from Singapore, says Australian Red + ship was in on 10th. Goods on sale in town – coconuts are selling in town at $5 so far, when available, they're $2.80 here. We find they are the best buy as a half amongst the three of us helps to add body to the half pint of breakfast 'pap' and the other half the evening meal.

15 April

Confirming rumours about the Red + supplies, all I know is that WE haven't got it!!! Feeling damned tired these days with aches and pains in the back and legs – weight now 8st 12 lbs. Hey ho it's a giddy life we lead – Talk about a bone yard, I have never seen so many skinny people in one place before.

Later. News just through that Red + supplies are released for consumption tomorrow.

16 April

Nip guard fired at believed escapee at 2200hrs last night with the result that a quarter of an hour after 'lights out' we were hauled out of bed and kept on roll call until 2315hrs, by which time they discovered that no-one was absent.

18 April

My share of the Red + 'comforts' parcels is a tube of brushless shaving cream. I was lucky in the draw, everyone got something, tooth powder, razor blades, toothbrush, latrine paper, pencil, comb, boot polish. This will be grand after months of camp-made washing soap.

20 April

Another roll call last night, this one from 2245–0030hrs damn silly really, it was known to be an Australian OR called Herman who was missing and that he was demented and threatened suicide. This morning his body was recovered from a bore-hole.

Have been doing some gardening when not arranging Ward shows – feel very weak. Issue of five 'Old Gold' cigarettes – what a joy to smoke Virginian tobacco after all these months.

21 April

We are to get the 10% rice cut-back starting tomorrow – this is excellent as is the news that a lorry load of Red + stuff came in this afternoon. Average loss of weight of British and Australian troops is something over three pounds for last period of one month – The Dutch are a pound and a half up! Much doovering!!

22 April

All gardeners are being turned onto digging a fire trench round the camp! It is not quite clear whether this is to be used for or against us, but it has to be completed by the 25th !! Ken gets radio cable from his wife lucky old stick.

<u>Later</u>. The sweet this evening was a chocolate éclair, pastry made from mashed biscuit, choc. sauce on top from slab chocolate and cream from butter and sugar.

24 April

Anzac Day etc., having a 'bash' mid-day, Eric Oram, Dallas MacMillan and the 'HAG Kongsi' pooling our stew adding tapioca root, coconut, blachang etc., and following it with a savoury rissole.

26 April

Four bags of mail in so far, no news of the dates. Many cases of malaria, BT and MT, particularly the latter.

28 April

Some gunfire heard last night although whether ack ack or shore battery is not known. About 1¾lb of wet rice been issued per head – should mean a big day tomorrow as it will have to be used. Some Red + books in tomorrow (actually ex–YMCA).

29 April

Making extra rice last, eleven days at two and a half extra ounces a day should help a bit. Have had a pair of Red + socks issued, Ken also, Tony a handkerchief. Donald Wise and Denis Pearl arrive with the goods!!

1 May

The YMCA books include a new style of up-to-date paper-covered novel published by an American non-profit organisation. Have just read CS Forrester's *The Ship*.

3 May

More Red + comforts – got a razor blade this time.

4 May

What an evening! Excellent meal using up remains of last Wednesday's Red + supplies (I got a 'leggie' cup with pineapple topped with cream!) two postcards one from Flossie dated 18 September '44 and one from Dot dated 8 October. Issue of five 'Old Gold' cigarettes and Dickie Laird's confab.

[*This was the last letter I received from my mother. I learnt of her death when I arrived home.*]

5 May

As well as malaria there are many cases of appendicitis due, it is thought, to the grit in the rice and greens. Owing to the lack of surgical gut, the substitute is causing a lot of infection after the operations.

We hear that Paddy Sykes was killed with five others in a slit trench from the effects of a bomb at Nong Ploduc, I am very sorry if it's true as he was a grand chap.

6 May

IJA say that the gaol cookhouse has to be converted to oil burning as supplies of wood will shortly cease. Those of us outside the gaol may have to feed from one communal cookhouse which wouldn't be so good.

Takahashi has told Newey that except in Czechoslovakia, resistance in Germany has finished.

7 May

Postcard from Frank dated August. The extra Red + rations don't seem to help my weight much. I am still 8st 12 lb – recent issues of prawns are playing havoc with our stomachs; they have jagged swords like a miniature sword fish which cut the mouth if you're not careful. Actually feel very shagged these days but 'Tiddapa'.

8 May

Some say good old!

9 May

Stomach not so good, hope it's not dysentery at this stage of the game, but rather suspect the prawns. Roll on freedom.

12 May

Amazing issue from Japs – nine lorry loads of tapioca root, sweet potato and pineapple came in early this morning at a rate of 2.07 lb, .488lb and .435lb per head respectively. Should help a bit!

Later. Vegetable issue to last three days, not so good as the quality leaves much to be desired.

17 May

My day! Get up at 0830hrs, shower and change. 0900hrs breakfast 0930hrs either gardening or arranging Ward Shows. 1300hrs tiffin. 1330–1600hrs read or sleep, 1600hrs tea. 1715hrs friends, 2300hrs lights out. On Wednesday and Saturday have Ward Shows at 1815hrs. Malaria still on the increase.

Later. Drew cake of toilet soap in third 'comforts' distribution.

21 May

Eight 'screamers' off in a hurry at 1230hrs – four carrying torpedoes, a new innovation. Have just read a Chinese saying that 'the stomach is the habitation of the soul'.

23 May

'Ullo, ullo' – raid on the aerodrome this p.m. – heard machine gunning, some faint thumps and the whine of bombs and apparently they 'ad it'.

Later. 'drome' party say a flying bat 'did over' the far end of the 'drome.

25 May

350-odd in from Sumatra, nearly all Dutch. A further 1,000 to come we are told.

26 May

Some planes over very high up – machine gun fire – definitely not B29s. Can they possibly be carrier borne? 'Screamers' have left here.

27 May
Watched an interesting attack by ants on a spider's web. In the angle of a table they pulled the web to bits, the spider fled and they ate all the eggs. 1900hrs plane over believed to be PB. Same as 23rd.

30 May
'Doc' Diver died last night after a great battle. He came up from Normanton Camp paralysed from waist down and then complications set in, heart, lungs etc., going. The treatment at this camp is very bad.

0940hrs siren goes first time for weeks – no raid developed. 'HAG Kongsi' may move to F.1 hut. We've all had to move up and are now more crowded than ever before in preparation for a party of 150 officers from either Java or Sumatra. Our move depends on whether or not we can keep together.

31 May
Sumatra party in last night, about seventy British officers, Army, RN, RNVR and RAF have had a rough time – the Jap is obviously the same the world over – just a bastard.

Later. PBY over, dropped leaflets in Malay on Singapore.

1 June
Moved to 'F' lines (mostly 18 Division) – the Colonel was keen for me to go so all the 'HAG Kongsi' have removed and are in a block together.

3 June
Last night RASC officers beat WOs and ORs at darts 2-1. Our celebration of 'Corps Week', fifty of them came out and we gave them tea and a 'doover'. It was not possible to arrange a service for Corps Sunday. Amazing to think that it is three years since our soccer games on the India Lines Padang.

6 June
A few facts and figures that may be of interest – Comparison of canteen prices. April '44 and April '45 – blachang $3.20 - $14.40, gula malacca $1.80 - $16.17, cigarette tobacco $24.80 - $70.00, cheroots $0.14c – $0.25c, coconuts $0.80c - $3.00. Nationalities in the Changi Gaol camp as at 1 June '45. British 3,843 – Australian 3,007 – Canadian 9 – South African 2 – New Zealand 8 – Americans 47 – Dutch 1,963 – Danish 3 – Norwegians 2 – Czech 1 – Italian 19 and French 1. Total 8,905. In one month 72,000 gallons of urine were put on the garden – not bad going, all the rice goes to water! (*One of my jobs. Mix one third urine to two thirds water!*)

Today being Derby Day, Suburbia ran a race meeting with tote and sweep on the Pacific Derby. Very good fun. I lost $1.

8 June

Rumours that officers may be going to Kranji!! Newey has asked me to take over entertainments in the playhouse if it reopens. It looks however, as if camp office really want to run the show and have everything their own way, have another session with him tomorrow.

9 June

Had two more sessions with Newey and have made it quite clear that I will only run the playhouse without interference – am still continuing putting on Ward Shows, but 'gloves are off' up aloft.

Watched at intervals, one Lieutenant Beet RNF play twenty consecutive chess games. He won sixteen, lost two and drew two – not bad on rice!

10 June

Following rat competition is to take place between 2300hrs Wednesday 13 June and 0800hrs Thursday 14 June. Awards will be made on following points:
a) Female rat is 'inpod' b) ditto not apparently 'inpod' but over 7 inches in length stem to stern c) Females under 7 inches d) Males over 7 inches e) Males under 7 inches. Captives to remain property of capturer (most necessary with rats fetching prices for human consumption). Moreno and Torres have a scrap – nice types.

11 June

Extremely interesting lecture by Squadron Leader Longmore on Parachute jumping – the leading living British parachutist with all his faculties. He has over 500 jumps to his credit and had many amusing and interesting things to relate.

Bathing for officers started again today and a late flash is that the Coconut Grove Theatre is to open on Wednesday. I have promised to do a turn in a variety show that Ward Booth is getting up. Incidentally I find he knows Uncle Harold very well, only discussed this last Wednesday. He also knew Hugh and Paddy.

13 June

Another of 'our day' surely to God this must be the last one to have us separated. Went to 0830hrs communion. Got issued with a Red + 'comforts' razor blade. Am spending most of today preparing for Ward show at 1815hrs and opening Show in Coconut Grove at 2000hrs.

Later. Show went well, my turn received a generous reception.

14 June

Rat hunt results in total bag of three. Great move from gaol area mooted, 4,000-odd to go with usual proposition (1 to 100). Rumour has it of course, that after the move all officers go into the gaol. Am told my turn last night was the best I've done which is gratifying. What are all the detonations we hear, particularly by night? Only explanation seems to be blasting.

15 June
Have borrowed an excellent book *Exercise without exercise* by S Arthur Devan, published by Methuens – Flossie, that permanently slim husband is a distinct possibility. I am going to make a damn hard effort anyway. Indian guards locked up inside gaol. Officers giving up 5g per day to make up supplementary diets in hospital.

17 June
Last Red + issue! Canadian parcels; as I sit after our evening meal I wonder when next I'll taste civilised food. We hear there are three bags of mail in with 15,000 British letters up to January '45. 200-odd in from Keppal Harbour in bad condition, the bed patients have gone to Kranji, these are all malnutrition etc., and look very thin.

19 June
Weighed today 8st 12lb. Yah skinny!

20 June
Rumour has it that there are another twelve bags of mail in. An IJA order forbids applause at concerts, lectures etc., 25 cents cheroots have gone up to 70c.
   Parties leaving Changi Gaol appear to be going to the Changi area only. Wise Guys?! My education grows apace – only discovered today by seeing for myself that the loofah one uses in the bath comes from a creeper and not the sea.

23 June
Postcard from Frank 2 Feb '45 all well thank God, but no word from me since May '44, that means the August postcard, cable and broadcast have all failed to get home so far. Hell! [*Actually postcards show they heard in July.*]

24 June
Rather belated, owing to lack of funds, the 'HAG Kongsi' today celebrated the Horner wedding anniversary with a coconut ($3) and quarter pound Gula Malacca ($4) with our breakfast 'pap' – the Gula melted with the Santan was 'Dei Itchi'.

25 June
Unidentified plane over at 0430hrs, 'screamers' (mit torpedo) off just before breakfast, did not return all day. Takahashi says he is leaving. 130 Indians put inside the gaol, I wonder why?

28 June
Plane said to be a Liberator over at 1415hrs. An Aussie private is missing.

30 June
All entertainment cancelled, presumably because of the escape. Read postcard from Flossie dated 27 Nov. '44.

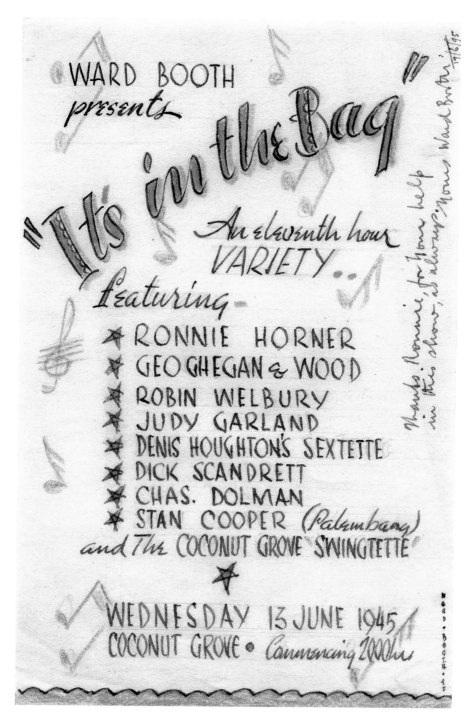

64. *It's in the Bag*

1 July
Seventeen drakes auctioned from hospital duck farm for $13.44 minimum $51.00 maximum $110.00 weights 1lb 8oz – 2lb 15oz.

2 July
1,000 party have now departed. There seems no doubt that all POW are being split up into small groups all over the Island and Johore. This means officers will have to find trailer parties to bring in wood – a round trip of some seven miles with the full trailer to be pulled almost entirely up hill.

3 July
Ref. above, have just completed my first trip in the traces! Hard work but some-what compensated by the mere fact of getting outside the camp and seeing a few civilians. Chinese, Malays, Tamils. Quite a lot of Jap activity. Have just read AG Street's *Country Calendar* with illustrations by Lionel Edwards – made one feel very homesick but was grand withal.

4 July
TAB injection today. No more Jap half holidays owing to state of emergency.

5 July
Repeat TAB stab played me up yesterday, gave me a fever last night. Queer, as they don't usually affect me, only shows how damned low one is in general health.

65. Trailer Party

Many rumours, 500 officers and 1,000 ORs going to KL, Krangi, coming here etc., etc. What does seem authentic is that Colonel Dillon is taking over from Newey as Representative Officer. All C. to leave.

6 July

My wee Iain's third birthday. It would be superfluous to say that I long to be home for his next, it goes without saying – but Oh hell!

7 July

During the year ending 30 June '45 the gaol workshops have manufactured: 2,172 mugs, 2,321 mess tins, 1,184 machine needles, 407 – 6 gallon containers, 392 – 3 gallon containers, 518 assorted containers, 104 rat traps, 482 watering cans, 442 latrine buckets. In addition over 20,000 articles were repaired.

8 July

Praying Mantis fighting bird. New camp commandant Lieutenant Muira.

11 July

Got 'Doc' Braganza to run the rule over me owing to increased number of 'blackouts' and excessive heart thumping when I exert myself. The result is simply general debility. The heart, although not A1 for an insurance policy, is OK by Changi standards and the cure, more food and food of the right kind – lack of protein causing anaemia. Hey ho, roll on freedom, I long to feel really fit again. Weight today 8st 10lb which is my lowest yet.

12 July

Ways of lighting one's pipe: Coconut coir, sheath of the coconut spathe / magnifying glass / kapok, electric transformer and filament wire, converted mag. Plane over this p.m. too high to discern what, but definitely Allied we think.

13 July

Plane over very high going at great speed – as yesterday attention seemed to be paid to this part of the Island. Thumbs up!

14 July

Food situation getting very difficult – no whitebait issued, blachang as a substitute – oil stocks low. Thank God for our own gardens which keep us well supplied with bayam, Ceylon spinach and occasional tapioca root. Assuredly our diet these days is greens and rice with a smattering of additional items such as coconuts, blachang, tamarin to give flavour. Wadsley the Messing officer, does very well with the limited stock available.

16 July
Out on wood trailers this afternoon – in evening a very interesting lecture by Squadron Leader Howell DFC and bar on the RAF organisation in 1940, bringing in the Battle of Britain in which he took part.

17 July
Plane over again – moving very fast and of medium size, powerful engines.

18 July
Just finished *Turnip Tops* by Ethel Boileau, a grand yarn, am next in line for another of hers *The Clansmen* – I will certainly read all her publications.

20 July
Two new canteen items have been on sale, both normally used as cattle or chicken food. One Copra after the oil has been removed and 'Misu', soya bean residue – how are the mighty fallen, we eat with relish both things intended for cattle. I am reminded of the ground nut cake sent to us by the Nips as manure in 1942 and consumed avidly for their vitamin B content.

22 July
Playhouse theatre being dismantled by order of the IJA.

23 July
Officers asked to volunteer to take over forestry. Don't feel fit enough these days, getting so easily whacked and with daily 'blackouts' at the slightest provocation, what about some of the people who have dealt in the black market or have sold things recently and do a lot of 'doovering'.

Later. Depressed tonight having written a 'just in case' letter to Florence. Party of fifty to sixty Dutch in from Sambawan in emaciated condition.

24 July
Rather interesting, a few of us worked out that our daily consumption is about 20oz all told, certainly not more and sometimes, if green issues include much red amargath or Ceylon spinach, whose stalks one can't eat, definitely less.

25 July
Two planes over at 1400hrs, very high but sounding powerful. They appeared to have the double body of the Lockheed 'Lightning' but at that height one can't be sure – they came in from the east. 1410hrs Short Sunderland over followed shortly by a Liberator. On the return of the 'Lightnings' they had come much lower, were easily recognisable and were joined by two more. The Liberator had fighter escorts of two planes.

26 July
Korean guard shot himself at 0810hrs this morning. Plane over at mid-day not identified.

28 July
'Lightning' over at 1220hrs very distinct – having a good look at Changi area.

29 July
Two 'Lightnings' over at 1000hrs – cloudy weather planes quite low.

30 July
Changing my meals today with John Crickmay, makes a spot of variety, the different technique in cooking helps to avoid getting stale on one type of meal. We decided to do this every Thursday. 1300hrs 'Liberator' over at about 1,000 feet. Had dysentery injection.

(Although only mentioned once, John Crickmay became a close friend and also godfather to his daughter Sally who was born after the war. Medical authorities had told POWs that it was doubtful whether they would be able to have any more children due to the lack of vitamin B. However, nine months later, they proved them very wrong!)

31 July
Thirty four today – my fourth in captivity – I refused to repeat previous hopes as never in my most pessimistic moments did I ever anticipate four birthdays away from my loved ones. However, sufficient unto the day – I am still alive and if the future is obscure, if it rests with me, I'll be back with them all once again.
    Later. Delightful surprise. Eric Adie produces a birthday pie –tapioca root, brinjal and beans and prawns) for my evening meal, made in a latex cup and baked, it was excellent and made me feel really full at the end of the meal instead of the usual unsatisfied feeling. In evening we noticed a fire in the direction of Singapore.

1 August
Drawn seventh in hut sweep. Two 'Lightnings' over at 1400hrs.

2 August
Two ' Lightnings' over at 1230hrs.

4 August
Out on wood trailer this morning, on way back seven Lightnings passed overhead going Singapore-wards, shortly afterwards they came back at 3–4,000 feet and proceeded to shoot up the 'drome'. A 'Zero' interfered and went down with smoke pouring from its tail.

5 August
Camp Commandant states that we are 'arrogant'. Electric heaters in officers' area confiscated for a fortnight owing to infringement of time schedule by Dutch officer.

6 August
'Sunderland' over at about 1330hrs, came right over the Gaol at about 6,000 feet.

7 August
IJA have offered (?) to buy food in exchange for watches. The suggested scheme is for watch owners who are willing to co-operate, will be given a receipt for value of watch, this to be repaid after War.

It is hoped that thereby it will be possible to buy rice so that heavy duty will be raised by 50g, light duty to present heavy duty and no duty ration to present light duty. If it means more food for the camp, then it's worth doing, but the whole scheme rather smells of being sold our own food.

8 August
Canteen purchases restricted by Lieutenant Muira as we've over spent (?!) already. New products in camp – alcohol for medical purposes made from washed out sugar sacks, pineapple skins discarded by Nips and Toddy – also cellulose from Lallang to be used in paper making.

<u>PRISON PAPER.</u>

This paper was manufactured in the prison at CHANGI Prisoner Of War Camp, Singapore.

The sole materials used were as follows:-
Lalang grass.
Wood ashes.
Lime.

The screens consisted of pieces of perforated zinc and mosquito netting.

The process was originated by Dr. Lob R.D.F., who together with Sgt Kemp S.S.V.F. & Spr. Braithwaite A.I.F. developed the plant and produced 500 sheets daily from 15 lbs of dried grass.

66. Paper Making

Had figures for July – Recieved from IJA, 13g of dried fish per man per day, as 70% of vegetables come from our own gardens we don't owe them much. No wonder we're perpetually hungry. Oh Lord how long?!

Later. Interesting lecture by Lieutenant Commander Clarke RN on the Narvik Show.

9 August

Lightnings over at 1300hrs – IJA offer tinned butter and cheese, 16 kilos sugar and 4 kilos coffee in exchange for watches! This smacks of Red + supplies and has been refused.

10 August

A new 'low' in weight 8st 8lb that puts me now just over 5st below my peace time 'all high' – much too fat of course. Am just recovering from a heavy cold which has pulled me down quite a bit.

11 August

It's **Over**, **Over**, **Over** – having an early breakfast at 0745hrs when news came in that to all intents and purposes the end had arrived. We duly did our wood trailer as the guards etc., don't seem to know yet.

At last we can breathe easily, knowing that unless things go wrong at the last moment we aren't going to have any last minute retaliatory action on us by the guards. Somehow the end has come so suddenly that one can't feel really excited, one can't grasp it that perhaps next week we may have left Singapore. Now my only wish is to let my dear ones know I'm OK and put an end to their worry – Oh God it's just too good to be true, I feel I can 'blether' on *ad infinitum*!

To feel that in the near future I'll be free of these filthy little yellow swine, I never thought I could loathe anyone so much as I hate them and how I've longed to write that down in the past, but have had to go carefully in case they were to discover the diary. Mistakes have been made in the past on that score – also about wireless news – what a joy to be able to write down that we've had the news all this time (excluding Thailand when it was only fitful).

Special. an order that has just reached us is that POWs will not smoke while urinating, this is apropos of a recent order that there would be no smoking whilst we walked about the camp or at work! 1445hrs got a JS Fletcher mystery from the library but can't concentrate, my thoughts are a whirl.

Later. Much digging up of tapioca roots gives us a good filler in the evening. I believe our days of hunger are over.

12 August

Today, my Flossie's birthday has been earmarked by the 'HAG Kongsi' for a 'bash' being also roughly half way between mine and Ken's which is on the 20th. Alan Gordon and Fred Wilkins the Australians have agreed to cook for us and we're having this evening, a 'doover' made of a quarter of our breakfast pap, tapioca flour and blachang. As the evening menu looks a good one we should retire with full bellies.

Couldn't sleep last night, was twice up for a smoke and dreams were fitful. And so today we hear that the Japs 'promise' has been agreed to, and all we wait for now is Lord Louis' circus!

Later. An air of complete quiet today, no Nip planes up. Somehow one can't help but feel anti-climax, a sweeping victory would in many ways have revenged February '42, but one wonders whether this way to the Nips, it may not be more degrading.

Anyhow it has saved many lives, both armed forces and civilians as well as ourselves, which we think of even greater importance. In the meantime, we wait and hope that there will be no hitch.

Evening. with the Nips not yet having accepted our final draft defining TH's 'sovereign rights' we are still 'at war' – somehow this waiting is more wearing than any of the last few weeks, so near and yet so far – it seems incredible to think that it's only 36-odd hours since the first news came through and I somewhat prematurely wrote 'it's over' – still, with Lord Louis' amphibious fleet standing by anyhow, our own release should not be long delayed. But I think they'll accept in Tokyo, I don't think they've any alternative. Will TH commit 'hari-kari'?

Later. This is farcical, here we know all about the negotiations etc., and as there's no intimation from the Nips, we have to carry on as usual. I'm on a wood trailer again tomorrow. Still they say good times are coming! SE Asia Command say 'Don't aggravate guards as they don't know'.

13 August
Most unexpected siren goes at 1330hrs and Nip fighters take off in a hurry, 'all clear' goes one and a half hours later. People very irritable, having bottled up likes and dislikes for months, this extra strain finds them venting their spleen when previously they would have held themselves in.

14 August
Wood trailer in morning. 1555hrs word in that Japs have expressed their willingness to sign! Hoorah, now we should see some action – overhead, a few Allied planes tomorrow perhaps and then the relieving force.

Now we won't have to reduce the rice ration, Dillon authorised, unknown to the Nips the issue of an extra 50 grams of rice as from last Sunday, this has given us one pint of pap for breakfast instead of three-quarters of a pint and an extra biscuit with an evening meal.

Tonight the 'HAG Kongsi' are having a 'bash' with Alan Gordon, Fred Wilkins and Alan Hamilton – well timed as it's turned out. We hear this evening that our relieving force now awaits only for General Itagaki's intimation that they are prepared to surrender. He is GOC Jap troops Southern Region.

15 August

Our 'bash' with the Aussies a great success, savoury buns with a hot chilli spread, sandwich biscuits with a gula malacca filling and ground sugar on top and coffee, santan and sugar.

For the first time there were no search lights up and all during the night there seemed little activity on the roads.

Just heard (0845hrs) that in the Attlee broadcast at midnight last night that the official surrender of Japan takes place today, exactly three-and-a-half years after the fall of Singapore, a day the Nips had intended to celebrate for that very reason. I hope they feel like hell today just as we did then. They haven't even had the satisfaction of having ever fought – even now I feel no change of sentiment towards them, I hope on leaving here never to see another Japanese and only trust that they will be relegated to the obscurity in world affairs from which they never should have emerged. The 'poached egg' [*Nip flag*] is still flying over the Gaol at 0900hrs.

The general pulling up of tapioca root and of green vegetables has made the officers' area look very different, quite naked in fact.

2245hrs – Just heard the Royal Rescript, now we await visible results. All guards were addressed by General Saito, Dillon is trying to get a report of this speech so that he can then approach Saito, tell him we know the surrender has been agreed and say "Wot abaht it?"

16 August

Two rifle shots at 0410hrs this morning – 'Hari Kari?' Reported that a Nip guard shot an Indian and then himself.

We hear that Lord Louis has ordered 'cease fire'. In the meantime all fatigues and working parties go out as usual and the trailer party reports usual Nip activity with a new guardroom by the Weng Loon Road. It's a phoney world. All we've seen is an unidentified plane over during the morning pretty high.

17 August

Senior officers called up to see Muira and told that all Singapore working parties are to stop and that those living down there are to come back. But as far as we can find out, no mention made about the end of the war; so the farce continues. Jones of the Sappers was told by Takahashi in Singapore yesterday that the war was over, so maybe they'll use that as a lever.

18 August

And so a week has gone by since we first got news that the Japs had agreed to unconditional surrender. The longest seven days of my life, up one day, down the next, having difficulty in concentration. Now I have decided the only sane course is to wait patiently and take it as it comes, impatience is foolish and only leads to shortened tempers.

The lure of the flesh-pots
Seen in the pouring rain 17 Aug 45

67. Unusual Sight

Our last working party, Singapore, yesterday report that at Durong the Nips are piling arms and ammunition in a wired enclosure and rubbing mud in the bolts etc. 1230hrs Allied plane, believed to be Beaufighter over Changi area. Ack Ack opened up when he was over Singapore and the Naval Base! So much for VJ day!! Apropos of yesterday's conference, it is now officially announced that the camp south of the gaol is now part of the camp again and that 3,000 are returning here from Singapore.

Later. At last things seem to be moving. Muira has told Dillon that we won't be here long and that he (Dillon) can utilise the food in the supply depot as he thinks fit – also Red + supplies are promised in a day or two.

The end really looks in sight at last and just in time, my towel is more like a diaphanous veil, my sleeping bag after grand service since March '40 is, in parts, as thin as the towel, socks, shirt etc., are all on their last legs whilst my pyjama trousers (I had no upper) are falling to bits, and having sold my sarong for $130 I have no other. This money has kept the 'HAG Kongsi' going the last ten days and enabled us to indulge in the various 'bashes' we've had.

19 August

Parties coming in fast. Nips unarmed with full equipment *en route* for Singapore. 1300hrs News is that Red + supplies have arrived and will be issued at the rate of twenty – one parcel <u>per day</u>, that's the same as we were having twice a week. Whacko! but what swines these Nips are to have had them all this time and not released them, apparently there are medical stores to come as well. Gosh it all seems too good to be true.

It is unfortunate for myself that since I had my cold it has left me with fever symptoms, headache, aching limbs etc., but no rigor – hope to shake it off soon. Half the POWs from Outram Road prison are in and the rest are expected this evening. Now we should get confirmation as to whether the Kempi took out American pilots and evacuated them following the bombing of Japan. Bruce Bowring in to see us, got back from Singapore this morning. Some of the working parties sound like Thailand all over again.

<u>Later</u>. Thanksgiving service at St. George's conducted by 'Bish Cordingly, I found it very moving. Issue of Red + cigarettes twenty Chesterfield. Nine lorry loads of Red + supplies have now arrived at one to twenty, that gives us twelve days. I hope we won't be here that long. Outram Road people confirm that they cannot account for thirteen American pilots and bomb-aimers who were removed from here.

An IMS Colonel says that 1,400 all nationalities have died there in six months and the B29 we saw come down over Johore had its tail taken off by a Nip fighter that was out of control. The seven crew who bailed out were either executed or picked up by friendly guerillas.

20 August

American airmen were over here in a B29, hit over Naval Base and came down seventy miles up the mainland. They had daily weather reports by wireless from Chinese or Malays and knew of at least four airmen who were safe with Chinese guerillas. This fellow does not confirm execution of Americans.

Ken's birthday, we're finishing up our flour and blachang and the 'Kongsi' is going in with four Divisional HQ lads and having 'chipolatas' and sweet coffee at 1100hrs and we, as a 'Kongsi' are having a sweet cake for tea (DV). Oh gosh I can't realise that the months of hunger are over, now comes the big test to try and maintain the slow eating I've been cultivating these last months.

More and more parcels continue to arrive, it's said that 47,000 are coming in today (American) are believed to be some from Sime Road issue of 1944. I wonder how many lives would have been saved had the yellow swine allowed this up to us before – however, this is a wonderful day, good food inside us, Virginian cigarettes. I only want some good tobacco to be able to view the world with the utmost complacency. This tobacco stalk is not so hot. 'HAG Kongsi' taking coffee this evening with Paul Holtzman of the NEI this evening.

Five-word wireless message to be sent.

Working parties returning today say that Singapore has gone mad, all the local population are shouting, singing and cheering. Blakang Mati party are back so I should see Freddie Holt with luck, although as far as we can find out, part were there and the rest at Keppel Harbour.

The cake turned out excellently, made of tapioca flour and palm oil and with ground sugar on top it was quite home like. Which reminds me that soon, soon I'll be back home and eating a real fruit cake.

A story brought in by Outram Road people is that seven MCS including Hugh Fraser the Federal Secretary were taken away and decapitated a short time ago, they were concerned in a wireless set discovery. Two marines are in the camp who have been masquerading as Eurasians since the capitulation.

Today's funny story – the Aussie OR who was always in trouble at Outram Road on working parties, stealing etc., got away with the Commandant's white riding breeches and was wearing them last night.

The Chinese have already started to settle accounts with the IJA when disarmed, the exact details aren't known, some say it was confined to Indians, at any rate fifty to sixty are said to be killed, rifles and machine guns being used.

21 August

Damn and blast, this damned fever has at last developed into Malaria. I'm not going sick, having 'friends at court' I'm getting quinine on the quiet.

Later. Pretty stiff bout of malaria has left me feeling sick and with a bad head. Driver Cornwall in to see me, he was in Outram Road gaol. Japs are amazing, after months of short rations etc, they are now delivering fresh pork, fish, wheat flour, eggs and clothes – do they really think our memories are so short that this is going to make us forget? I expect the eggs will go to the hospital, there was some fresh pork (.7oz) in our evening meal, although I felt too sick to eat anything.

It looks now as if we won't see any relieving force at least until the weekend.

22 August

Fourteen lorry loads of supplies including yak meat arrived last night. The clothes are Nip stuff but will nevertheless be most welcome. 8,000 pairs of boots are in, with working parties going out bare footed now that these are stopped this 'presento' loses a lot of its attractiveness. Nip 'Zeros' making a show this morning.

I hear MOs having recommended that the wheat issue be reduced from 2oz to 1oz per day.

Yank airmen up from Outram Road say the 'Lightnings' we saw were actually 'Black-Widows' – they also say what a wonderful job Lord Louis did in Burma and are high in his praise.

Feeling very groggy today, were it not for the fact that Red + supplies are now a daily issue and one has the vision of proper food to follow, that it would break my heart to refuse these meals. Refuse is actually wrong as the 'Kongsi' benefits. They are insisting that until I'm OK I have all the breakfast issue of milk.

<u>Later</u>. General Saito has officially told Colonel Dillon that the final surrender of Japan will shortly be signed.

Dillon asked for wireless sets so that we could get real (!) news. Medical authorities have advised against an increase in rice ration (325 grams) although this is available; the reason is that the present available food doesn't give a balanced diet and there have been several deaths from beri-beri in recent days.

An item I forgot in General Saito's interview was that he regretted there had been some deaths during the fifteen months we had been here – between sixty to seventy here alone is the figure and many of these would have been prevented had more effort been made to give us something more than the near-starvation diet.

<u>Later</u>. We hear on the news that on or after 25th 0800hrs we may get supplies dropped by parachute.

23 August

Late flash last night. Count Terashi who is in charge of all Southern Region has ordered 'Ceasefire' with effect from 12 midnight 22–23 August. Weight 8st 6lb, this bout of fever has pulled me down a lot.

The Nips have brought in so much clothing that they can't sort it all at once. Every OR, there are well over 10,000, is getting a shirt, vest, pair of shorts and towel – nice people with fellows going round in rags for months. There are also thousands of G-strings and boots, size eight and under, gosh it makes one furious – do they really think that this supreme act of generosity is going to help? It only makes the case against them all the blacker. All their protestations that there were no stocks of clothes available are shown to be just another lie to add to the long record.

'Doc.' Braganza, who is treating me for my malaria, is giving me a course of Attabrin after the quinine which, with luck, should clear my system of the bug.

<u>Later</u>. Just heard that there are to be no more roll calls. Two ORs buried today, one Australian ate two and a half pounds of sugar, blew up like a balloon and died – on the break-up of camp south of the gaol, everyone was issued with 4lb sugar – how the folks at home could do with that.

24 August

Funny how we've dropped back into the old routine. The first week after <u>the</u> news was hellish, but now that we know that we've got to wait a bit longer and have got the extra Red + food, we're just sitting back and waiting quite patiently – after all, after three and a half years a week or so means little and of course the big thing is the extra food and that glorious knowledge that it's not just a 'flash in the pan' but will now continue.

1400hrs General Saito sent for Colonel Dillon today and told him all that had transpired in Japan, Singapore and elsewhere. Requests for towgay, rice polishings and shore bathing and access to other camps on the Island have all been granted. Having the first two means that an increase will be possible in the rice ration.

After 1700hrs today, parachute supplies and medical personnel may be dropped. A request for a wireless set was parried by Saito saying that we would then get only our side of the news. Dillon replied by saying that at the moment we were only getting his. The request has been granted!!! Damn funny when after these items of local news we were then to read an eight page screed gleaned from all over the world.

One item thrilled to bits, the arrival of letters from home as soon as possible. 1630hrs the biggest sell yet. Eight large planes escorted by one fighter circled round, came down low directly over the camp, everyone out and frightfully excited as they were twin-engined bombers. Issue of Red + soap, a half tablet per person. Supplies continue to pour in. A lorry load of pineapple brandy has been returned on medical grounds. A small issue of meat, fresh fish and cigarettes have also arrived. Just goes to show doesn't it?!

Later. Now reported that Allied planes are expected as from 0500hrs tomorrow. Brand new blankets have been issued to the hospital, this after fellows have had to lie under tattered rags, rice sacks sewn together and often nothing at all.

They had a 'float' of thirteen for malaria cases, this ward holds over 200. Two Korean guards who behaved abominably to POWs in the camp at Keppel Harbour are now running around trying to persuade people to write them good conduct chits. Needless to say none have done so.

25 August

British bugle calls for first time today, sounded grand. Issue of fresh fish and meat. And what of the day, do we see Allied planes dropping supplies?

I'm putting on a show in the Hospital Area this evening, they have the largest open space. Issued with pair of shorts, fanoochie, white vest, pair of socks, sweat rag – ever so pansy!

Later. No Allied planes appeared over Changi anyway. Show in Hospital Area went off okay a huge crowd of 2–3,000 sang their heads off.

26 August

Took part in concert in the gaol in the evening, otherwise an uneventful day. We hear that tomorrow the International Red + representative is to visit us. When Dillon was told this by Muira he replied 'he's just three and a half years too late'.

27 August

With the addition of soya bean paste, towgay and 20g rice polishings, the medical authorities have agreed to the rice ration being increased from 325g to 400g per man per day, also Red + parcels are to be issued at fifteen to one parcel instead of twenty as heretofore.

I find I have to go very carefully with the extra food to avoid tummy upset – this is very prevalent in the camp and also a tendency for an increase in beri-beri owing to the increase in carbohydrates and none in vitamin B until today's issue.

There has been an issue of pullovers, boots, laces and boy scout hats! I only need the laces, but to see a 6ft 4in ex guardsman like Barry Walker in a scouts' hat should be grand. Issue of fresh butter working out at 10oz per head. We are also getting an

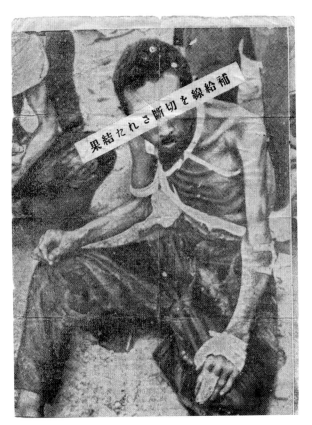

68/69. Two leaflets dropped on Singapore by Allied aircraft. The first drew attention to the fact that the Nips were losing the battle in Burma. The other gives instructions to the Nips that when they capitulate, they should not take it out on the POWs or words to the effect! Have I got it the right way up?!

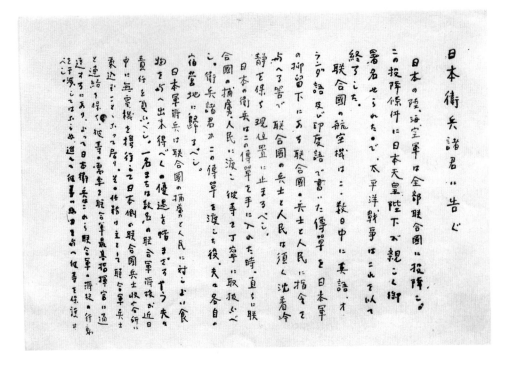

issue of twenty cigarettes a day. One day 'kooa' which are good, the next day some local make done up in old '3 Castles' packet.

28 August
Issue of cheese, something like 8oz per head, also sugar. The butter issue yesterday was grand.

Our 'official' wireless set has arrived today, it's not certain whether they'll be able to fix it up so that all can listen, it largely depends on the power.

Starting a 'Road Show' tour of the camp on Friday with a mixed cast of British, Australian and Dutch artists. 1400hrs 'Liberator' came low over the gaol and dropped leaflets in Japanese addressed to guards. It's funny, last week I could read and felt quite settled, now I find I can't settle to anything. Books have lost their attraction and bore me, even the entertainments are a real effort which all leads to the one conclusion, the sooner we get out of here the better.

1700hrs. Another Liberator this time dropping leaflets in Urdu and instructions to POWs in English – their advice re. medical items is amusing in view of the strict supervision of diet here. Probably the MOs after three and a half years experience of food know more than those outside. I suppose however, that if ORs were on their own with no medical supervision, the advice may be necessary. They tell us to eat small quantities if we have been starved, make broth using water the rice has been cooked in and so on. Anyhow it was a great thrill actually seeing the fellow standing at the door waving and throwing out the leaflets.

The Australians under 'BJ' are quite amazing, he has them out every evening on Company drill – this does not prevent their discipline being far worse than the British. Two Aussies were found half way to Singapore the other day and two more stole a pig from a local Kampong.

29 August
A great increase in beri-beri in spite of medical efforts to balance the diet – puffy faces and legs is the most prevalent. Took part last night in a show to Australians in the gaol.

Later. News has come over wireless that MOs and supplies are to be dropped on Changi airfield tomorrow.

30 August
0730hrs Liberator over dropping eleven parachutes that we could see, but from here not whether they were men or supplies.

Alexandra Hospital has been handed over to us if we want it. Actually it has been decided not to (a) because the Allies have asked for us to be collected in one area (b) there are many people too ill to move (c) there are not the facilities there now that we have here. Good thing the plane was over early because at 0830hrs the rain started with real tropical intensity.

Later. We are told six people were dropped by parachute, two MOs (Captains), two Lieutenants and two orderlies. 1100hrs Just seen the two MOs, all six are British, they left Columbo this morning and say a medical Colonel and Captain, with supplies are expected this afternoon.

A Colonel with transmitter was dropped some days ago and should have been there to meet them but wasn't. They say 300 POWs have been flown out of Thailand already and that conditions in Hong Kong are very bad. It's amazing what an inferiority complex seeing these fellows gives one – we have all noticed it and it makes one wonder what our reactions are going to be like when we are free. It's only natural I suppose, the Nips to them are a beaten and inferior army – to us they have been oppressors, lords and masters for three and a half years.

Apparently the impression from aerial reconnaissance was that this camp would hold 6,000, they didn't know how the Nips pack us in.

My bed space is as follows: Right up against my left hand neighbour, one foot between myself and my right hand neighbour and with 2ft between the end of my bed and the bed opposite.

70. Our Bed Space

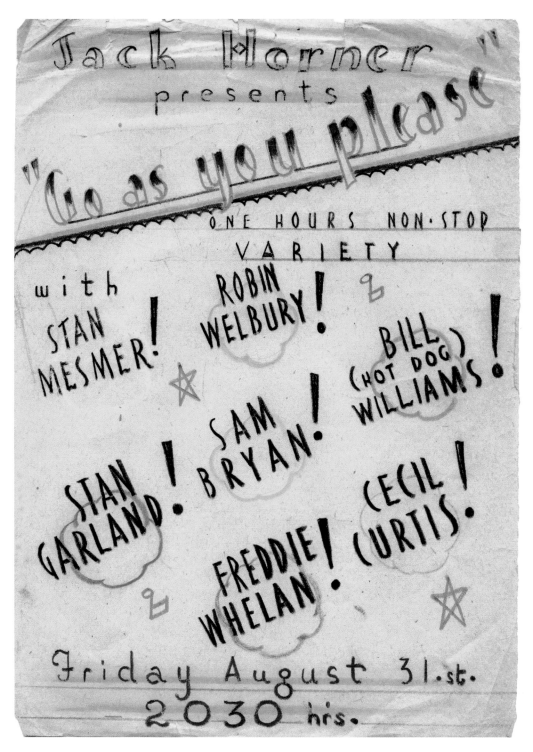

71. *Go as you please*

1400hrs Liberator over 'drome' low down, couldn't see if anything was dropped.

Later. Two planes arrived and were seen to drop more parachutes, but what they contain is not known yet. Issue this evening of cigarettes, gift of International Red + and one tin of pineapple between two, Jap issue. It is now confirmed that supplies only were dropped this afternoon.

Apparently the new arrivals don't think much of our food. Just seen a *Daily Express* of June this year, first British paper we've seen for three and a half years.

Tomorrow I start a Road Show *Go as you please*, first night in the Officers' area, on Saturday in Hospital Area and Monday to Australians in camp south of the gaol. This of course depends on what arrivals we get in the meanwhile.

31 August

Mosquito plane over this morning. Sixty parcels and cannisters etc., dropped by three Liberators during the afternoon.

Lorry loads of Red + supplies continue to arrive, almost all 1942 South African supplies that have been in Singapore for the last three years. A Swiss Red + representative told Ken Archer that when representations were made to the Nips, they had their faces slapped and told to mind their own business. What swine, they could have made such a difference to our feeding during the past twelve months.

The Mosquito over this morning was forced down at Kalang and the two occupants are now in the camp. One is a New Zealander, a flight Lieutenant and the other a British WO they came from the Cocos Islands. During the afternoon two ORs with a transmitter were landed.

1 September

Show went off very well, in fact some people reckon that it was the best show that had been on at the 'Coconut Grove' – gratifying, as it should be our farewell performance to the Officers' Area. Weight today 8st 11lb, up 5lb which, considering I have had a bout of malaria is satisfactory. I certainly don't get blackouts now and the extra food makes one feel much stronger, no weakness in the knees which was so prevalent before.

I still have difficulty in realising that this is no 'flash in the pan', but that our days of hunger are really and truly over. One wonders now how one stuck it with a continuous empty belly.

An official South Eastern Asia Command newspaper is now circulating; it came in one of the canisters dropped yesterday.

Later. Have just been looking at a *Picture Post* of June 24th this year, a *London Opinion* and an *Answers* and *Tit Bits* – after nearly four years it is wonderful to see these again and to see that fashions etc., are not too altered as to make one feel a stranger in one's own country.

Two Mosquitos over the Gaol so low that they almost touched the tower, one we think was the one that force-landed yesterday as the pilot promised to 'Beat Up' the Gaol before he went off.

Incidentally both of them came to the show last night and were apparently considerably amused at an item I introduced 'That the mosquito that landed at Kalang today was definitely not of the Anopheles variety.' We are now having daily wireless relays from London and Delhi.

<u>Later</u>. Show in Hospital Area attended by huge crowd and received very enthusiastically.

2 September

Colonel Stewart, who was dropped recently with a transmitter, arrived early this morning with a band of Guerillas and Private Fairbrother who escaped from here recently and was able to make contact through the Chinese.

1050hrs Have just heard the signing of the Japanese surrender over the wireless, we were glad to hear that General Percival was present behind General MacArthur when he signed, a wonderful moment.

At 1200hrs the Union Jack, Stars and Stripes and Flag of Holland are to be broken from the gaol tower and our freedom is assured. The two members of the Mosquito who saw my show on Friday night said afterwards that they had no hesitation in saying that it was better than any ENSA show they had seen.

1200hrs Breaking of the flags postponed as they were unable to get the flag posts up in time. Liberators over all morning dropping supplies, coming over very low waving and taking photos.

Amongst the party that came in this morning was an Aussie Captain who got away from here on the official escape party of 13 February '42 and volunteered to come back some months ago – also a Chinese Captain and two Chinese Sergeants and an MO who was second in command to Colonel Neil and also got away from here.

1245hrs Mosquito 'Beat Up' the Gaol in no uncertain fashion, we're pretty sure it was our two friends back again, one of them was in the bomb aimer's compartment in the nose and could easily be seen waving.

It's all very disconcerting, but these newcomers say we smell! Presumably it's the fact that we've been living on native food and oil so long that we smell like them. I hope that we will have got over this before we get home, even my very best friends otherwise will keep their distance. 1515hrs Just heard London direct, very thrilling – we're exactly eight hours in advance of GMT.

A story brought in from internees at Sime Road is that the Bishop of Singapore when in Outram Road Gaol was treated abominably. One of his punishments was to kneel for twenty four hours on a grating. Like a true Christian he bears them no malice.

Apparently Fairbrother is not yet in the Camp, apparently he has been contacted at Kota Tingi. We are now in constant touch with Kandy, Ceylon, by wireless, things should really start moving soon. According to Colonel Wylie, another Guerrilla who has arrived here, the attack on Singapore would have been a terrific affair.

The planes that have been over, Liberators, also come from the Cocos Island. The comforts they are dropping have been subscribed by all ranks and services on the Island, so stated a letter dropped today. We have had to put out a 'plus' sign if being received okay or 'minus' if not – our reply is +. Got a razor blade 'Kova' and a tin of pineapple today. Had some fresh pork today and as from tomorrow we receive parcels at ten to one parcel. Life's pretty good, but happy as I feel, it will not be complete until I'm with my loved ones again.

2315hrs And so a wonderful day is over aptly concluded by listening to a broadcast from London and hearing 0215hrs struck from Big Ben.

3 September

1205hrs – following a fanfare of trumpets, the flags of the three Allied nations represented here were broken on the Gaol tower – a most impressive moment. The ceremony was performed by Colonel Holmes for the British Empire, Lieutenant Colonel van de Hoogenband for the NEI and Lieutenant Miles Barrett of the US Marines for the USA.

It is a sad fact to have to record that there are quite a number of people who have, during the last few weeks gone mental – some to a lesser degree than others. I only hope it is a temporary state, but as most are of advanced years, one has one's doubts.

Issue of two Players and one Craven 'A' cigarettes, magnificent.

Three Public Relation Officers dropped today, one broke a leg on landing. They will commence getting things going here and at Singapore – according to them we may expect the Cruiser HMS *Sussex* off here today and troops by air (Aussie) today and land tomorrow 5 Indian Division.

Anyhow things begin to move. Lucky boy! I've drawn a bag of Red + toilet requisites including a towel, face flannel, handkerchief, comb, razor, five blades, shaving soap and brush, toilet soap, toothbrush and a pencil. I feel like a child on Christmas morning. This was amongst those comforts dropped by parachute from 99th and 356 squadrons RAF and RAAF from Cocos Island.

I'm becoming civilised again, instead of having to use a towel you could see through in its best places and holey in its worse, ordinary soap to shave with and use a blade that's been sharpened and resharpened in a marmite jar and toothpowder that's not just camp-made ash, I have the real commodities at last.

4 September

Went down to the beach this morning for a walk. Didn't bathe as I'm still taking Plasmaquin, very pleasant to get out of the camp. We hear that HMS *Cleopatra* is in and the *Sussex* is expected this afternoon.

The RAPWI people are taking over the Cathay building today, our press representatives go with them, lucky devils.

5 September

It has just come over the camp radio pick-up service (1545hrs) that troops of the 5 Indian Division have begun landing at Singapore. Things progress slowly, but I still

'Wanna go home'. Two 'Seafires' over, the first single-engine Allied planes we've seen since the capitulation.

We're gradually being weaned off rice, rice reduced to ten and a half ounces as from tomorrow, ten to one parcel per day and in addition 1oz each of sugar, coffee, wheat flour, salt and soya beans, palm oil, 2oz milk and mixed meats 3oz and vegemite half an ounce. Total calories 4,448 – so even if we're still in our POW camp we're on the road home as I cannot see them loosing us on a hard world until we can 'take' normal food and we certainly can't yet.

At the moment my tummy has gone back on me slightly, nothing much, but a definite warning that all is not well and that even with slow eating, our digestive organs aren't by any means 100%.

Listened in to the St Leger from York. RAPWI Colonel who landed with occupational forces says that we should start embarking in about four days time. We expect to have the pukka occupational troops up here tomorrow.

6 September
Been out all morning to the air strip and down to the Straits where we saw a destroyer and two mine sweepers starting to clear a passage for the Navy. Many people in from the occupational forces – press representatives both male and female, photographers etc., all very exciting. In fact getting outside the wire was grand, a real feeling of freedom again. So far none of the occupational troops have arrived to disarm the Nips, but the guards present arms to all officers! 1800hrs – Just been talking to the war correspondents of the *Daily Sketch* and *Daily Mirror* – they couldn't believe that we actually ate blachang.

Later in the evening we were issued with an airmail letter card.

7 September
Have got the job of transport officer in charge of lorries doing a bus service into Raffles Square and Sime Road internment camp. I'm going in on the former this evening.

Things seem very muddled, there are supposed to be cigarettes and tobacco for us, but so far we haven't seen any – also as far as we know, no cable has gone for us. RAPWI are now known here as 'Retain All POWs indefinitely'.

Going in tomorrow to Singapore as was too busy to get in today. Talked to two Red + nurses – they can't understand why we're not on our way from here. What a joy to talk to a member of the opposite sex. Admirals Holland and Power were up today.

8 September
Had a wonderful day, been in Singapore all day. The enthusiasm of the civil population was most moving. Beflagged streets, cheering crowds were grand to see. The shipping lying off in the roads is like old times.

There are three hospital ships, the *Sussex* and two transports off Keppel Harbour. Had lunch at Tanjong Payar POW camp who are receiving supplies from the Navy.

Had bread, <u>real</u> bread, butter, tinned tongue and fish. It is hoped that they will help up here as RAPWI seem to be in chaos and such comforts, cigarettes etc., are all mouldy.

General Christianson was up here today and spoke over the camp radio. Still no sign of our going home and anyhow rumour has it that 18th Division go last. The band of HMS *Sussex* are up here this evening, there's no doubt there's something about the Navy! But really they do seem to have made a mess of things, our supplies are running low and unless things alter radically, rice will have to be increased on Monday again – efforts are being made to prevent this at all costs. The Navy's language about RAPWI is in the true tradition.

These nurses are magnificent, they allow themselves to be bombarded with questions by hundreds of troops and although absolutely whacked still keep cheery and smiling. It does one good to see girls again and hear them talking, but it's only a stop-gap – Come on Lord Louis what about all those promises about early repatriation.

9 September

Richard Sharpe, BBC commentator up today. I wish we could get some pipe tobacco, I'm fed up with this stalk, it seems farcical not to have any yet.

As from today we should be coming on Indian Army scale rations, this still includes some rice but is far nearer European diet to anything we've had so far. Several lorry loads of comforts etc., in this morning from HMS *Activity* one of the destroyers – a gift out of their own store.

Admiral Power has stated that had he had the evacuation of us we would be half way up the Straits of Malacca by now, he would have utilised the aircraft carrier that is at present lying in the Roads.

<u>Later</u>. Things are beginning to move, some people flying out tomorrow and more by transport. There is a Kampong just outside the wire to which we are taking 'lagi' rice of which they are in great need, one Chinese girl aged about nineteen hasn't walked for three years following a bashing by Nips in an endeavour to get information of her husband who was a communist.

10 September

We are beginning to realize more and more how lucky we are to be alive. It is now definitely established that had the Nips not capitulated when they did, all officers were to be sent to Kranji. Here, Colonel Stewart the guerrilla has documentary evidence that POWs there, working on the tunnels, were to be shot and that the fate of all POWs in that area, which certainly would have seen some fierce fighting, was very much in doubt.

Drawn a quarter ounce of Capstan Navy Cut from HMS *Activity* comforts and ten Players.

Lady Louis pays the camp a visit this afternoon.

Sent off a cable today, at last. As it's a set message we had hoped it had gone off days ago.

1630hrs: Just seen quite a cheery ENSA show, also Lady Louis looking, I thought, very attractive. She has an excellent way with the men and was very popular. Also in the camp was the Deputy Allied Commander, an American General who is second in charge to Lord Louis. Lady Louis has just broadcast over the camp radio.

A film unit has just arrived in the camp. All very nice, but I still 'Wanna go home'.

A great kick seeing the Nips working in Singapore under Sikh guards. I only saw one party when I was in, but reports today say that large crowds of locals and ex POWs are watching all the time.

2200hrs Just seen my first 'flick' for four years, the mobile unit operated this evening. It was grand to see the Gaumont British News again, the other film was called *A Thousand Cheers!*

11 September

Kampong Chinese and Tamils having the time of their lives collecting discarded food, clothes, bedding etc., we hear that some mail is in. I hope like blazes there's some for me. In the *Straits Times* today it states that General Saito has been put in prison – good show!

12 September

Today is the day for Singapore. Planes of all types, Liberators, Dakotas, Catalinas have been 'beating up' the Gaol. 1200hrs – Just heard the Singapore surrender including Cyril Wilde's broadcast.

I did not know that the flag we had broken here was the one that had been over Command HQ although Cyril had told me some time ago the full story of the flag's retention for further use.

Have just sent off a hurried letter to Flossie via a Naval bloke who, incidentally, gave me a tot of brandy. The first real alcohol I've tasted for months, nay years.

When in Singapore the other day I noticed that our old HQ at 29 Newton Road had been gutted, it now turns out that this was where 300 Nip officers committed 'Hari Kari' by blowing themselves up with grenades.

The camp this afternoon is lousy with British Generals. Cinema show in 'Coconut Grove' this evening by Naval mobile film unit.

13 September

Went down to Singapore today. Drew new green tropical kit for journey home, or first part of it, and also sent off my second 'official' lettercard. Tonight I sleep between sheets! And take leave of the sleeping bag that Frank gave me in March '40 and which, now on its last legs, has given me such wonderful service.

14 September

Lord Louis Mountbatten accompanied by Lady Louis paid camp a visit today and addressed four different groups including officers in 'Coconut Grove'. What a terrific personality, no wonder all his troops think so highly of him.

15 September

Saw a Bob Hope film last night *Princess and the Pirate*. Ken sails today, Tony left a few days ago. These days are dragging horribly – heaven only knows how we'll exist until Wednesday.

Later. Have just got a Jap sword – Philip Sayer and I heard there was a Jap camp in the Ooloo, so we set off, found some Jap wine and Asnanty beer. I took the sword from a 'Gunsa' – on our way back he sent five Nips armed with spades and cudgels to get it back. I stood them up and harangued them, told them to go away and they went. [once we had rounded the corner, we ran like hell!!] My biggest moment as a POW apparently they were duly impressed when I said I was a 'Tai Shoko' (Captain) officer. Philip reckoned it was the best turn I've ever put on!

16 September

There's mail in but I've been through all the H's and there's nothing for me. The food has deteriorated these last few days. For breakfast we're back on rice pap and the other two meals are a sort of stewed steak with no issue of vegetables, and biscuits, butter, jam and cheese. Drew £5 advance of pay.

72. RMH with Jap sword (the diary is also featured)

17 September

Had a grand day in Singapore today. Got a lift in in two stages – managed to persuade the Field Cashier to give me a further advance of $100 and then for the first time for three and a half years, walked out shopping with money to spend – a wonderful feeling of freedom. Bought silk pair of 'Chuplis' and a new wrist watch as we're told they're unobtainable in England. Then, after, an ice cream, whew!

I called on a Chinese family called Wee Hong Kee and spent the rest of the day with them and two young Eurasians who had been in the internment camp. After a dinner of 'Mahmee' fresh pineapple and bananas they drove me home. What a wonderfully happy and kind race are the Chinese – they were embarrassingly hospitable.

18 September

Did little all day, saw a Jack Oakie film in the evening.

19 September

Just as I was off to bed last night I was dragged off, not very reluctantly, to a party being thrown by Australian officers, to Royal Naval Officers – it didn't break up until late and was a riotous affair. I have a thick head this morning.

Australian occupational troops have now taken over supplies and messing. It's amazing how much more one feels the heat getting meat every day.

73. Postcard of *Sobieski*

1330hrs – Have just heard we're not embarking tomorrow. This continual putting off is absolutely maddening, we've had enough nerve strain during the last three and a half years without this. There is only one redeeming feature – we've had much more kit and equipment issued to us than those who went off earlier.

20 September

We now hear that we're definitely not embarking tomorrow – all the AIF that remain go tomorrow and we <u>may</u> go on Saturday, but nobody really knows. Really I do think we're getting a raw deal, we're still living in the same conditions as we were under the Japs.

Food has improved considerably, but it is the fact of being in the same surroundings, thirteen miles from Singapore and having practically no money that is so galling.

21 September

Went down to Singapore last evening and visited the 'Great World', had several dances with 'Taxi Girls' – am just as bad as ever, but my impassive dancing partners didn't seem to mind.

Rumour last night says that we may not now go for a week! It does seem absurd when the German internees are living in villas in the town, we are still stuck out here at Changi.

Where <u>is</u> the *Sobieski*? Nobody knows. She's supposed to be at Port Swettenham – we think she's sunk with all hands. General Dempsey round today – couldn't give us any idea when we're going.

23 September

Had a good afternoon and evening in Singapore – did some good shopping, had a meal and saw an ENSA show, getting back in a jeep. The latter was a lucky break.

24 September

Red + supplies are pouring in. Up to 'tiffin' today we've had the following issues: Halex toothbrush, bottle of hair cream, two tins of sweets, a new Australian blanket, cigarettes.

In evening saw an excellent British film *Candlelight in Algeria*. We're to embark on Wednesday on the Anchor Line *Cecelia* unless the *Sobieski* comes in before. Is this another disappointment? I don't think so somehow. 1000hrs. It is just announced that we embark on Wednesday on the *Sobieski* which is either in or definitely coming in.

2230hrs Went down to Singapore with Macfarlane of the Forresters, had a Chinese tiffin (Mee Hoon) did some shopping, had tea at Toc H, home in a jeep with the incoming AIF. DAQMG and so to a film show back in Changi – a punk film called *Brazil* with Virginia Bruce. Had a Chinese haircut in town which included massage.

25 September
Had an easy day, packed my kit and saw a Peter Lorre film *The Face Behind the Mask* in the evening.

26 September
Am writing this, on board the *Sobieski*. From 0630hrs I was in charge of a convoy of twenty four lorries taking the troops down in two lifts. The third lift of ten trucks took the officers. So here we are at last – we sail, I understand, tomorrow. We have internees, male and female and Dutch on board. My cabin mates are Denis Pearl, Bill Bowie, Mark Drinkwater and Eric Hinde. Have just had a <u>hot</u> shower. The first hot water I've bathed in for, oh I don't know how long, over three and a half years anyhow.

27 September
Weighed anchor at 1320hrs, went out westwards through the Straits and so into the Malacca Straits heading for Ceylon which we expect to reach on the 1st October.

What a joy to sleep on a mattress, but oh so hot! Doubt if there will be much to record daily as I intend to take things very easily, sun bathe and generally relax. Have agreed to help on entertainments after we leave Colombo.

The French battleship *Richelieu* passed us at 1645hrs proceeding towards Singapore.

30 September
Just heard that the *Richelieu* hit a mine in the Malacca Straits. Makes one think a bit.

2 October
Arrive at Colombo about 0800hrs – the organisation for disembarkation was excellent and we were taken ashore in landing craft and bussed to the Officers' Club.

Bill Bowie and I then went to the Echelon Barracks where I drew twenty seven rupees and sent off a cable. Then we went to the Galle Face where we met up with three blokes who insisted on standing us lunch. Then back to the Club for tea and back on board at 1630hrs. Altogether most enjoyable – we are due, I believe, to weigh anchor this evening or tomorrow morning. The whole organisation at Colombo was first class, the Dogra pipe band played us into the quay-side and bands were playing continuously at the barracks as well as every facility available for all you could need.

3 October
Weighed anchor at 0715hrs and now we're set for the Suez. Nothing much to record as I'm taking things very easily – we get a free tot of brandy or whisky each evening.

M. S. SOBIESKI

LUNCH.

Pea Soup

*

Boiled Chicken, Curry Sauce

*

Boiled Rice

*

Carrots Purré

*

Tinned French Compote

*

Coffee

*

Tea

21st October, 1945.

GDYNIA - AMERICA SHIPPING LINES, LIMITED

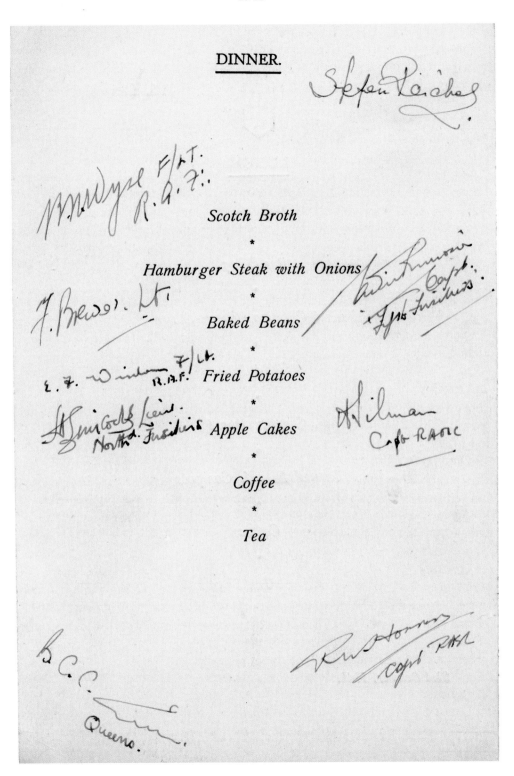

74/75. Ship's Menu, plus inside

4 October

We're certainly making up for lost time with Red + supplies, cigarettes, soap, chocolates and tobacco as well as vitamin pills to build bonny boys. Working on a ship concert.

5 October

Was vaccinated today.

7 October

Vaccination seems to be taking, feel lousy and my arm is rather sore. Gosh how slowly we seem to be going, that's nonsense of course, but I'm so longing to get home that I feel unnecessarily impatient. Saw some whales today. We enter the Gulf of Aden some time this evening.

9 October

Now we're into the Red Sea, terrifically hot, the sweat simply pouring off. My vaccination still making me feel lousy.

Quite a lot of shipping about include two submarines which passed to starboard at 0800hrs.

11 October

Show went off quite well last night. A strong head wind today with definitely a nip although the sun still very strong.

12 October

Docked at Adabuya this morning, train six miles out to Ataka where heavy kit was drawn. In afternoon sent off cable and did some shopping. In evening Donald Edge BBC pianist and Suzette Odell entertained first and second class passengers in the lounge. No mail or cables.

13 October

Weighed anchor at 0730hrs – lay off entrance to Suez Canal until 1145hrs and then started off on the 100 miles journey up it. Bum-boat men most amusing. Spent several hours in great Bitter Lake, started up second leg of Canal at 1800hrs – quite impressive with search lights sweeping the water ahead.

Very cold this evening, shades of things to come!!

14 October

We dropped anchor at Port Said at 0100hrs this morning, took on mail and an interrogation officer and then set sail again. Exact time of sailing I don't know as I had then gone to sleep.

16 October
Put on show for troops last night, I hope that this is my last public performance.

18 October
Some £60-odd collected by 19th Division personnel for charity institutions includes £20 for NCH. [*My grandfather was one of the three founders of the National Children's Home*] 1745hrs: The first glimpse of the coast of Europe – that sounds nearer home! Spanish coast just visible on the starboard bow. We reach Gibraltar tomorrow morning and pick up mail.

19 October
Reached Gibraltar at 0745hrs, took on mail – got cables from my Flossie and St Albans but no letters. Still they're okay and that's the great thing.

   Weighed anchor again at 0845hrs. As I write it's 1800hrs, the coast of Spain is faintly visible on the starboard side – there's a swell on but nothing to worry about – was sunbathing again this afternoon, at Gibraltar it was damp and cloudy but cleared up at midday and is now grand.

   I'm still in 'greens' and don't intend to put on my heavy kit until I've got to.

   We are due at Liverpool on Monday evening around 2200hrs. Next stop England. What a thrill to be able to write that.

* * *

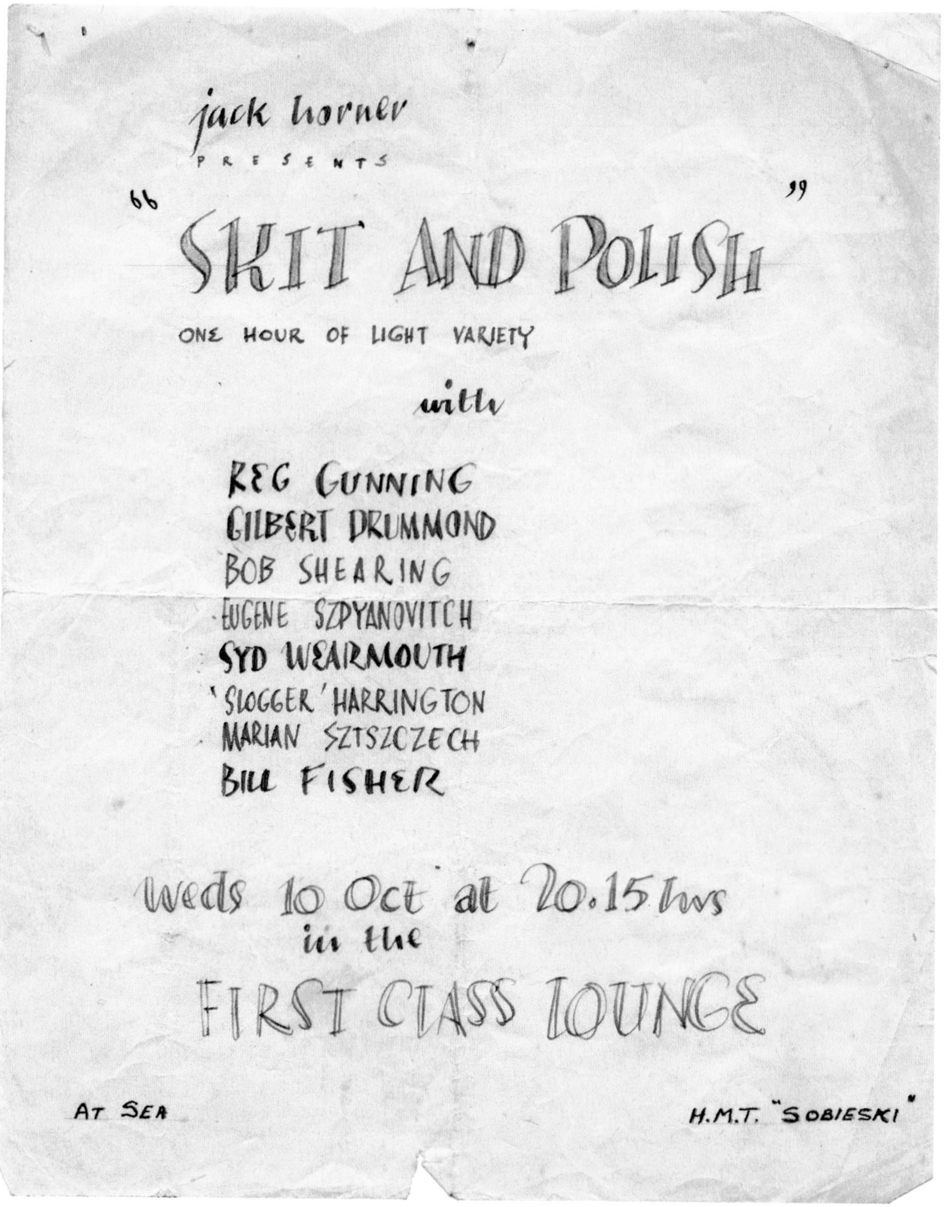

jack horner
PRESENTS

"SKIT AND POLISH"

ONE HOUR OF LIGHT VARIETY

with

REG GUNNING
GILBERT DRUMMOND
BOB SHEARING
EUGENE SZPYANOVITCH
SYD WEARMOUTH
'SLOGGER' HARRINGTON
MARIAN SZTSZCZECH
BILL FISHER

Weds 10 Oct at 20.15 hrs
in the
FIRST CLASS LOUNGE

AT SEA   H.M.T. "SOBIESKI"

76. *Skit & Polish*

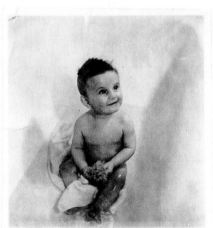

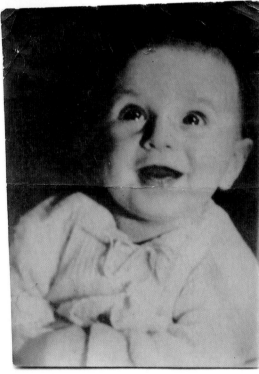

77. Photos of Flo, Beth and Iain. The larger of the two 'baby' photographs was the first I received of Iain, with the other following several months later. The top two photographs were my inspiration to survive at all costs.

78. RMH

Postscript

On the 15th August 2002, a 30-metre length of the original Thai/Burma Rail Track was dedicated at an open-air service held at the National Memorial Arboretum, near Alrewas, Staffordshire.

Attended by many FEPOWs (Far East Prisoners of War), families and friends, it was a very moving occasion and, for those of us who have not been to Thailand, the length of track acted as a tangible symbol of the sacrifice made by so many.

Frank Champkin, an ex-FEPOW, successfully negotiated with the Thai Railway Authority to purchase this stretch of track and return it to England. (I say *return* because it was later found that this track had in fact been made in Middlesbrough!).

I went back to the Arboretum with my family on the 15th August 2005 to mark the 60th anniversary of VJ Day, and to attend the opening of the FEPOW Memorial Building. Championed by COFEPOW (The Children and Families of Far East Prisoners of War) and the Arboretum, this impressive building has been designed to provide a permanent exhibition space, and uses photographs, drawings, archive newsreels as well as eye-witness interviews and donated artifacts to tell the complete story of all aspects of life as a Far East POW.

It also includes the names of nearly 57,000 men from the British Armed Forces who were captured. To see my father's name highlighted was a very poignant moment.

COFEPOW was founded in 1997 by Carol Cooper with the aim of ensuring that the story and memories of all FEPOWs are never forgotten. I hope that the publication of this diary will help towards that aim.

* * *

For further details please go to:
COFEPOW   www.cofepow.org.uk
National Memorial Arboretum   www.nationalmemorialarboretum.com

BUCKINGHAM PALACE

The Queen and I bid you a very warm welcome home.

Through all the great trials and sufferings which you have undergone at the hands of the Japanese, you and your comrades have been constantly in our thoughts. We know from the accounts we have already received how heavy those sufferings have been. We know also that these have been endured by you with the highest courage.

We mourn with you the deaths of so many of your gallant comrades.

With all our hearts, we hope that your return from captivity will bring you and your families a full measure of happiness, which you may long enjoy together.

George R.I.

September 1945.

79. Letter from the King

Index of Names